THE LEGACIES OF SLAVE TRADE, SLAVERY AND INDENTURED LABOUR IN POST-SLAVERY SOCIETIES IN THE CARIBBEAN

THE LEGACY OF SLAVERY AND INDENTURED LABOUR

edited by

MAURITS S. HASSANKHAN AND FARZANA GOUNDER

LIST OF PLANNED PUBLICATIONS

1. *Social Aspects of Health, Medicine and Disease in the Colonial and Postcolonial Era,* edited by Henk Menke, Jane Buckingham, Farzana Gounder, Ashutosh Kumar and Maurits S. Hassankhan
2. *Women, Gender and the Legacy of Slavery and Indenture,* edited by Farzana Gounder, Kalpana Hiralal, Amba Pande and Maurits S. Hassankhan
3. *Collective Memory, Identity and Legacies of Slavery and Indenture,* edited by Farzana Gounder, Bridget Brereton, Jerome Egger and Hilde Neus
4. *Localization and Globalization of Religions,* edited by Maurits S. Hassankhan, Narinder Mohkamsingh, Goolam Vahed and Radica Mahase
5. *Ethnic Relations in Plural Societies: Social-economic and Political Dimensions,* edited by Maurits S. Hassankhan, Hans Ramsoedh, Brij V. Lal and Goolam Vahed
6. *Post-emancipation Indenture and Migration: Identities, Racialization and Transnationalism,* edited by Maurits S. Hassankhan, Kalpana Hiralal, Cristiana Bastos and Lomarsh Roopnarine
7. *Historical and Contemporary Aspects of Indian Indenture and Migration,* edited by Maurits S. Hassankhan, Rachel Kurian, Lomarsh Roopnarine and Ashutosh Kumar
8. *The Legacies of Slave Trade, Slavery and Indentured Labour in Post-Slavery Societies in the Caribbean,* edited by Michael Toussaint, Hillegonda M.A.E. Neus-van der Putten, Jerome L. Egger and Eric R. Jagdew
9. *Slavery, Indentured Labour, Migration and their Legacies in the Americas and Africa,* edited by Karwan Fatah-Black, Michael Toussaint, Hilde Neus and Hans Ramsoedh
10. *Historiography, Theory and Philosophical Aspects of Slavery and Indenture,* edited by Maurits S. Hassankhan, Brij V. Lal, Vijaya Teelock and Goolam Vahed

THE LEGACIES OF SLAVE TRADE, SLAVERY AND INDENTURED LABOUR IN POST-SLAVERY SOCIETIES IN THE CARIBBEAN

Edited by
MICHAEL TOUSSAINT,
HILLEGONDA M.A.E. NEUS-VAN DER PUTTEN,
JEROME L. EGGER & ERIC R. JAGDEW

MANOHAR
2025

Cover illustrations: Map of the Tribal Areas in Central and South-Pamaka Tribal East Suriname; and the Image of Enslaved Woman, *Report of the Female Society for Birmingham*, Birmingham, 1826.

First published 2025
First eBook edition 2025

ISBN 978-93-6080-571-5 (hardbound)
ISBN 978-93-6080-536-4 (eBook)

Published by
Ajay Kumar Jain *for*
Manohar Publishers & Distributors
4753/23 Ansari Road, Daryaganj
New Delhi 110002

Cover design by Kamal Purna Jammual

Typeset by Ravi Shanker, Delhi 110095

Printed and bound in India

Contents

Figures

List of Tables

Preface from the Series Editors

This book is the eighth in a series of ten volumes on the theme 'Legacies of Slavery and Indentured Labour'. The series is an output of the 2018 conference Legacy of Slavery and Indentured Labour, organized by the Anton de Kom University of Suriname, with participation of scholars from all continents. The aim of the conference was: 'to connect historical specificities of slavery, indentured labour and migration to contemporary issues of globalisation, diaspora, identity formation, nationalism and transnationalism' and 'to promote new perspectives and approaches in the study of forced and free migration and their impact on society'.

Some of the questions which were addressed in the conference and the volumes of the series are:

- What are the legacies of slavery and indentured labour in social, economic, cultural, and political fields?
- How did post-slavery identity formation occur in different parts of the world in general?
- What has been the psychological impact of slavery and indentured labour on contemporary societies?
- How are transnational identities developing in the world of today?
- How is the process of identification related to the imaginary with the country of origin and with other 'partners in distress' in the diaspora?

- In the case of the second migration or the twice-migrants, which is perceived as a country of origin? In other words: What kind of homeland perspectives do people have, and how does this impact on their relationship with the former homeland?
- In which ways did the various Diaspora groups adapt to their new environment? What has been the policy or attitude of the receiving countries or societies?
- How are localizing processes ('creolization') expressed in migrant cultures?
- What kinds of transnational ties exist among descendants of immigrants in the Caribbean and other countries? Are alternative transnational identities in the Caribbean real or an imagination?
- How are transnational ties and identities recognized and institutionalized by the State in the former homelands?
- How and why are local processes of identity formation related to emotional and practical identification to the countries of origin? In which ways have the country of origin and the 'new' host country played a role in promoting or discouraging these relationships?

The themes for the conference included the following:

- The legacy of slavery and indentured labour: historical and current developments, with particular reference to the psychological legacy of slavery and indentured labour.
- Ethnogenesis and interethnic relations:
    - The role of ethnocentrism, ethnic labelling and stereotyping in the process of creating and maintaining ethnic boundaries.
    - Ethnicity and politics.
    - The role of religion and religious organizations in identity formation.
    - Identify formation, boundary maintenance and interethnic marriage.
- Transnational networks and identities:
    - Relations with the country of origin?
    - Transnational families.
    - Popular culture.

- Language development in migration societies/migrant communities:
  - Origin and development of creolized languages.
  - Development of multilingual societies.
- Localization and globalization of religions.
- Social and cultural problems of people in Diaspora.
- Health issues in historical and contemporary context.
- Reparations: moral, legal and practical aspects.
- Diaspora policy: past, present and future.
- Role of people in diaspora for the development of their country of origin.

This book consists of revised versions of selected papers from a few panels, supplemented by additional papers from scholars not present at the conference but who are well-regarded in these fields. The chapters in the volume have all undergone rigorous peer-review and revision to provide high calibre discussions on the volume's theme.

As the series editors, we would like to thank all authors who have done their utmost best to meet the deadlines and for their patience in the long process of review and editing.

We also thank the editorial team members of this volume, who have done an excellent job by reviewing the submitted papers and editing them to ensure that the publication is of a high standard. A special word of thanks goes to the external reviewer of the manuscript and the copy editor of Manohar, who provided critical remarks and comments that have contributed to the quality of the articles in this book.

We are grateful to the management and the editorial staff of Manohar Publishers for critical guidance during the editorial process. Our sincere thanks go to late Shri Ramesh Jain Ji, who showed keen interest in the subject of the history and culture of the Indian Diaspora.

Finally, we would like to thank Anton de Kom University's Institute for Graduate Studies and Research, the Faculty of Humanities, and the Board of the University of Suriname, who gave us the opportunity to work on this series.

The preparation of the manuscript for publication has been delayed by the onset of the COVID-19 pandemic, which has affected the entire world from early 2020 to mid-2022. We thank the individual authors and editors for their patience. Ultimately, we are very proud to present this publication because the book consists of well researched papers and the topics are of interest to both experts and the general public.

We congratulate the authors and the volume-editors for the good work they have done.

Paramaribo and *Wellington*
January 2023

Maurits S. Hassankhan
Faculty of Humanities, Suriname

Farzana Gounder
IPU, New Zealand

Introduction

MICHAEL TOUSSAINT,
HILLEGONDA M.A.E. NEUS-VAN DER PUTTEN,
JEROME L. EGGER & ERIC R. JAGDEW

The present and future generations, it has been contended, will persist in scrutinizing the past, seeking further understanding and refining perspectives. reflects an interconnectedness between the past, present and future. This understanding highlights the symbiotic and interdependent nature of these temporal dimensions leading to several significant implications. It is not simply that each day, by way of historical inquiry, the past extends itself further, albeit more broadly and deeply, into its own recesses. It is relatedly inarguable that all that is known about the present depends on what is known about the past. Remarkable complementarities present themselves when it is understood that comprehension and conceptualization of the future rest, not merely on that of the present, but invariably on historical experiences. It is not accidental that extension of the frontiers of knowledge regarding the future has always been concomitant with the push further back in time of the boundaries of our knowledge regarding what has transpired before. The driving force behind the evolution of our understanding of historical spaces is the scrutiny of what is presumed to be known and the emergence of new reckonings regarding them. 'New light' in historiography maintains its fundamental consistency, while also challenging established ideas.

In some instances, the veering is towards support for traditional lines of thought and in other times it questions long-held beliefs. In essence, the key to human progress lies in re-imaging our historical records through valid perspectives. By examining the past in the light of contemporary cicumstances and envisioning the future of global civilization, we can better understand the present and envision a better future for humanity.

The papers published in this volume form part of the contributions made to the mammoth conference titled 'Legacy of Slavery and Indentured Labour: Linking the Past with the Future' held from the 18 to 23 June 2018, in Paramaribo, Suriname. The conference focused on slavery, indentured labour, and aspects of the resultant migratory processes, including diaspora formations and identity materialization at their various levels.

The conference subtitle clearly indicates that the organizers recognized the essential link between the inevitability of the connectedness between the present and the future. With this awareness, the conference aimed to offer deeper insights and understanding. The vastness of the conference proposal, its wide-ranging themes, and the multitude of geographical regions, thematic areas it sought to incorporate, the number of geographical regions it aimed to cover should be expected. These contributions would not only shed light on the historical realities of slavery and indentured labour but also explore their enduring legacies shaping today's complex and multi-ethnic nation states. As was expected, it raised novel questions, introduced new perspectives, and posed new challenges. It illuminated two of the most enthralling themes in modern history, resulting in the publication of 10 volumes. The present volume covers the post-slavery period of the nineteenth century and its continuities into the greater part of the first half of the twentieth century.

The articles inevitably delve into the background or origins from which nineteenth or twentieth century developments emerged. Like other volumes in this series, this publication covers a broad range of topics. From a geopolitical perspective, the essays collectively cover the French and English Caribbean as well as Latin America. In nearly every essay, a wide range of complex issues are highlighted. The authors deserve credit for providing thorough historical and historiographical backgrounds that contextualize the situations discussed, enhancing the reader's understanding. The themes raised cover a broad spectrum, the First Nations, European colonization, Africa, enslavement in the New World, and resistance, including marronage, and debates about the abolition of slavery. There is also data on emancipation, post-slavery migrations, indentured labour and the intersection of African, Hindustani and Jewish diasporas. The essays also address issues of continuity, adjustment, and present-day challenges, such as social group integration and the role of the nation state. Readers have been offered multi-disciplinary analysis, with the essays encompassing disciplines such as history, sociology, anthropology, philology and literary criticism.

One of the main focuses of the conference was to take a comparative approach to slavery and indentured labour. There has long been a long-standing argument that discussions on indenture have often been influenced by issues more relevant to the discourse on slavery, and accordingly, there is a need to analyse indenture on its own terms. The argument is not unfounded, as the similarities often mask the significant differences between slavery and indentured labour. Therefore, it is essential to apply the same level of scrutiny to the notion of similarity as well. Far from being an unjustified claim, the argument validates itself on the basis that more often than not, the sameness reflects considerable differences. Therefore, its even more important to apply the same scrutiny to the notion of similarity. Scalability based on perspectives can churn out huge differences. To a considerable extent, such understandings permeated the organization of the conference, the presentations made, and the essays generated for publication. The result of all this has been a re-analysis and clarification of familiar concepts and groupings, leading to the identification of both older or even new niches of micro and macro contextualities in the history of the New World. In this sense, if accused, the conference could be deemed guilty of seeking to liberate history by fostering new possibilities and ensuring that the papers are published with faithful adherence to the context in which they were presented, debated, propitiated or harangued. By the same logic, throughout the series, every attemptt was made to prevent the arbitrary exclusion of presentations based on personal pedagogical interpretations of the volume editors. The value of the author's work largely rests for the most part on the interpretation of their original contributions. It is this shared awareness that allows other scholars and students of history to interpret and evaluate each contribution effectively. Editors inevitably play a crucial role in determining the content of each volume, especially if random selection and organization are to be avoided. The volume of contributions, the overarching themes they address, and their significance with respect to historical understanding all influence what goes into a volume and how its contents are organized internally. It is worth noting that the volume and quality of the conference presentations made the selection process at both these levels challenging. While it is the prerogative of the editors to make decisions, they should do so with care. Novel approaches may introduce new synchronicities and syntheses that may not immediately align with a reader's expectations, yet they are far from being disorderly. The present volume decidedly embraced the challenges of bringing to the fore fresh approaches assembled from perspectives forged in the spirit of new enquiry into the history of slavery and indentured labour. It focuses on aspects of the story that still remains significantly underexplored or untold. Likewise, and of necessity, it deliberately embraces the challenge of linking the past to the present. Given this, the present volume is divided into three sections.

Section One. 'Legacy of Slavery and Indenture', focuses on these two institutions in an overall comparative context, beginning with the then official classification of these labour systems. Additionally, it also explores issues as they emerged as challenges for imperial authorities and colonial administrators in the face of the coterminous existence of enslaved society, as well as newly legally emancipated communities, and the continuing debates between protagonists of both slavery and free labour regimes, including indentured labour. The next two sections explore bequeathed experiences, examining for the most part, what can be considered as representative samples of the implications of the past, not only formerly enslaved cum freed men, but also other groups, including the post-emancipation White creole and Jews. Thus, section two, 'Slavery's Legacy in the Caribbean' samples new classifications of post-emancipation African-descended workers against the background of both challenges and opportunities posed to them in New World communities during and after slavery. It also elaborates on developments regarding maroon communities and Afro-Surinamese. The third section explores representations of 'French and Jewish Entities and Experience' in the Caribbean.

The discussions presented in this volume, and change within continuity, and in some instances, these are contextualized in relation to the challenges and complexity of present-day living, inclusive of the integration of social groups and consolidation of the nation state. Readers have been treated to multidisciplinary analyses. The essays subsume the disciplines of history, sociology, anthropology, philology, explanation and literary criticism. It is hoped that the general reader and the academic community material provided in the text will stimulate further interest in the history of the issues discussed.

Section One: Legacy of Slavery and Indenture

For imperial overlords and their colonial administrators, once a reasonably common awareness that slavery had run its course and its dismantling by official decree was inevitable, there must have been profound consideration regarding what life would be without it. For many stakeholders, there would have been much uncertainty concerning what the future held for the maintenance of the compliant labour in the sugar estates and related social changes. For many of them it was necessary to turn to the experience of nations already engaged in experiments with alternative systems of labour. Not surprisingly, their decisions were shaped also by preceding debates which informed the legal emancipation of slavery, but, in turn, and more importantly, by how the experiment with freedom was unfolding in various New World territories. The way these influences impinged on imperial and colonial policies on the threshold and implementation of a new system of labour, are explored in the essays presented in this section.

David Leconte's research delves into the crucial discussion surrounding the evolving classifications of immigrant labour sourced from subjugated provenance societies. In order to assuage the anxieties of both anti-slavery onlookers regarding evolution of a new system of slavery, and New World sugar planters in dire straits resulting from labour shortages in their plantations. In the aftermath of slavery, such a discussion would have been imperative. Colonial and metropolitan imperial authorities, along with competing imperialist nations, and the newly arrived immigrant labour classes, would have needed assurance of a clear distinction between slavery and its proposed replacement or alternative labour providing system, such as Indian indenture. The differentiation was essential for various stakeholders to navigate the complexities of post-slavery labour arrangements.

In discussing the issue in relation to Mauritius, La Reunion and British Guiana as host societies, and both French and British India as source societies, Leconte has provisioned a useful exploration framework of the then running conversations on the classification of indentured labour. His discourse is couched, however, in an international context wider than that between an imperial mother country and its colonial composites, and equally important, against the background of an understanding of the reality that while discussions on slavery helped to influence the conversations on indentured labour, deliberations concerning the latter assumed an orientation and character of its own. Accordingly, Leconte's offering provides a useful template for further exfoliation of the comparative nature of slavery and indentured labour.

Eric Jagdew's essay is also set in a comparative context. While it has been fashionable to compare slavery with apprenticeship, or to compare the latter across British territories, or even to compare post-emancipation scenarios in the context of differentiation between the experiences that unfolded in various Atlantic New World empires, Jagdew opted for a more direct and particularistic approach, focusing instead on the similarities and differences between developments in Suriname and neighbouring British Guiana. In the process, however, Jagdew provides a welcome exposition of the historical spaces of emancipation in British Guiana and Suriname, the former a hitherto Dutch colony, which, in consequence of its implementation of British emancipatory measures, largely provided the model for what was subsequently proclaimed and implemented in nearby Suriname. Further, Jagdew's study is complemented overall by analysis of the debates surrounding the causal factors driving the emancipation of slavery in the Caribbean and Latin America. This includes examining the impact of capitalism and slave resistance, and their implications in the emancipation process—from its official proclamation and essential legal frameworks to implementation and, ultimately, its practical outcome in Suriname, which experienced emancipation some two and a half decades after British Guiana. Jagdew's contribution illuminates not merely the unfolding of the post-emancipation systems in two colonial territories, each belonging to one of two different imperial powers, and distinguished by different linguistic, administrative and cultural systems. It elucidates also the interconnectedness forged by their geographical proximity and contiguity, highlighting the cross-border assimilation of political policies fashioned additionally by three decades of hindsight, influenced by one imperial power's from the experience of another operating in a colony near its own. Jagdew's presentation forms an important contribution to the implications of time and space considerations regarding the evolution of post-emancipation labour systems.

Section Two: Slavery's Legacy in the Caribbean

Marten Schalkwijk's discussion of the early history and geography of the Pamaka[1] community and the road they have travelled to experience freedom and ancestral community, constitutes a telling example of the extremely close proximity that can exist between the past and present. Schalkwijk's meticulously detailed account offers a recounting of the history of this comparatively small, under-historicized Surinamese Maroon community. He tests the validity of existing written accounts of their historical and geographic origin and movement using archival and oral sources, as there are members of Pamaka communities still able to provide oral testimony. However, because historically they lived mainly on the riverine islands of the Marowijne, before moving to the mainland, Schalkwijk uses maps of the rivers and coastal areas surrounding the mainland territories to chart their movements. The study focuses on their movement

[1] Pamaka is one of the Maroon tribes/communities in Suriname.

during the nineteenth century, the motivation behind their migrations, including their relationship with other Maroon communities. In addition, readers are exposed to the internal conflicts between different Maroon camps and the Pamaka migration to the French side of the river and back during the 1950s and 1960s. This is an immensely valuable contribution to the study of the evolution of Maroon communities as a legacy of slavery.

Nicole Burrowes directs readers' focus to the complex and long-standing interplay of the inhibitive and disabling legacies of slavery and indentured labour. These legacies, including underdevelopment, violence and racism, established from the beginning of European contact and interactions with labouring classes in the Caribbean. Burrowes presents the resistance of the labouring classes to these European tenets as a legacy in its own right. While the history of the region speaks in general about both colonial oppression and resistance to it, the site chosen by Burrowes for discussion is British Guiana, where, starting with the strenuous colonial attempts at political and socio-cultural erasure of the Amerindians, the imposition of the exploitative and dehumanizing logic of European economics and racism was followed by and concomitant with African enslavement and Indian indenture. Burrowes offers a theoretical exposition that taxonomizes labour resistance as a primary bulwark against European displacement, treated from incipience to successful Amerindian confrontation of efforts to enslave them, and supported by the colony's difficult geographical terrain. Burrowes explores this resistance energy through its transformation into working class consciousness and culmination into headwinds generated against colonialism and its persistent pauperization and dispossession of the masses by the time of the labour riots in British Guiana and the Caribbean during the late 1930s. This notwithstanding, Burrowes acknowledges modern lingering limitations: legacies bequeathed by Amerindian erasure, African enslavement and Indian indenture.

Chan Choenni's research on Afro-Surinamese offers a provocative, summative assessment of the nature and character their integration into their country's national community over the hundred years marked by emancipation in 1863 and ascendency of an Afro-Surinamese Prime Minister in 1963. The study provides extensive coverage of their demographic and socio-economic situation at the time of emancipation, and periodizes what Choenni presents as key phases of Afro-Surinamese integration subsequent to the proclamation. Choenni advances data that purports co-variance between race and colour discrimination on the one hand and urbanization patterns and processes, class distinctions, employment options and economic prospects on the other. While Choenni emphasizes the traumatic and negative impacts of enslavement on the development of black communities and the economic prospects over the centuries, the study also acknowledges certain self-imposed limitations, which it deems to be self-debilitating and based on what, when examined against the background of the economic progress and prospects of the Hindustani and Javanese populations, these limitations are seen as hindrances to Afro-Surinamese integration style. Choenni's analysis of the closing phase of the period demonstrates that that in former colonial societies, access to political power does *not* necessarily coincide with or guarantee the empowerment of formerly exploited classes. Further, in plural societies forged out of diverse ethnic diasporas by metropolitan powers, the post-colonial integration of these groups remains a formidable challenge.

Section Three: French and Jewish Entities and Experience

Noémi Marie-Rose, in her essay, draws attention to the evolution in Martinique between 1848 and 1880 of a category of labourers who became classified as 'attached workers'. The emergence of this group represented the transitional and mutational inevitabilities that framed the interstices generated in the period immediately subsequent to the proclamation of emancipation and precedent to greater realization with the progress of the century. For Marie-Rose, the attached workers carried two distinctive identity markers: first, they received remuneration for the work they did on the plantation; second, they were allowed to occupy a hut and cultivate a garden on the plantation. The hut and garden were continuities of the indulgences provided during slavery. On one hand, the arrangement bound the formerly enslaved, newly freed African workers to the plantation and maintained varying degrees of servitude by fostering dependence on the planter for sustenance. On the other hand, it imposed obligations on the planters, compelling them to provide for these workers, ultimately giving rise to the evolution of contract labour. These contracts were contingent upon the level of negotiation between the planters and the formerly enslaved individuals, theoretically granting them the legal right to choose how to utilize their labour, even if other options were somehow rendered less practical by prevailing circumstances. On the other hand, the attached worker framework checked the right to planters to the labour of the ex-slaves on the scale that existed before. In short, the attached worker system checked both the freedom of the formerly enslaved and the power of the planter, bracing itself on elements of and change and constituting workable palliatives for the various stakeholders: the metropolitan interests, colonial authorities,

Adélaide Marine-Gougeon explores the experiences of the Creolized White population in Martinique, shedding light on a group that has historically received insufficient attention. The long-held fear of the arrival of emancipation, had threatened the sense of security concerning economic and social status they had held as a historically dominant minority. The 1848 revolution in France and the outbreak of a slave rebellion on island that same year, together with memories of the bloody Haitian revolution, increased their apprehension concerning their personal safety and status. For Marine–Gougeon, once emancipation was proclaimed, they came to fear even more intensely that their position in society would be overtaken by professional, wealthy middle-class mulattoes. Accordingly, two key strategies were adopted to protect their safety and professional and economic prospects. One effort was the protection and preservation of their family name and genealogy. However, this was closely tied to the second strategy: the development of what Marine-Gougeon conceptualizes as archipelago-based geographic mobility. In response to the post-emancipation in Martinique, the island's White Creole families turned, not for the first time, to a strategy of migrating and developing homesteads in other French West Indian islands, while retaining, however, close contact with their families on the different islands. Also, because many of them were anti-republican partisans who had intermarriage connections with lower rank noble personnel and officials and functionaries in France, they sought consistently to maintain their genealogical lineage and close contact with family members in the metropolis. Marine-Gougeon explores how these efforts and strategies have left significant records for exploration of the White Creole families in a number of West Indian islands; records which dates back to the seventeenth century and which family generations continued to update as recently as the 1980s.

Poignant criticism emanates from Kathleen Gyssels concerning the literary outpouring of a number of notable French literary luminaries, from whom better might have been expected than of the mere obscurity to which they have relegated the many meaningful parallels and complementary experiences that relate to the historicity of the people of African and Jewish ancestry, with respect to forced migration, displacement and ethnic discrimination. Gyssels bewails the extent to which even some Caribbean novelists, through their silence in their own work, portray a contrived sense of non-connectedness to a status of situational reality, contrary to what deeper and more probing analysis reflect. Included in these connections are the many interethnic relations. For Gyssels, the nonchalant and cavalier treatment has contributed to continuing discrimination and the many political, social and economic problems that have persisted over the centuries. Behind Gyssels' assessment lies the inclination that a change of approach on the part of writers will contribute to a more dignified and empowering global society.

Concluding we can say that all of the eight contributors illuminated the themes in this volume on the legacies of slave trade, slavery and indentured labour in post-slave societies in the Caribbean. Their contributions cover not only a period from slavery and apprenticeship, to indenture but also developments in the twentieth century. They cover developments among people from different ethnic and racial background and territories that were ruled by the French, British and Dutch empires. Geographically the contributions cover not only the Caribbean, but also Indian ocean territories. In that sense the volume contributes to understanding of a part of World History.

Part One

Legacy of Slavery and Indenture

ONE

The Free and Regulated Migration
Legacies from Slave Trade and Slavery to the Indentured System

DAVID LECONTE

Introduction

In the aftermath of the publication of H. Tinker's work, *A New System of Slavery* (1974), many historians attempted to demonstrate that indenture was, to a certain extent, a perpetuation of the slave trade and slavery. However, legacy is not simply the replication of a phenomenon by successors. Legacy also implies adaptation and appropriation. This chapter focuses, not on illustrating whether or to what extent certain continuities were apparent in the new practices, but rather, on how the debates concerning indentured migrations were framed through references to the slave trade and/or slavery. The comparison of three configurations of interdependent actors, in Mauritius, Reunion Island and the French West Indies, will shape this discussion.

In *Melancholy Order*, A. McKeown (2008) analysed state regulations against Asian immigration at the end of the nineteenth century (in the United States of America in 1882 and in Australia in 1901). He depicted the transformation of free migration into a category throughout the long nineteenth century. This category was constructed in opposition to slave trade and indentured migration. Nevertheless, McKeown's analysis underestimated the legacies of the slave trade and slavery to another categorization—indentured migration.

During the first half of the nineteenth century, slavery and slave trade were gradually delegitimized. In this context, the various migration experimented in the British and French empires were closely monitored and sometimes criticized for one reason or another. The advocates of migration and the colonial states found it necessary to categorize a new form of migration—free and regulated migration. To legitimize indenture, this new migration had to be disassociated from slave trade and slavery by state regulations. But there were also other influences regarding the categorization of mobility in a colonial context.

In this paper, I will examine how, between the 1830s and the 1840s, slavery and slave trade influenced the framework of indenture and its regulation by the British and the French states in their respective colonial empires. Through research in the public archives of colonial administrations and scrutinization of imperial newspapers, I will foreground three arenas of controversy surrounding the regulation of indentured migration. First, I will describe how Indian migrations to Mauritius were discussed within the British Empire between their first prohibition in 1838 and the overturning of this prohibition in 1842. Exploring the consensus between migrations' partisans and opponents within the British Empire will be an important element in this scenario. Then, analogous to this, I will analyse the French debates about Indian migrations to the Bourbon Island between their first prohibition in 1839 and the suppression of this prohibition in 1848. Underscoring the tensions between La Reunion (Bourbon) and the French India administrators on one hand, and the difference with the Mauritius situation on the other, will be necessary. Finally, I will also investigate how European migrations towards the French West Indies were discussed between 1845 and 1852. Comprehending the continuities in respect of European migrations, their roles and attendant regulations, before, during and after the abolition of slavery, is significant.

The First Prohibition of Emigration to Mauritius (1838-1842): Imperial Debates and Consensuses

The Denunciation of the Coolie Trade: A New Public Issue in the British Empire

On 6 March 1838, Lord Brougham, a leading abolitionist and anti-slavery advocate, condemned in the House of Lords the recruitment of labourers from British India. These migrations were based on contracts, and the migrants were being lured to colonies where the economy was based on slavery (Geoghegan 1873, 10). He strongly criticized the order in the Council on 12 July 1837, a decision that authorized recruitments to British Guiana. In May 1838, the parliamentary debate led the Lieutenant-Governor of Bengal, Auckland, to suspend the recruitments for the British West Indies. As pointed out by Madhavi Kale (1998, 24-8), this development followed the publication of a number of articles in homeland newspapers. The articles of John Scoble, a member of the British Anti-Slavery Society, seemed to have played a major part regarding the issue. His description of the living conditions of migrants in British Guiana helped in making the matter a public one. However, the debate morphed into a wider imperial issue, because recruitments to Mauritius were also strongly criticized in Great Britain and in British India.

In Calcutta, the first article which condemned the recruitment to British Guiana was published in May 1838, and 5 July 1838 saw yet another article, published in the *Asiatic Journal*, denouncing the 'kidnapping and coercion by recruiters for Mauritius' (Kale 1998, 29-31). Consequently, on 10 July 1838, a petition was addressed to the Government of British India. It directly mentioned the criticism developed and propagated by Lord Brougham. In consequence, the very next day, Bird, the Superintendent of Police in Calcutta, suspended the recruitments for any British colony that was not governed by the East India Company (EIC). These two spheres of verbal and written protestation, one in London and the other in Calcutta, contributed to the prohibition of indentured migrations to the British Empire colonies.

Whereas the first sphere of engagement seemed to mobilize the abolitionist networks in London, the second seemed to have amalgamated a group of concerned public figures in Calcutta. Both groups of actors shared the same goal, dependence on the same means (newspapers, petitions, parliamentary debates) and similar arguments. For Madhavi Kale, their arguments were strongly inspired by anti-slavery strategies:

> Paternalism towards vulnerable and ignorant Indian natives, hostile familiarity (spawned in the struggles over abolitions) with sugar-planters' reputations, and free-trade liberalism were crucial elements of the debate on the export of Indian indentured labourers to British colonies overseas, as contexts but also as weapons (1998, 31).

Moreover, the words used to denounce the coolie trade were borrowed from the British abolitionist slavery debates.

The Metamorphosis of the Abolitionist Arguments

There was cause for concern: 'The system was radically bad and contained in itself the elements of a new species of slavery' (Kale 1998, 3). Accordingly, the petitioners condemned coolie trade in order to defend the well-being of the labourers from India. They criticized the recruiters' practices, although acknowledging the bandied about notion of 'the free agency and civil rights of the emigrants'. For the opponents and the administrators of the East India Company, this free agency meant the 'workers' right to sell their labour at the most favourable terms' (Kale 1998, 29). However, for the petitioners, this right was limited by the ignorance of the Indian labourers. They were described as not being 'capable of understanding the loss they sustain in separation from their families and country, and the nature of the contract into which they enter' (Kale 1998, 31). The consequence of this incapacity was therefore espied as a vulnerability to abuses from the recruiters and planters.

By 23 July 1838, however, a second petition was addressed to the Government of British India. It gathered the names of twelve merchants engaged in business with planters in Mauritius They refuted the analogy between the slave trade and what they called 'the export of Indian workers'. For them, 'the rights of British subjects (in principle, all British subjects) to carry their manual labour to the most productive market' had to be respected (Kale 1998, 31). They advanced an economically comprehensive justification for emigration: It had its benefits—better wages for the Indians who would quit a miserable homeland; cheaper labour costs for Mauritius which would be saved from its labour shortage; cheaper sugar and bigger profits for the Empire, which was in expansion. To top it off, they publicly justified their position as being in defence of the Indians' rights and the promotion of free-trade. Moreover, in that sense, the immigration protagonists ultimately shared ideologically with the abolitionists the same free-trade liberalism and paternalism towards the so-called inferior Indians. But so too did many representatives of the imperial state.

In 1839, Vernon Smith, the Under Secretary of State for War and the Colonies, declared that it was 'unfair to the coolies to prevent their seeking their future where they wish and thereby raising at home the price for labour for their class' (Carter 1995, 22). If administrators were careful about practices similar to the slave trade or slavery, they were also sensitive to the defence of the Indians' rights and the promotion of freetrade. At any rate, the nature of empire itself was altogether a serious obstacle to any determined denunciation of indentured migrations. As with other colonies, the Mauritian economy was export-oriented and organized around the plantation complex. Accordingly, for planters, merchants and administrators within the empire, this was an obvious basis for consensus. Even British abolitionists approved of this colonial project. They wanted to reform rather than to abolish it.

On 12 November 1844, Thomas Clarkson sent to the Prime Minister, Robert Peel, a memoir about migration. He opined that:

> the prosperity of the British West Indian colonies should be a matter of concern to anyone, and even more so to members of the Abolitionist Society than others, given that this prosperity should stimulate the other nations to abolish slavery (quoted in: *Ministère de la Marine et des colonies* 1844, 515).

The defence of the Indians' rights and the promotion of free-trade was by then a rhetoric shared by pro-immigration partisans and their opponents alike on the subject of indentured migrations. And, in a similar manner, they held in common a perception of the post-slavery colonies as export-oriented economies regarding which expansion had to be supported.

The Legitimising of a Free and Regulated Immigration

On 15 January 1842, an Order in Council concluded the imperial debates. The Colonial Office and the Board of Directors of the EIC choose not to prolong the interdiction nor a return to the initial situation. The Order in Council authorized once again the recruitment from British India only to Mauritius. However, the emigration to the post-slavery colony had to be regulated by the state. Each administration in India and Mauritius had to control the practices which could contain abuses: the recruitment in India, the crossing, and the sojourn in Mauritius. Two new agents were instituted to organize these regulations: An Emigration Agent in each authorized port (Calcutta, Madras and Bombay) and a Protector of Immigrants in Mauritius. They were the main actors of the new controlling mechanism which had to demonstrate the necessary practical expressions of respect for emigrants' rights and freedom.

Marina Carter (1995, 22) argues that the new migration after 1842 constituted a compromise between the humanitarian and the capitalist perspective: 'The desirability of large-scale immigration was not simply a principle of economics adhered to by cultivators and colonial theorists. It was also turned into a moral argument.' This compromise authorized state-regulated migrations within the Empire. The new regulations adopted in British India and Mauritius during 1842 and 1843, aimed to put certain practices under greater administrative scrutiny. Recruitments and crossings were specially regulated, because the practices most denounced were with regard to these operations. If suspicions were more often against recruiters and captains, it was because they were given to targeting migrants, who, as has been pointed, were recognizably vulnerable. But Carter (1995, 23-4) has highlighted how state regulations also invaded the personal life of the working population:

The extension of controls over the personal life of the working population was explained in terms of supposedly prevalent vices such as indifference to sanitation, fear of medical care, proneness to violent disputes, jealousy, drunkenness and even absence of marital fidelity or maternal feelings!

Great Britain, towards the end of 1844, found itself still engaged in debates regarding the renewed phase of the recruitment in India of migrants bound for the British West Indies. Consequently, once again the British and Foreign Anti-Slavery Society confronted the British Government. In a text sent to the Prime Minister in November 1844, Thomas Clarkson explained the Society's position on migration. He described what for his Society constituted a legitimate migration: the spontaneity of the emigration and the free choice of the worker and employer, which had to be guaranteed. Still, he opposed this legitimate migration as it was being undertaken, comparing it to the previous migration experiments in the British West Indies in the 1830s. He acknowledged the regulations developed by the colonial administrations in the Indian Ocean, but he pointed to their inefficiency:

> The regulations adopted for the emigrants' protection are violated daily. The emigrants' recruitments are made, as in the past, by indigenous brokers who sent agents in all direction to seduce Indians with false promises and to constrain them to sign engagements which they cannot break (quoted in: *Ministère de la Marine et des colonies* 1844, 515-17).

For the abolitionist movement, the principle of state regulation was fair, but its application, it was felt, needed to be discussed and addressed. In consequence, therefore, the principle of a free and state-regulated migration in the post-slavery colonies was shared by the different actors.

By the end of the 1830s, indentured migration had become an imperial issue of opposition between the British abolitionist networks on the one hand and the planters and their allies on the other, but they shared the same paternalistic view of the Indian labourers, the same free-trade liberalism and the same belief in the benefits of state regulation. In the 1840s, though, compromise arose from the imperial debates, and it was about new recruitments but under state regulation. Indentured migrations in the British Empire were framed by actors mobilizing the abolitionist rhetoric, though essentially through the necessity to distinguish more clearly slave trade and slavery and from other bonded work and migration, and by concomitantly conciliating plantation economies' interests and the new norms for mobility and work.

The First Prohibition of Emigration towards Bourbon (1838-1842): Imperial Debates and Tensions

A Different Configuration of the Opposition to Indentured Migration

In March 1839, the Governor, de Saint-Simon, prohibited emigration from French India. This decision was in response to a request of the British Governor of Madras. The members of the Conseil Général discussed the eventual abolition of this decision on 7 January 1842.[1] The councillor, Couard, supported the prohibition, underlining a distinction between good and bad emigration. Like Thomas Clarkson, Couard defined the legitimate migration as individual and spontaneous, and based on the status of free men possessed by Indians. In the same way, the migration he tried to ensure remained prohibited was associated with deceptive recruitment strategies, 'fallacious promises', speculation and harsh management. The councillor, De Rosières, supported the perception that rural Indians could not be in a rational state when facing a recruiter:

> each of us knows the ignorance, the credulity and the greed of country dwellers leaves them helpless before the suggestions of anyone who offers them a better position in the future.[2]

Consequently, the councillors argued that Indians had to be considered as minors by the gubernatorial administrators. Like the

[1] The Conseil Général was a local council, the members of which were designated by the Governor from within the local elites.

[2] Archives Nationales d'Outre-Mer (ANOM). Fond Ministériel-Série Géographique-Réunion (FM-SG-REU)-406, D3862.1842.01.07. Procès-verbal des délibérations du conseil général des Établissements français dans l'Inde.

British abolitionists, French India's elites justified their peculiar patronage of Indians because of the latter's supposed vulnerability to a more damaging patronage, that of indentureship and the abuse to which the indentureds could be exposed.

In November and December 1838, members of the Bourbon colonial council discussed and amended aspects of a decree that was being prepared by the local administration.[3] The ambition of this text was to control the indentured migrants themselves during their sojourn on and outside the plantation. By the end of December 1838, Frémy, the Director of Interior, the decree's author, disapproved of some of these modifications in the presence of the Governor's Privy Council. In his opinion, they would endanger the decree, because homeland authorities and others were not likely to accept the new dispositions: 'one will not hesitate in the homeland to assimilate indentured labourers to slaves'.[4] This assimilation of the Indian migrants to slaves would harm a project developed since the first migration experiment in 1828: the coexistence of slavery and free labour in the same colony. Guarding against the French protagonist of abolition, the Bourbon administrators desired to oppose a progressive reform of slavery, thanks to free labour at an attempted level. Although the influence of the French abolitionist movement was weak in the French homeland, the Bourbon administrators did not want to give the abolitionists any opportunity to criticize the government's policy on slavery (Jennings 2000, 142-192). That is why Troquet, the colonial inspector of Bourbon, gave a harsh report about these modifications to the Minister:

> 'Will they not, [the opponents to colonies], see in that the revelation of feelings which, [..], will uncover a spirit of domination seeking to extend itself upon the frail class of the colonial society?'[5]

Despite their support for new recruitments from French India

[3] This Colonial Council was similar to French India's, but it lasted longer.

[4] ANOM. FM-SG-REU-406, D3836. 1838.12.24. Procès-verbal du conseil privé de Bourbon.

[5] ANOM. FM-SG-REU-406, D3836. 1839.01.03. Rapport de l'inspecteur colonial au ministre de la Marine et des colonies.

to Bourbon Island, some administrators adopted a cautious stance against any kind of assimilation in homeland between indentured labourers and slaves.

In March 1843, the French India privy council discussed one more time a request from a Bourbon captain to recruit some labourers for the island. The Governor, Du Camper, and his council opted to reject the request, because the Bourbon administration did not draft or forward proper legislation regulating the indentured migrants. And, on this occasion, the Governor offered to contact his British colleagues to explain how the French authorities would regulate these migrations in their territories. He wanted to assure the British authorities and the potential emigrants that:

> [the British emigrants] who would come to embark in Pondichéry to Bourbon Island would find in this colony the same management and the same guarantees that [is] in British countries.[6]

His councillors, however, refused to let the British authorities dictate or seem to dictate the French regulations. However, he reminded them of the fact that the British authorities could effectively obstruct the emigration. Since the restitution of French territories in India in 1816, French administrators had to accept the reality of the superiority of the British domination in the subcontinent. The dispersion of the territories, the limited and constrained armed forces, and the shortage of material and human resources forced them to maintain good relations with their British colleagues (Weber 1988, 943-62). As such, the French India Governor was always mindful of the precarious situation and his duty to navigate between French sovereignty and acknowledgement of the practical superiority of British sovereignty. Contrary to some of his administrators and his colleagues in Bourbon Island, he acknowledged the international nature of the issue.

[6] ANOM. FM-SG-REU-406, D3863. 1843.03.16. Procès-verbal d'une séance du conseil d'administration des EFI.

The Arguments of the Debates about Indentured Migration

When de Saint-Simon prohibited emigration, he did not terminate entirely the mobilities in progress but obstructed new projects developed in Bourbon Island. Consequently, emigration's opponents and partisans did not discuss current migrations except the migration experiments in Bourbon Island between 1828 and 1838. A total of 3,211 Indians had emigrated from Yanaon to Bourbon Island between 1828 and 1831. Their work was framed by contracts established in Yanaon. These migrations had generated many conflicts: those between migrants and planters about wages, others related to harsh management and desertion; some between planters and Bourbon administrators and also between Bourbon and French India administrators about money transfers towards French India; and issues between French India administrators and migrants' families about these money transfers (Weber 1988, 948-53). In French India and Bourbon Island, local elites and administrators shared the same belief regarding the failure of these migrations. If the Bourbon actors distributed almost equally the blame between planters and migrants, French India actors blamed the first at least more than the second. When Du Camper explained to his successor that he did not believe that the emigrants' rights would be respected in Bourbon, he referred to past actions of Bourbon planters.[7] As a result, the different players did not then share the same priorities when they discussed the conditions for new recruitments in French India. The previous migration experiments framed differently the concerns of the imperial debate regarding indentured migrations.

In 1838 one of the most troublesome issues between the planters' representatives and Bourbon administrators was the source of the discipline to be imposed on Indian immigrant and the general condition of its application on the plantation. Articles 14 and 15 of the decree proposed by Frémy, the Director of Interior, served to aggravate the tensions. These articles stipulated that a planter had to employ a minimum of five indentured labourers. One of them would

[7] ANOM. FM-SG-REU-406, D3867. 1844.11.15. Extrait du mémoire du gouverneur Du Camper à son successeur.

supervise the discipline and consequently the sanctions outside of the planter's control. The Director had thus proposed an indigenous and autonomous source of discipline: 'they have a caste chief, who gives more guarantees to the planters, and allows to constrain them to the discipline of their country.[8] Some councillors rejected this autonomy and proposed that the planter could formally demand sanctions or measures from the caste chief. For the Director, submitting the migrants to a kind of Indian discipline would have solved three objectives: prevent any physical sanction, comfort the potential migrants and, just as well, the homeland authorities. However, his proposition failed to convince the planters' representatives, the Governor and the rest of the Privy Council. The planters, though, did not want repetition of the same desertions and resistances experienced since 1828. They were the ones who, it was thought, would have been comforted by this decree, which, at any rate, failed to achieve the required consensus.

For the Bourbon administration, four concerns had to be conciliated: providing to the planters an efficient discipline, preventing any similarity with slavery, limiting the expenses for the local budget, and maintaining public order. During the 1830s, the Bourbon administration paid for the managements of Indians who deserted their employers. In consequence, the administrators encouraged, however best possible, stronger control over migrants so that public order and the local budget would remain safe:

> 'First and foremost, guarantees had to be given to the public order and it was crucial not to involve the interests of the Treasury, while also ensuring the Indian workers respected their commitments'.[9]

Likewise, all key decision-makers agreed on the need to distinguish indentured labourers from slaves. However, they shared

[8] ANOM. FM-SG-REU-406, D3836. 1838.06.22. Procès-verbal du conseil privé de Bourbon.

[9] ANOM. FM-SG-REU-406, D3836. 1838.06.22. Procès-verbal du conseil privé de Bourbon au sujet du projet de décret concernant les gens de travail libres de l'Inde et de l'Asie.

neither the same priorities nor the same interpretation of the possible similarities.

During the period from 1840 to 1848, the French-Indian administration faced opposition to proposed legislation from various actors, stemming from the lack of assurance regarding efficient regulation by their counterparts in Bourbon Island. The General Prosecutor highlighted the repercussions of this negligence and its adverse effects.

> But I will say more, and I think that without a collective and uniform legislation, the precautions adopted in Pondichéry would be without effect in Bourbon Island.[10]

Most of the Bourbon administrators seemed to be interested mainly in other objectives. Until July 1848, tensions and misunderstandings, no less engaging or easy to comprehend in an environment of revolution, characterized their exchanges about indentured migrations. Even the homeland administration did not really understand the disagreements between the two administrations and the two colonial societies:

> How is it possible that the publications of the Navy Department, the many documents proposed to the colonial administrators, did not arouse the attention of the Bourbon privy council so that it would understand that such an operation would not be authorised until the freedom of the labourers introduced in the colony was guaranteed?[11]

For French India administrators, the best solution for the French empire was to adopt a Mauritius-like regulation. Against this background they posited:

> In the manner of what is promulgated by the new British legislation, this demure and weak population, powerless to protect themselves, need protectors where they are recruited and furthermore where they are moved.[12]

[10] This carefulness was expressed by the general prosecutor, Gibelin. ANOM. FM-SG-REU-406, D3863. 1843.03.16. Procès-verbal d'une séance du conseil d'administration des EFI.

[11] ANOM. FM-SG-REU-406, D3847, 1843.06.14, Note interne au ministère de la Marine et des colonies.

[12] If the proposition was expressed by the general prosecutor, Gibelin,

But the Bourbon administration did not accept the necessity for any such regulation, although Roujoux, the then Director of Interior, was sent to investigate the situation in Mauritius in 1843.[13] Moreover, Bazoche, the Bourbon Governor, tolerated the initiatives of many captains who tried to be especially authorized to recruit Indian labourers. In March 1843, the council of the French India Governor discussed and rejected the request of the Mazagran captain. In explanation of his opposition, which he offered to the homeland administration, Du Camper, the Governor, did not hide his irritation with the initiative. This latter was supported by a letter from the Bourbon Governor in which there was no reference to any new regulation in Bourbon Island, and in which he defended the interests of his colony, but excluded any British opposition, leaving it up to the French India administrators to decide on any precautions in the recruitment.[14] It was challenging to identify and address all the political, bureaucratic and ideological factors of the tensions between the administrators.

Since the dispatch of June 1840, the Minister of the Navy and the Colonies informed the new French India Governor that the interests of Bourbon Island were more important than those of French India. But that was not enough to reduce the tensions between the two administrations. The French India administration portrayed its opposition as plainly based on respect for ministerial instructions, whereas the Bourbon administration ignored the need to give guarantees to the British Indians and British India authorities. The Revolution of February 1848 and abolition of slavery transformed the situation in the French Empire. From then on free labour was no longer an exception, but the future labour regime for all inhabit-

---

it was shared by other members of the privy council. ANOM. FM-SG-REU-406, D3863. 1843.03.16. Procès-verbal d'une séance du conseil d'administration des EFI.

13 ANOM. FM-SG-REU-406, D3847. 1843.06.14. Lettre du gouverneur de Bourbon au ministre de la Marine et des colonies au sujet de l'introduction d'indiens engagés et de la mission de Roujoux à Maurice.

14 ANOM. FM-SG-REU-406, D3847. 1843.01.14. Lettre du gouverneur de Bourbon au gouverneur des Etablissments français dans l'Inde afin de soutenir le projet du Mazagran.

ants of the colonies. This new principle was obviously exaggerated, for the abolition of slavery did not dissolve the main *raison d'être* of these territories: to produce tropical goods, especially sugar cane, at minimum cost. Although French abolition did not implement a transitional period of forced labour like the British apprenticeship, some initiatives were similar in Bourbon Island. Sarda Garriga, the new republican head of the colony, quickly formulated and implemented a legal obligation to work. The Order of 24 October 1848 established formally for the newly freed people the obligation to contract a work engagement and to satisfy this by submitting and adhering to a required document, 'otherwise to be judged as vagrants and to be forced into discipline houses'.[15]

The new recruitment initiatives in French India were the products of a frail arrangement. Pressed by the Minister, the administrations of the two colonies quickly produced a new legislation regulating the migrations. But the need to dissociate the migrants from slaves continued and the French authorities pretended that there was no issue when it came to the emigrants' origin. It is noteworthy that primarily they were once again from British territories and the British authorities tolerated these migrations.[16]

In the French Empire the prohibition of 1838 was an answer to a British India request, but there were also choices to be made to limit new conflicts inside and outside the empire. The French imperial debates were framed differently from that of the British. The external opposition, although more presumed than active, was important: but the conflicts between each colony were more tenacious. Antagonistic interpretations about the similarities between the slave trade or slavery and indentured migrations were, after all, not the only factors explaining the tensions and misunderstandings between the administrators.

[15] ANOM. FM-GEN-235, D1665. 1849.12. Note sur les engagements de travail et les ateliers de discipline aux colonies.

[16] Archives départementales de la Guyane (ADG). 1M-57. 1856.03.14. Immigration indienne - Privilèges sollicitées par diverses Compagnies dans nos colonies en France.

The European Migration to the French West Indies or the Civilization of Free Labour (1845-1852)

Two Projects of European Migration to the French

West Bourbon Island's certainly was not the only chamber where locals and homeland administrators discussed how migrations would support the colonial economies and societies. 19 July 1845 saw the passing of legislation with the support of De Mackau, the French Minister of the Navy and the Colonies. It promoted four measures: the introduction of European workers and labourers in the West Indies; development of agricultural establishments supporting free and paid labour in the colonies; the evaluation of proprieties in French Guiana; and the repurchasing of slaves by the colonial administrations.[17] These measures were part of the French project to gradually reform the slavery system. Conceptually, this legislation was similar to that of July 1845, which would have been explained by the Minister's admonition that:

> It is the duty of the law and the Government to soften slavery everywhere, to ensure the negro recovers through education and comfort, from his moral degeneration, so that when his emancipation will come, he can enjoy his freedom, without trouble nor injury to society.[18]

As in Bourbon Island, the homeland administration also thought that free labour and slavery could coexist in the same colony and the first could influence the second. Moreover, they believed that state intervention could be both necessary and efficient, given that 'The idea was to open the way, by assigning legislatively the state assistance to experiments which would prepare the transformation of colonial labour'.[19]

With the law of 19 July 1845, the homeland administration

[17] ANOM. FM-GEN-149, D1252. 1845.08.29. Instructions sur l'exécution de la loi du 19 juillet 1845.

[18] ANOM. FM-GEN-149, D1253. 1845.04.19. Intervention du ministre de la Marine et des colonies à la Chambre des députés.

[19] ANOM. FM-GEN-149, D1252. 1845.08.29. Instructions sur l'exécution de la loi du 19 juillet 1845.

therefore tried to stimulate new migrations towards the French West Indies. These migrations had to be defined, supported and monitored by the state agents in homeland France and in the West Indies. Accordingly, a budget of 120.000 francs was established for the years 1845 and 1846. It was to serve as a subsidy to pay the expenses of emigrants from any homeland port towards Guadeloupe and Martinique. The payment was made, before the crossing, by the agent of the Minister of the Navy and the Colonies. The emigrant had to present an individual contract with a West Indies employer. Moreover, the municipal authority where the contract was signed had to confirm it and inform the minister. Finally, the repatriation to homeland France could be paid for by the state if the migrant and the employer submitted a request.

In March 1848 when the homeland administration decided to assess the policy, the modest results it showed were considered a failure. Between July 1845 and March 1848, less than one hundred labourers participated in this migration experiment.[20] The subsidy was suppressed for the year 1848. The administrators and planters had failed to convince the homeland French people to try agricultural labour in the sugar islands. They had failed to develop successfully a new migratory system towards the West Indies, despite having developed tools to control and support the labour emigration.

After the Revolution of February 1848 and the abolition of slavery, the West Indian planters strongly sought to impress upon the local and homeland administrators the necessity for new immigrants. Despite the modest results of the experiment between 1845 and 1848, some planters and administrators asked for new European migrants. For example, in June 1849, Bois, a merchant of Le Havre, made a related proposal to the Minister which involved the gradual introduction of 50,000 migrants into the West Indies. The expenses were estimated at 10 million francs, and the project was not discussed further.[21] Between 1848 and 1852, supporters of labour migration

[20] ANOM. FM-GEN-148, D1244. 1848.03.29. Note sommaire sur le travail européen aux colonies.

[21] ANOM. FM-GEN-135, D1145. 1849.06.13. Mémoire de Bois au ministre de la Marine et des colonies.

to the post-slavery colonies discussed different ways of organizing migrations and recruiting migrants of diverse origins. Certain objectives of 1845 now seemed obsolescent, but operating on the basis of the transformation from slaves to free men was still a very important and challenging issue for administrators and planters.

The old tools were quickly mobilized by the administrators. In August 1848, the Directory of the colonies within the homeland administration proposed to the Minister the maintenance in 1849 of the budget as had been established by the law of 19 July 1845. The proposition was accepted, and the annual budget was raised to 100.000 francs (against 120.000 francs for seventeen months).[22] Moreover, French Guiana joined the destinations financially supported by the state.[23] Thus while certain previous initiatives were maintained, local administrators in the West Indies became more important. From 1850 onwards, planters had to submit their requests to the local administration. Consequently, the latter were now required to investigate their financial situations and the hygiene of their plantations, and submit a report to the Minister. In Martinique, the local administration decided that 'an allocation of six months rations would be given to each labourer contracting for more than a year'.[24] Some 1,200 European labourers, mainly from homeland France, emigrated to the West Indies between 1848 and 1852. The experiment was soon denounced by planters as a failure, and over a period colonial and homeland administrators came to share this assessment for this policy. In November 1851, in a report to Governor, Blanc, the Director of Interior of Guadeloupe, condemned European migration, requesting, notwithstanding, that homeland administration should not give up its support to immigra-

[22] ANOM. FM-GEN-148, D1244. 1848.08.08. Proposition de maintenir l'allocation qui figure au budget de 1849 pour immigration aux colonies.

[23] ANOM. FM-GEN-148, D1244. 1851.0.11. Immigration européenne dans les colonies en 1850 et 1851.

[24] ANOM. FM-GEN-135, D1145. 1849.09.08. Emploi du fonds de 100 000 francs pour encourager l'immigration européenne.

tion to the post-slavery colonies. Following the British and Bourbon migratory experiments, what needed to be done to procure migrants was that they had to be recruited from different places.[25]

From the Promotion to the Disqualification of European Migrants

For planters, administrators and even migrants, free labour and European migrants were naturally associated before and after the abolition of slavery in 1848. In the contexts of how this issue was envisioned and discussed, there was a slight adjustment after abolition, although some continuities are apparent. In 1845, for homeland administrators, it was considered that the number of European migrants should remain modest, because it was never planned that they were to replace slaves. For them, the European migrants had all the qualities that African slaves lacked. The Minister considered slavery as a moral degeneration for African people.[26] In consequence, before granting them freedom, planters and administrators had to find methods to moralize them. Freedom and free labour would be the results of a moral education. The methodology was not new and seemed justified by many gradual emancipations such as the British apprenticeship. Within the project of 1845, the agent of moral learning was the European migrant. The coexistence of African slaves and European migrants in the same colony and same workplace was to stimulate the African slaves. For administrators, imitation would be the key to a civilizing process on the plantation, and the medium through which current tensions between planters and slaves could be reduced. Furthermore, it was understood that 'it would be in these plantations that the Government, by bringing closer the coloured

[25] ANOM. 2400-COL-78/2. 1851.10.07. Rapport du directeur de l'Intérieur de la Guadeloupe au gouverneur.

[26] ANOM. FM-GEN-149, D1253. 1845.04.19. Intervention du ministre de la Marine et des colonies à la Chambre des députés.

class and the white class, could efficiently continue eliminating the prejudices which have separated them for so long'.[27]

European migrants were envisioned as instruments to safeguard colonial rule against the troubles arising from future emancipation efforts. When the abolition of slavery came about, these migrants were expected to assist plantation owners in mitigating the perceived difficulties stemming from the newly emancipated population, they would once again help planters limit the troubles supposedly caused by the emancipated. This was the plan of Delluy, for example, a planter of Case-Navire in Martinique, when he proposed to the minister, in April 1848, to introduce around one hundred European labourers. In his opinion, this migration would be beneficial for all, because, he averred, 'these European labourers will give good example to Negroes by their intelligent working manners, their stable and moral behaviour, and, by this doing, will help strongly to their civilising'.[28] However, if local and homeland administrators supported this objective, few were the migrants to come or to play the planned role.

For administrators, the other main issue about European migration was their acclimatising to the colonies. Promoting the 'white labourer' in the sugar colonies was a clear goal of the law of 19 July 1845, and a fundamental justification of state intervention:

> [the administrative intervention] will help advanced planters to oppose with success against the prejudice which lead to consider the employment of Whites in colonial rural labour, as absolutely incompatible with the physical obstacles resulting from the climate and the speciality of the plantations.[29]

To be sure, the history of the delegitimization of the European labourer in the tropical colonies had been ancient and was associated with the legitimization of the African labourer. The status quo about slavery was becoming at least increasingly less easily arguable for the

[27] ANOM. FM-GEN-149, D1253. 1845.06.10. Exposé des motifs de la loi du 19 juillet 1845.

[28] ANOM. FM-GEN-135, D1145. 1848.04.24. Lettre du planteur Delluy (Martinique) au ministre de la Marine et des colonies.

[29] ANOM. FM-GEN-149, D1252. 1845.08.29. Instructions sur l'exécution de la loi du 19 juillet 1845.

French government and its administrators. As a result, promoting once again the 'white labourer' became part of a larger discussion of the colonial categories used by planters, slaves, administrators and homeland labourers. Still, as might have been expected, the process was slow, because, ultimately, the discussions were aimed primarily at preserving the colonial rule and the organization of the colonial societies. In view of this, and towards this end, after slavery's abolition, planters became more engaging towards administrators, and even asked for stronger and more supportive regulations where European were concerned:

> Reaching the colonies, the indentured should not be abandoned by the Government. General rules about hygiene should be defined, as well as food supply and working hours; newly arrived migrants should not be left to their own devices, preys to the fervour of their boldness and ego. They must not work too much; and need to avoid the hours when the sun is the most burning.[30]

Planters and local administrators supported regulations protecting European migrants against the so-called climatic difficulties. But, gradually, however, the legitimization of the 'white labourer' failed again when planters lost trust in European migrants. For planters, the acclimatizing challenge regarding climatic conditions per se was the main explanation of this new failure. They did not highlight the conflicts with the migrants who asked for higher wages or did not act according to the role planned for them.[31]

The Principle of a Regulated Migration

A notable specificity of the European migration to the French West Indies was the financial support of the homeland authorities. This assistance was another signifier of the greater and strategic appli-

[30] ANOM. FM-GEN-148, D1244. 1849.11.05. Journal *L'Avenir* (Guadeloupe).

[31] These factors were highlighted by the directeur de l'Intérieur in Guadeloupe, but he never criticized the planters. ANOM. 2400-COL-78/2. 1851.10.07. Rapport du directeur de l'Intérieur de la Guadeloupe au gouverneur.

cation and implication of the homeland authorities' power and influence. Also noteworthy is that such an intervention was not seen in Bourbon Island or French India during the same period. The failure of the experiment between 1845 and 1847 led homeland administrators to suppress the related budgetary allocation for 1848.[32] But after the abolition of slavery, however, local and homeland administrators approved allocations and adoptions of resources to experiment with new migration initiatives. The adjustments and adaptations were requested by local planters, indebted or not, who called for more help from administrators. Finally, the state's financial support was ratified by the decrees of 13 February and 27 March 1852. Gradually, the local administrators of the post-slavery colonies came to be responsible for management of the financial support.[33] In consequence, the assistance justified also more bureaucratic control on planters and within local administration.

If state-regulated migration was justified in Mauritius and Bourbon Island because of the abuses similar to slavery or slave trade, protecting the European migrants against the climate was yet another way to justify it. If some dispositions were developed between 1845 and 1848 to look after the health and working conditions of migrants, the most important efforts were actually made after the abolition of slavery. On 31 August 1849, the Privy Council of Martinique discussed the use of the subsidy and how to organize the European immigration. Bourgoin, Director of Interior, highlighted the need to control in homeland ports not only the physical, moral and fit for work qualities of emigrants, but also the ability of the contract to preserve and protect them against illnesses or accidents.[34] Furthermore, he requested within the colony, the assistance of local medical state agents. He did not want a repetition of the failure of

[32] ANOM. FM-GEN-148, D1244. 1848.08.08. Proposition de maintenir l'allocation qui figure au budget de 1849 pour immigration aux colonies.

[33] ANOM. FM-GEN-141, D1202. 1855.06.15. Circulaire sur la constitution d'un compte spécial pour la concentration des recettes et des dépenses de l'immigration.

[34] ANOM. FM-GEN-135, D1145. 1849.08.31. Procès-verbal du conseil privé de la Martinique.

the recent Madeiran migration experiment, which had inspired the following comment:

> For having neglected such measures towards Madeiras [...], we observe today that most of these unfortunate workers, abandoned by the planters because of their debility and their bad health, fall in the care of the colony, which will be happier to get rid of them paying the cost of their repatriation.[35]

The Madeiran migration was one of the experiments embarked on previously in the British West Indies. It should be noted, however, that planters and administrators did not categorize migrants from homeland France and Madeira islands in the same way. The latter were looked upon as racially more acclimatized to the tropical climate than the first. This notwithstanding, prejudice regarding Madeiran migrants did not preserve them from the harsh management on the plantation. Although the death and illness of these migrants justified more attention from administrators, the said phenomena provoked less trust and reliance of the planters regarding them. Moreover, European and Madeiran migrants in the French West Indies were not coerced to the same extent via particular regulations as was the case regarding Indians in Bourbon Island and Mauritius.

For the partisans, European migrants were to participate in the reforming of slavery, its consequences, and the ex-slaves. But Europeans were not discussed in the same context as Indian migrations. The so-called free migration of European was supported by its own framework of state regulations. And in all respects, the intervention of the homeland administration was more important than that of administrators in the Indian Ocean. Although the debates about European migrations were not directly determined by parallels with slavery or the slave trade; they contributed to the shaping of the debates about migrations to the sugar colonies after slavery's abolition. Perceptions, arguments and mechanisms mobilized in these debates survived, and but they were adapted when administrators and planters looked for new immigrants.

[35] ANOM. FM-GEN-135, D1145. Ibid.

Conclusion

In the situations analysed above, slavery and the slave trade influenced, directly or indirectly, the debates about migrations under contract. The recruitments in British and French India were described by those opposed to it as similar to the purchasing of slaves. Deception was the tool of local recruiters and ignorance of the Indians were among the explanations for emigration and its negatives. For its opponents, the harsh management on board the vessels and the deaths during the crossing constituted evidenced that the so-called coolie trade was similar to the slave trade. The denunciation of the harsh crossing conditions played a role in redefinining of the mobility norms on ships. The description of the working and living conditions in Mauritius and Bourbon Island also yielded evidence to draw some parallels to the living and working conditions of slaves. By emphasizing such aspects, the opponents contributed to a concentrated focus on the migrations, and the debates surrounding the various issues and, just as well, state interventions regarding them. But, in each area and in each Empire, opponents shared with the proponents of migration a paternalistic view of the labourers, a free-trade liberalism and a belief in the potential and benefits of state-regulation. Given the necessity for plantation labour, pro-immigration partisans found that they could support the Indians' right to seek better wages and living conditions, and even asked for and encouraged regulations to strongly distinguish between indentured migrations and slave trade. They were also able ultimately to acquire the support of homeland and local administrators who, at any rate, were committed to defending the export-oriented economies of their respective Empire.

But the debates about indentured migrations, and especially about state-regulations, were not framed only on the basis of Western or other parallels drawn with the slave trade or slavery. Often overlooked, is the configurations of the relations between the decisive players involved: Each situation was also characterized and influenced by the particular configuration of administrators' relations. Within the British Empire, with emancipation having been finally proclaimed in 1838, it was still mostly the abolitionist movement that was influencing the decisions of the British government. Meanwhile, French situations were influenced also by the homeland's project to gradually reform slavery system through the introduction of so-called free labourers. Until 1848, slavery co-existed with indentured labour, however interrupted this last might have been, and the difference between them was maintained, even though it meant striving to do so, India immigration having been initiated since 1828. The negotiations between British India and Mauritian administrators were quicker and easier than that between French India and Bourbon administrators, as the last arena was shaped by its peculiar context. In the French colonies of the Indian Ocean, it was the fear of the British India administrators and more directly the cautiousness of French India administrators, but that was rooted more in geopolitical practicality than philanthropy. In the French West Indies, planters were among those who initially eagerly solicited European migration, which failed unmistakably, despite the special supportive mechanism implemented for its realization. The intervention of the French homeland administration was more direct in the European migrations than in the Indian. French authorities always saw distinctions between European and Indian immigrations, and between these two and slave labour. The coterminous existence of all three was seemingly more amenable to the French than the British.

Various other dynamics would no doubt have helped to frame the debates on Mauritius, on Bourbon as well as on the West Indian islands. But the multiple state-interventions in the post-slavery colonies also point to adaptations and adjustments of colonial rule. In all of this, Indian immigration was evolving its own trajectory and character. As with institutions and practices involved, arguments and perceptions mobilized in these debates on Indian indentures survived, but were adapted when administrators and planters looked for new migrants, when opponents contested against these migrations, and when migrants tried to accommodate, resisted or could not function in accordance with the metropolitan design or what was expected to be delivered in respect of plantation interest. Moreover, in each empire, the debates about indentured migrations played an important part in the framing of successive debates and the organization of post-slavery societies. Much more than just the solicitation of parallels or comparison with the slavery, Indian indentureship came to map its own influence on the intricacies and complexities of colonial character and development.

Bibliography

Books and articles

Carter, Marina. 1995. *Servants, Sirdars and Settlers: Indians in Mauritius, 1834-1874*. Delhi: Oxford University Press.

Geoghegan, J. 1873. *Note on Emigration from India*. Calcutta: Office of Superintendent of Government Printing.

Jennings, Lawrence C. 2000. *French Anti-Slavery: The Movement for the Abolition of Slavery in France, 1802-1848*. Cambridge (UK) New York: Cambridge University Press.

Kale, Madhavi. 1998. *Fragments of Empire: Capital, Slavery, and Indian Indentured Labor Migration in the British Caribbean*. Philadelphia: University of Pennsylvania Press.

McKeown, Adam. 2008. *Melancholy Order: Asian Migration and the Globalization of Borders*. New York: Columbia University Press.

Ministère de la Marine et des colonies. 1844. 'Enrôlement de Coulis pour les Indes occidentales', *Revue Coloniale, t.IV*. Paris: Imprimerie royale.

Tinker, Hugh. 1974. *A New System of Slavery: The Export of Indian Labour Overseas, 1830-1920*. New York: Oxford University Press.

Weber, Jacques. 1988. *Les Etablissements français en Inde au XIXème siècle, 1816-1914*. Paris: Librairie de l'Inde Editeur.

Archives

Archives départementales de la Guyane (ADG). 1M-57. 1856.03.14. Immigration indienne - Privilèges sollicitées par diverses Compagnies dans nos colonies en France.

Archives Nationales d'Outre-Mer (ANOM). 2400-COL-78/2. 1851.10.07. Rapport du directeur de l'Intérieur de la Guadeloupe au gouverneur.

ANOM. Fond Ministériel-Généralité-135 (FM-GEN), D1145. 1848.04.24. Lettre du planteur Delluy (Martinique) au ministre de la Marine et des colonies.

ANOM. FM-GEN-135, D1145. 1849.06.13. Mémoire de Bois au ministre de la Marine et des colonies.

ANOM. FM-GEN-135, D1145. 1849.08.31. Procès-verbal du conseil privé de la Martinique.

ANOM. FM-GEN-135, D1145. 1849.09.08. Emploi du fonds de 100 000 francs pour encourager l'immigration européenne.

ANOM. FM-GEN-141, D1202. 1855.06.15. Circulaire sur la constitution d'un compte spécial pour la concentration des recettes et des dépenses de l'immigration.

ANOM. FM-GEN-148, D1244. 1848.03.29. Note sommaire sur le travail européen aux colonies.

ANOM. FM-GEN-148, D1244. 1848.08.08. Proposition de maintenir l'allocation qui figure au budget de 1849 pour immigration aux colonies.

ANOM. FM-GEN-148, D1244. 1849.11.05. Journal *L'Avenir* (Guadeloupe).

ANOM. FM-GEN-148, D1244. 1851.0.11. Immigration européenne dans les colonies en 1850 et 1851.

ANOM. FM-GEN-149, D1252. 1845.08.29. Instructions sur l'exécution de la loi du 19 juillet 1845.

ANOM. FM-GEN-149, D1253. 1845.04.19. Intervention du ministre de la Marine et des colonies à la Chambre des députés.

ANOM. FM-GEN-149, D1253. 1845.06.10. Exposé des motifs de la loi du 19 juillet 1845.

ANOM. FM-GEN-235, D1665. 1849.12. Note sur les engagements de travail et les ateliers de discipline aux colonies.

ANOM. FM-Série Géographique-Réunion-406 (SG-REU), D3863. 1843.03.16. Procès-verbal d'une séance du conseil d'administration des EFI.

ANOM. FM-SG-REU-406, D3836. 1838.06.22. Procès-verbal du conseil privé de Bourbon.

ANOM. FM-SG-REU-406, D3836. 1839.01.03. Rapport de l'inspecteur colonial au ministre de la Marine et des colonies.

ANOM. FM-SG-REU-406, D3836. 1839.01.17. Délibérations du conseil colonial de Bourbon publiées dans le journal local, *Le Conservateur*.

ANOM. FM-SG-REU-406, D3836. 1838.12.24. Procès-verbal du conseil privé de Bourbon.

ANOM. FM-SG-REU-406, D3847. 1843.01.14. Lettre du gouverneur de Bourbon au gouverneur des Etablissments français dans l'Inde afin de soutenir le projet du Mazagran.

ANOM. FM-SG-REU-406, D3847. 1843.06.14. Note interne au ministère de la Marine et des colonies.

ANOM. FM-SG-REU-406, D3847. 1843.06.14. Lettre du gouverneur de Bourbon au ministre de la Marine et des colonies au sujet de l'introduction d'indiens engagés et de la mission de Roujoux à Maurice.

ANOM. FM-SG-REU-406, D3862. 1842-01-07. Procès-verbal des délibérations du conseil général des Établissements français dans l'Inde.

ANOM. FM-SG-REU-406, D3867. 1844.11.15. Extrait du mémoire du gouverneur Du Camper à son successeur.

TWO

British Guiana and Dutch Guiana in the Post-Emancipation Period, 1833-1873

Historiographical Notes on Emancipation and Apprenticeship

ERIC R. JAGDEW

Introduction

In 2014, I wrote and presented a paper about the impact of revolutions related to wars and the Congress of Vienna on the Dutch colonies in Guiana, South America between 1799 and 1832. The conclusion of that paper was that while the revolutionary situation in Europe and America resulted in the British annexation and division of the Dutch colonies in Guiana, its liberalist ideas had little impact on British Guiana and Suriname.[1]

In Caribbean history, the period between 1833 and 1873 was

[1] The International Conference on the Congress of Vienna and its Global Dimension: 200 Years of History and Historiography, organized at the University of Vienna, in Austria, 18-22 September 2014. The organizers of this conference were: the Association of Latin American and Caribbean Historians (ADHILAC), the Faculty of Historical and Cultural Studies of the University of Vienna and the Society for the Study of Continental America and the Caribbean (FGKK).

shaped by the abolition of slavery by the British in 1834, the French in 1848 and last by the Dutch in 1863. With the ending of the slavery system, the British authorities introduced an Apprenticeship System in their colonies in the West Indies. This system was instituted to regulate the transition of the former enslaved workers to free wage labourers within the plantation societies. Antigua was excluded from this experience, but in British Guiana, as elsewhere in the Anglo-Caribbean, the Apprenticeship period lasted until 1838. In Guyanese history, Apprenticeship is described as a New System of Slavery, that was certain to collapse because both the planters and the newly freed men were against it. The Dutch authorities were quite late with the abolition of slavery, but in their colonies they too experimented with a similar post-Emancipation system, called 'Staatstoezicht', translated as 'State Supervision', between 1863 and 1873. What is interesting, is the extent to which Dutch Emancipation and State Supervision was influenced by the British experience in the West Indies, but especially in British Guiana, after 1834.

In this article, the primary focus is on how the British abolition of slavery and the post-Emancipation developments in British Guiana after 1833 influenced the Dutch Emancipation and State Supervision between 1834 and 1873. The year 1833 is selected as the starting point of this research, because the British emancipation marked, directly or indirectly, the beginning of a new era for the plantation economy all over the Caribbean. Likewise, the developments in the Caribbean, Guyana and Suriname are discussed up to 1873, when the Dutch State Supervision period came to an end.

The British Abolition of Slavery

Two conflicting scientific schools contributed intensively to the historiography on British Abolition of the Slave Trade and the Abolition of Slavery in the twentieth century. The first school is represented by what Claudius Fergus (2013: ix-x) termed 'The Clarkson (1836)-Klingsberg (1926)-Coupland (1933) combination'. The representatives of this school argued that humanitarianism or the 'moral ideology' was not only the basis, but also the driving force of a growing anti-slavery movement. The second, and an opposing school, is that which we will refer to as the Ragatz (1928)-James (1938)-Williams (1944) triad, to which Eric E. Williams also contributed within the Third World Philosophy paradigm. The scholars within this school explained Abolition of the Slave Trade and Slavery in terms of capitalist interests, decline of the plantation economy, and the growing industrialization in England.

In the post-war period, with the publication of the second and third editions of his book, the 'decline theory' of Williams became, as Gad Heuman (2006: 98-9) described it, part of a larger discussion. Roger T. Anstey concluded in 1975 after his own study that there was no reduction in the average profitability of the trade in enslaved Africans in order to necessitate an abolition in 1808. David B. Davis reasoned in 1975 that the British abolition of the slave trade was possible, because the anti-slavery humanist ideology in a pre-industrial era was in harmony with the interests of the new emerging class. Following Anstey, Seymour Drescher posited in 1977 that the West Indian plantation economy, contrary to what Williams claimed, was not suffering from economic decline before and after the abolition of the slave trade. David Eltis stated in 1987 plainly, like Drescher, that the Atlantic slave trade was abolished during a period in which the West Indian plantations were flourishing and in a great need of more enslaved workers.[2]

In May 1984, followers and defenders of the Williams' thesis, from Europe, North America and the Caribbean, came together at a conference on 'Caribbean Slavery and British Capitalism' in Italy. In the introduction of the subsequently published book (1987, 10-13) the editors, Barbara L. Solow and Stanley L. Engerman, summarized the essays: 'Williams story of plantation profits [...] (and) the Industrial Revolution does not hold up'; and 'On the decline issue the conference came to no clear-cut consensus'. Some years later, the, debate, now additionally leveraged as 'Capitalism and Anti-Slavery' debate, now between Thomas L. Haskell ('market consciousness') and David B. Davis and John Ashworth ('class interest'), was brought

[2] For a good summary of books and articles regarding to this historical topic, see the book chapter of Gad Heuman in Juanita de Barros, Audra Diptee and David V. Trotman (2006).

together in another publication, edited by Thomas Bender (1992). In between both positions, Robin Blackburn (1988), arguing from a Marxist perspective, provided more insight in the accumulative development of the anti-slavery movement, by connecting the class struggle in Europe to the revolutionary activities in the colonies.

At the end of the twentieth century, Franklin W. Knight concluded in the *General History of the Caribbean, Volume III* (1997, 339-40) that: 'The schools of thoughts are sharply divided, with each producing overwhelming evidence to support its position'. At the same time, however, he made it clear that the conventional humanitarian story as explanatory ground for the Abolition of the Slave Trade and Slavery was not holding. In his view, there would have been an economic powerplay, because eventually the British parliament approved several millions for the compensation of the West Indian planters. Not long after this publication, Selwyn H. H. Carrington (2002) illustrated once more, that the prosperity of the West Indian plantations was linked to trade relations with the North-American colonies. With extensive data, he showed that, as such, the American Revolution of 1776 had a damaging effect and led to a recession of the sugar industry up to the 1790s.

Apprenticeship in the British Caribbean

Almost a century after the British abolition of slavery, William L. Burn (1937) published a study on the policymaking, *Emancipation and Apprenticeship in the British West Indies,* with special focus on Jamaica. He argued that Apprenticeship as a transitional experiment from slave exploitation to open labour was understandable, but not well thought out, and too much a system created by the planters' lobby. In his view, the success of this system was also too dependent on the Special Magistrates, an important institution that was not well organized to oversee the important work of policy implementation and enforcement. The real problem was essentially that while the policies were created based on different interests in London, England, the local governments in the West Indies colonies determined to some extent the application of the Abolition Act of 28 August 1833.

Eric Foner (1983, 16-18) in his book on the American Emancipation, reminded us that the British authorities were 'Caught between an antislavery public, a beleaguered planter class, a commitment to the idea of "free" or voluntary labor, and their own fears about the reliability of black labor after emancipation, [...]'. Comparatively, he concluded that in the Emancipation period after 1833, in every West Indian colony there was animosity, controversy and rivalry among the parties involved about 'labor control or [...] class formation' (p. 10). He reasoned further, that the labour relations in the several colonies during Apprenticeship were so complicated that not everything could be processed within a generalizing description. Still, he was able to see some similarities in the plantation colonies, like passive and active resistance by the apprentices, but also beatings, cheatings and detentions by the planters and colonial officials.

James Latimer (1964, 52-3) stressed that both the planters and the apprentices used the system 'to defeat, rather than advance the Imperial Government's idea of giving the slaves more useful spiritual, and educational preparation for final emancipation'. In reality, the problems began immediately after the promulgation of the Abolition Act on 28 August 1833.[3] In general, the Act meant that all enslaved persons had to be registered and categorized into three groups, namely 'praedial attached, praedial unattached, and non-praedial'. The non-praedial and praedial labourers were obliged to stay in Apprenticeship until 1 August 1838 or 1840 respectively. Other details of this law were that the apprentices now had to work 45 hours per week, not only for food and clothes but also some payment, mostly or especially for overtime. To compensate, the apprentices were also allowed to redeem themselves through self-purchase, stay together in one place as a family unit, and farm provision grounds.

Claude Levy (1980), in his book on Barbados between 1833

[3] Bill 3 & 4 William IV, cap 73: 28th August 1833: An Act for the Abolition of Slavery throughout the British Colonies; for promoting the Industry of the manumitted Slaves; and for compensating the Persons hitherto entitled to the Services of such Slaves. *Source:* https://pdavis.nl/Legis07.htm

and 1876, presented figures regarding Apprenticeship in the British West Indies. Based on these figures, the British government paid nearly £20 million in compensation for the abolition of a total of 667,925 African-descended enslaved individuals in 17 British colonies throughout the Caribbean. The largest sum was paid to the slave owners in Jamaica (£6,149,955 for 311,070 persons), followed by British Guiana (£4,295,989 for 82,824 persons), and Barbados (£1,719,980 for 83,150 persons). According to Levy, the average compensation per enslaved person was not the same in each colony: in Barbados, the cost (some £20.69) was still higher than that in nine other colonies. Barbados in 1834 had the largest number of apprentices, (501) per square mile, and, besides British Guiana, was the only colony with a positive increase in sugar production between 1835 and 1838, compared to 1831-4.

Apprenticeship in British Guiana

Ten years before the British abolition of slavery, British Guiana was shaken by a massive rebellion in Demerara-Essequibo. It involved almost 12,000 of the estimated 74,978 enslaved labourers. After analysing the Demerara Rebellion of 1823, Winston McGowan (1998, 107, 135-6) concluded that this rebellion was special in that it led to increased attention in Britain to the anti-slavery movement. According to him, although their rebellion was repulsed, the rebels still achieved their ultimate goal of liberation in 1834, or, more fundamentally, 1838. From the figures of Levy (1980), we know that the planters or slave owners in British Guiana received a total compensation of £4,295,989 for 82,824 persons in slavery, on average the highest per enslaved (£51.87) after British Honduras (£53.34). Based on this information British Guiana, from among all seventeen British colonies in the West Indies at that time, was, after British Honduras (0.2), one of the least densely populated colonies with 0.9 person per square mile.

What were other differences in Guyanese Apprenticeship? William A. Green (1969, 44-6) determined that the situation in this British colony on the mainland of South America was quite different, because of the high fertility of the land, sufficient rainfall, and thus a high level of production of sugar. As mentioned by Levy (1980), British Guiana (after Barbados) was the only British colony in the West that realized a positive volume change in sugar production between 1835 and 1838, compared to the period 1831 to 1834. The high sugar production was also a result of the introduction of 'improved machinery', but especially, as Green espoused, from the strict ruling of the military officer, Sir James Carmichael Smyth. He described Smyth as 'an unflinching champion of the rights and entitlement of the emancipated population [...]' (p. 48), who acted as such because he got all the support required from his superiors in England. As an appointee of the British monarch, William IV, Smyth had to adjust the existing judicial system, in order to also serve the new class of free black workers. Given this, what Smyth did first was to secure the passing of legislation for the establishment and implementation of a local judiciary to adjudicate in matters regarding apprentices. It consisted of almost 82 Local Justices. Smyth was very rigid in his approach to these judges, selected from the local white population, as he also was to the 15 Stipendiary Magistrates, who, sent from Britain, were also to be held accountable for their own actions.

Thomas N. Tyson, David Oldroyd and Richard K. Fleischman (2005, 223-5) noted that the Apprenticeship System was '[...] a social system which was built on a hierarchy of accountability' of workers, planters, justices and magistrates, and the Colonial Office. This notwithstanding, in British Guiana the planter class was still able to secure their control over the labour of the apprentices, by developing 'Scales of Task-work'. These labour standards, as required by Smyth, were developed by a committee of planters and were incorporated in contractual arrangements that emerged. The planters in British Guiana were able to enforce further their ownership rights within the system, by implementing weekly examinations by practitioners, and a 5-days week of 9 hours per day. Sunday was a mandatory rest day and there were to be regular assessments of the goings-on by the magistrates. But, as Tyson et al. point out, in the final analysis the planters were able to get a grip on the possibility of redemption by the apprentices, by participating in the so-called 'appraisement tribunals' in which they had a majority of two to one judge. The valuation of the apprentices was especially necessary, as planters still had the option to sell or lease out apprentices, though, admittedly, not now in public (pp. 210-18). Smyth also regulated the penal system by transferring the authority to determine and administer punishment from the planters and overseers to the magistrates. In the end, though, flogging, the treadmill, hard labour, and other forms of penalties were still applied. Between August 1834 and May 1836, out of 72,000 apprentices, 16,230 (22.5 per cent) were punished, 2,666 by flogging, with a total of 53,360 lashes (p. 219).

British Guiana after Apprenticeship

In 1838, at the end of Apprenticeship, the apprentices in the several British West Indian colonies left the plantations in greater or lesser extent to establish themselves as independent small farmers or wage workers. Barbara P. Josiah (1997, 109-10) stated that in British Guiana the foundation for this post-emancipation movement of free labourer's was laid during the Slavery and Apprenticeship period itself. After all, starting from the 'Amelioration Act of 1825', the enslaved persons were allowed to redeem themselves, to own property and to get married. At the same time, ill treatment and poor provisions, also forced them to grow supplementary food and to keep poultry and livestock. In British Guiana as elsewhere, the enslaved individuals were also engaged in selling activities and thus able to accumulate some money for themselves. Based on the African tradition they were able to organize a cooperative saving method known as 'esusu' or 'boxhand', by which the partners involved borrowed money in rotation.

William A. Green (1976), in *British Slave Emancipation: The Sugar Colonies and the Great Experiment 1830-1865,* emphasized that British Guiana, as indeed Jamaica and Trinidad, had a relatively large peasantry class, but a shortage of estate workers because of a low labourer to land ratio. Even before Green, Rawle Farley (1954, 91-2) affirmed that '[...] peasant freehold and village development were possible only because of the existence of one basic condition and that was the abundance of land over and above what could be developed by the existing population. The end of Apprenticeship thus marked the emergence of a class of independent small farmers in village settlements in the coastal area of British Guiana. What should not be overlooked is that after 1838 'squatting' on uncultivated lands along the banks of the main rivers in the hinterlands by ex-slaves who had no or little savings, was also a normal phenomenon. As such, the number of 'freehold properties' in Demerara, Essequibo and Berbice jumped from 2,943; 379 and 1,187 respectively in 1842 to 5,672; 2,254 and 3,226 respectively in 1852, and amounted to a total value of at least £1 million (pp. 101-2). It is beyond dispute that the above-mentioned 'money club' made it possible for the newly freedmen to buy land individually and collectively after Apprenticeship. That the ex-slaves were able to acquire that much land was also, however, a result of the economic recession of the 1840s and the subsequent misery it spelt for many plantation owners in the colony.

O. Nigel Bolland (1981, 592-3) believed that 'the availability to land' or 'population density' would not have been the most important factor underlying the emergence of the new peasantry class. He was convinced, after studying developments in several British West Indian colonies after 1838, that this explanation was not workable. He pleaded for a dialectic approach and comparative study, in which land control and labor control should be considered as equally important but mutually influencing factors (pp. 612-13). Regarding British Guiana, he was able to determine that in this colony, within a decade after Apprenticeship, only a third of the ex-enslaved population was active as wage workers. That in 1844 30 per cent were still living and working on the plantations probably had to do with the fact that in British Guiana, as in Jamaica, but unlike Barbados, housing and gardening on the plantations were still free and the wages were comparatively high (pp. 599-600). Thus, in British Guiana the former enslaved workers were pulled away from the plantations, because of the desire to live completely free as a small farmer on their own plot of land. Brian L. Moore (1987) analysed British Guiana after 1838 and saw the dreams of the Creole population for economic independence shattered in the 1850s because of the negative reinforcement generated through government policies. What successive governments did was to frustrate the further acquisition of land by groups and isolate these peasants in the plantation belt. As a result, the Creole petit agriculture collapsed within decades.

Suriname in the 1830s and 1840s

In 1979, the Surinamese historian Jozef P. Siwpersad published a study entitled *De Nederlandse regering en de afschaffing van de Surinaamse slavernij (1833-1863).* From this revealing volume (pp. 1-41), it becomes clear that developments in Great Britain kept the tempers in Suriname on edge and as such two emancipation proposals were developed in 1833. The retired civil servant W.H. Lans, believed that with the new situation in British Guiana the abolition of slavery in Suriname was unavoidable. He, therefore, advised the colonial government to ransom the enslaved population, and to use them as vassals in some new less labour-intensive production sectors. The old consul, Th. J. Travers, was afraid that the enslaved persons would emancipate themselves. Therefore, he proposed the implementation of palliative measures such as strengthening the military power, improving the slavery system, and the establishment of an amortization fund. Initially, the Minister of Colonies, Johannes van der Bosch (1834-9), decided to adopt a wait-and-see policy, especially because he was reluctant to use Dutch money for this exercise. It is partly because of this that the Dutch authorities declined a proposal by the economist L. van Rossum to ransom the enslaved population with a bond loan to the planters.

In a later publication (2009, 125-7), *Behavioral Patterns in a Slave Society (Suriname, 19th Century),* Siwpersad emphasized again that despite the threat in British Guiana, it remained rather peaceful in Dutch Guiana, at least in the 1830s and 1840s. The colonial authorities in Suriname were confronted with only a few conspiracies, primarily in 1836 (this was led by Colin), 1841 and 1850, to flee the colony (Hira 1984, 165-8).[4] According to Siwpersad (1979, 23-4),

[4] Meanwhile, quiet strategically the colonial government in Paramaribo renewed the 18th Century peace treaties with the pacified Maroon groups in the interior of Suriname in 1835, 1837 and 1838. According to Jagdew

it was remarkable that even so, especially between 1840 and 1844, there were more runaway slaves, a total of 1299, from the so-called old part of the colony to the interior. He came across no effective solution to the problem, and blamed the fleeing of the enslaved persons, especially those in the westerly divisions of Suriname, on the policy and attitude of the authorities, planters and even newspapers journalists in British Guiana. As such, he concluded (pp. 27-32) that 'the indifferent attitude from the 1830s', together with the news of developments in British Guiana, including those after 1838, was not helpful to the cause of abolition.

Siwpersad (1979, 155-88) also explored the impact of the French Abolition of Slavery in the Dutch colonies in the West Indies. He determined that while there were serious disturbances in some territories of the Dutch Antilles, for example, St. Martin and St. Eustatius, it remained more or less peaceful in Suriname in 1848. Nevertheless, one effect of the 'French danger' was that the Ministry of Colonies instructed the plantation owners, by a circular of 15 May, 1848, to follow an 'active fate improvement policy' (pp. 157-8) towards the enslaved population in Suriname. As a result, improvements, which should have been implemented since 1828, were made to the penal system, requirements for housing, food provision, clothing supply, working hours, religious education and medical treatment. Noteworthy, the then incumbent minister, J.C. Rijk, who had been a governor in Suriname between 1839 and 1842, also developed an emancipation plan for Suriname. In outline, it boiled down to the Dutch government guaranteeing a bond loan to release the enslaved persons, but in return the planters had to pledge their plantations and stay in Suriname. In the end, however, this plan was rejected, because, to a significant extent, there were too many financial risks involved for the Netherlands. Accordingly, with this disapproval the discussion was once again postponed for several years.

(2014, 389-416) with this renewal of the peace treaties, the Ndyuka's, Saamaka's and Mattaway's lost their independent status and more of less became dependent on the colonial government in Paramaribo.

Dutch Emancipation in 1863

Compared to the British and French, the Dutch were quite late, almost five decades after the abolition of slave trade in 1814, with the abolition of slavery in 1863. Moreover, this issue was not dealt with for a long time in historical and historiographical debates in the Netherlands. It was only after a comparative paper by Seymour Drescher in 1992, titled 'The Long Goodbye', that the debate took off in a conference convened by the KITLV in Leiden in 1993. As a result of this conference, Gert Oostindie (1995) edited a volume in which the papers presented by ten scholars were compiled. In the main paper presented by Drescher (pp. 50-1) he asserted that the Dutch case, as he framed it, '[...] offered an ordinary rather than an exceptional goodbye to slavery'. He also claimed '[...] that Dutch capitalism, whether mercantile or industrial, whether in oligarchical or revolutionary phases, created no significant anti-slavery moment.' He formed this conclusion based on his study of developments in the Netherlands from as early as the beginning of the seventeenth century until the abolition of slavery in 1863. On the basis of his comparative research, he concluded further that the major North Atlantic revolutions, both the American and French, did not result in any mass anti-slavery movement in the Netherlands, and that, as such, the Dutch resembled the other countries on the European continent (pp. 37-8).

In 1978, in an article carried in a Dutch historical journal, Maarten Kuitenbrouwer had already dealt somewhat with the question of the late Abolition of Slavery by the Netherlands. In this article (1978, 69, 74) he elaborated further on Van Winter's (1953) conclusion that abolitionism was not a popular movement in the Netherlands, and was very poorly discussed in the Dutch society at least until the 1840s. In the summarized version for the Leiden debate (1995, 67-8), he argued that '[...] the lack of popular abolitionism can best be explained by the gradual character of Dutch capitalist development and political change.' Oostindie (1995, 143-4) attributed the late Emancipation by the Netherlands to '[...] the economic insignificance of the Dutch Caribbean, and particular the major colony, Suriname, to its metropolis'. That slavery at last was abolished in 1863 in the Dutch colonies was, according to him, attributable to 'the eventual emergence of a modest abolitionist lobby and, indeed businesslike, to the rising income from the Dutch East Indies and the simultaneous substantial decrease in the number of slaves in the Dutch West Indies, [...]'. Van Stipriaan (1995, 138) noted that at the end of the 1840s it was clear in the Netherlands and it's colonies that slavery needed to be abolished, but that in the end '[...] the Suriname interest on both sides of the Atlantic, united for once, [...]' led to a delay of at least one decade.

In the last chapter of his first book, titled '1853-1863: The Last Episode', Siwpersad (1979, 217-99) described in detail the final developments in the Netherlands regarding the belated Emancipation in 1863. From this chapter it becomes clear that in 1853 the abolition issue became relevant again because of the publication of the famous anti-slavery literary work, *Uncle Tom's Cabin* (1852). M.D. Teenstra and W.R. van Hoëvell, anti-slavery protagonists who themselves wrote passionately about slavery in the Dutch colony Suriname, played an important role during these years. It is partly because of their efforts that a State Commission was appointed under the leadership of the former Minister of the Colonies, J.C. Baud. The report and proposal subsequently put forward by Baud and P. Mijer generated a lot of opposition in the Netherlands and Suriname and consequently were rejected in 1858. This rejection had mainly to do with recommendations such as the compensation of the planters, the state control of the plantations, repayments by the freedmen, and the establishment of negro communities. As was described by Siwpersad, the changed public opinion and increasing parliamentary pressure for Emancipation in this period was related mainly to the improvement of the financial position of the Netherlands as a consequence of the increased revenues from Java in Dutch East India.

Staatstoezicht in Suriname, 1873

Rudolf van Lier (1977, 132-3), one of the few Dutch and Surinamese writers, addressed, in his social-historical study of Suriname, the issue of Staatstoezicht or State Supervision. He noted that although the first bill for abolishing slavery was drafted in 1856, it was only on 9 July 1862 that the Dutch parliament accepted what amounted to a fifth draft. Dutch legislators were well aware of the negative developments in the British West Indies after 1834, and determined to develop their own Apprenticeship system, one that would work in Suriname. E.J.G. Slootweg (1987, 7-9), in his thesis, *Het Staatstoezicht in Suriname (1863-1873)*, wrote that finally three important amendments were made in the last draft bill of 1862. First, the mandatory length of ten years was dropped; second, an earlier discharge from the system was accordingly made possible; and third, special wage arrangements between employers and workers were allowed. Pieter C. Emmer (1993, 87-8), in an article based on the thesis of Slootweg, answered the important question of the uniqueness of the State Supervision System in Suriname. He mentioned in this respect:

'the political stalemate on this issue in the Netherlands [...];
the absence of important slave rebellions in Suriname [...];
improving the living and working conditions of the slaves [...];
the conditions during the period of apprenticeship or 'state supervision' [...];
the immigration of indentured labourers [...] remained uncertain until the very end [...]'

Another important feature of the Dutch Emancipation was that the Netherlands Antilles were excluded from the seeming Apprenticeship system. The compensation paid to the slave owners in these island colonies in the Caribbean (fl 50 to fl 200) was also less than what was paid to the slave owners in Suriname (fl 300). Heinrich Helstone and Joop Vernooij (2000, 15-16) were unable to account for the difference in compensation for the territories.

The Dutch Emancipation Act of 8 August 1862 consisted of five chapters with 39 articles, but breathed nevertheless the spirit of the British Abolition of Slavery Bill of 1833 (66 articles) (pp. 37-43).

In Chapter 1, the four principles (4 articles) were stated, namely: the abolition of slavery within a year, the compensation of the slave owners, the state supervision of the system, and the promotion of free colonization.

In Chapter 2, the guiding rules for the compensation (13 articles) were described. This chapter came down purely to registration of the enslaved persons per plantation and slave owner, a procedure also obliged in the British West Indies; and, additionally, it incorporated the proviso that the interested parties could object to the findings.

In Chapter 3, the special supervision by the state (3 articles) was regulated. The purpose of monitoring by the state was to protect and train the freedmen to function properly within the new colonial society. Through these articles, the colonial government made regular work compulsory, encouraged education and religion, and provided resources to care for the poor. Stipulated in this chapter, and this too was copied from what the British had ultimately implemented, was that supervision was placed in the hands of local officials, namely, District Commissioners.

In Chapter 4, the ground rules for the freedmen were established (4 articles), and elaborated (12 points), inter alia, the registration with a family name, the application of civil and criminal law, residency without full civil rights, and the obligation to hard work. Like the British, the Dutch also made a distinction between praedial and non-praedial workers, but in Suriname only those between 15 and 60 years were obliged to enter an agreement, respectively for 1 to 3 years and 3 months to 1 year.

In Chapter 5, general provisions (15 articles) were laid down regarding matters such as the working hours (300 days a year, 8-10 hours a day), deterring idleness and vagrancy, free housing, medical services, care for orphans, and penalty's for breaches on the part ex-enslaved (fines, penal labour, public labour), etc.

Ten Years of State Supervision, 1863-1873

Based on the Colonial Records of 1863, the free population in Suriname, both white, coloured and black, consisted of 17,129 persons, 8,143 males and 8,986 females. Of this number, 14,015 persons (82 per cent) were living in Paramaribo and its suburbs and only 1,241 persons (7.2 per cent) in the fifteen districts. As recorded, 30,952 emancipated former enslaved persons (14,518 males and 16,434 females) ended up under State Supervision in that year (for a comparison of the regulations in British Guiana and Suriname, see Table 2.1 on page 68). This amounted to 63 per cent of the total

TABLE 2.1: COMPARISON APPRENTICESHIP IN BRITISH GUIANA AND STATE SUPERVISION IN SURINAME

	Regulation	*British Guiana*	*Suriname*
1.	Abolition of Slavery	Act 28th August 1833, 1 August 1834.	Act 8th August 1862, 1 July 1863.
2.	Apprenticeship	Praedial and Non-Praedial Labourers 6-4 years work.	Praedial and Non-Praedial Labourers 10 years labour.
3.	Compensation	£4,295,989 for 82,824 enslaved persons.	fl 9,864,360 for 34,394 enslaved persons.
4.	Registration	All enslaved persons, in Apprenticeship 6 years and up.	All enslaved persons, under State Supervision 15-60 years.
5.	Contract	Oblige to work for former masters 1-3 years/3-12 months.	1-3 years (Praedial) or 3-12 months (Non-Praedial).
6.	Discharge	Voluntary: employer liable; and involuntary: appraisement.	Possible (moral behaviour and hard work).
7.	Removable	Transferable property (praedial by consent of 2 SJ).	Praedial: first 2 years same division.
8.	Working Hours	45 hours a week (not Sunday), scales of task-work.	8 (field) and 10 (buildings) hours per day.
9.	Payment	Only a quarter (or overwork 15 hours a week).	All work for wage or at rate (tax deduction).
10.	Mobility	Vagrancy laws (around the plantation).	Booklet/pas ('livret'), only with permission.
11.	Food	Food supply and/or provision grounds (and time).	Food rations and/or provision grounds (and time).
12.	Other Material Facilities	Clothing and lodging.	Clothing and lodging.

13.	Children	<6-12 years attached to mother (can become apprentice).	Up to 15 y (p) or 12 y (np) part of mother (paid for work).
14.	Elders	Under Apprenticeship.	>60 years, attached to family, can do light work.
15.	Penalty	Extra labour, fines, imprisonment and flogging (stripes).	Fines (wage reduction), hard labour, public work.
16.	Supervision	Local Justices and Stipendiary Magistrates (punishment).	Civil Servants, District Commissioners.
17.	Military and Civil Services	No exemption or disqualification.	Government authorized.
18.	Social Services	Standards of behaviour (vagrancy laws).	No dwelling, help for orphans and people in need.
19.	Education	3-6/12 years, moral and religious education with grants.	All children, subsidy to religious missions.
20.	Religion	Free to attend services of several denominations.	Roman Catholic and Moravian churches.

Source: J. Latimer (1964), W. A. Green (1969), E.J.G. Slootweg (1987); B.P. Josiah (1997), M. Lenders (1996), H. Helstone & J. Vernooij (2000) and T.N. Tyson et al. (2005).

population of 48,932 inhabitants. By 1872, the group under supervision had decreased to 28,774 persons (2,178 persons less), while the group of free persons had increased by 3,755 persons.

As indicated earlier, immigration was one of the provisions of the Emancipation Act of 1862, and in consequence the number of immigrants grew from 296 in 1863 to 2,230 in 1872, and to 4,415 in 1873.[5] The increase in the immigrant population was due largely

[5] Koloniale verslagen (Colonial Records) 1863-1873, consulted in the National Archive Suriname, Paramaribo-Suriname, in the year 2020.

to the immigration of Chinese and West Indian workers, some from British Guiana to Suriname. It is worth noting that the birth rate among the ex-enslaved population increased slightly, not significantly, from an average of 3.2 per cent between 1858 and 1862 to 4 per cent between 1868 and 1872, while mortality during this period dropped slightly from a total of 6,662 to 6,057 (Slootweg 1987, 129).

Sandew Hira (1984, 181-2), commenting from a Marxist perspective, pointed out that the class structure of the colonial society in Suriname remained upright, with the planters as the exploitative class. In his view, the role of the state had changed in the sense that it had now to supervise the transition from slave labour to wage labour and eventually indentured labour. He argued, however, that with this change in the role of the state the repression system changed also, retreating somewhat as the planters lost their power to punish the new wage labourers. Slootweg (1987, 79, 124) could unravel that, starting from 1863, the District Commissioners reported various violations of the law by the ex-slaves; and, according to him, this was a sign that the new legal system worked. Notably, the percentage of freedmen breaching the law increased from 1,320 cases in 1863 to 5,275 in 1867, and then decreased to 3,602 in 1872. From a total of 39,297 breaches, under eleven different rubrics, 15,644 cases (39.8 per cent) had to do with absence from work and only 1,735 with actual violence. At the same time also, 1,190 cases of vagabondage or dwelling were recorded. On average, during the ten years from 1863 to 1872, 13 per cent (between 4.2 per cent and 17.0 per cent) of the total ex-slave population was punished for minor to mayor offences.

Van Lier (1971, 135-8) acknowledged that 95 plantations were sold between 1862 and 1864, while in total during the entire period of State Supervision, 77 plantations were liquidated. From the 225 plantations counted in 1853, at least 163 were still in production in 1891. The decreases in the production and export of the main crops and the negative trade surplus starting from 1863, made him conclude that the colony of Suriname in 1873 was in a severe state of discomfort and decline. From the attachments in the thesis of Slootweg (1987, 120-1) it becomes clear that in 1864, compared to that of 1862, the production of sugar and coffee fell to 55.5 per cent and 22.9 per cent respectively. Over the whole period, from 1864 to 1873, only the production and export of cacao and cotton increased. Van Lier therefore concluded (pp. 100-2) that the State Supervision mechanism softened the 'system shocks' and spared Suriname from becoming a chaotic state as in Guyana, but failed to retain the ex-slaves as wage labourers for plantation cultivation. In the end, from a total of 16,758 ex-slaves as fieldworkers on 30 June 1873, 25 per cent (4,199) left the plantations during the following six months, and only 8,864 were active on the plantations *circa* 31 December 1876.

Conclusion

Within the Commonwealth, but especially Anglo-America, there is an ongoing discussion about the British Abolition of the Slave Trade and Slavery between the representatives of the 'moral ideology' and the 'decline theory'. Although starting from the late 1970s several Dutch, but also Dutch-Surinamese writers, were influenced by the writings of the proponents and opponents of these scientific schools, a debate about the belated Abolition of Dutch Slavery only took off in 1993. From this debate, it became clear that, to some extent, the above-mentioned theories do not apply to the Dutch situation. As Drescher (1992) and Oostindie (1995) concluded, the Dutch Abolition of Slavery was not as exceptional as the British Emancipation, but more ordinary, like that executed by other continental powers. As I previously concluded in another paper in 2014, the liberalist ideas, coming out of the revolutionary situation in Europe and America after 1796 resulted in the Abolition of the Slave Trade in 1814, but not in the Abolition of Slavery in the Dutch colonies in the West. In summary, it is justified, following Kuitenbrouwer (1978) and others, to state that the belated abolition of Dutch slavery was related to the fact that the modest development of capitalism ideology in the Netherlands did not fuel a large abolition movement within Dutch borders.

Regarding the impact of the British Abolition of Slavery (in

1833), and to a lesser extent the impact of the French Abolition of Slavery (in 1848), it became clear, especially from Sewpersad (1979), that:

1. First, starting from 1833, several abolition plans were written, but none of them were implemented, especially because of the poor financial position of the Netherlands.
2. Second, the decline in British Guiana after Emancipation and Apprenticeship enlarged the reluctant and laggard approach of the colonial authorities and the strict attitude of the planters.
3. Third, with a delay from 1828, but finally in 1848, the living and working conditions of the enslaved population in Suriname were improved.
4. Fourth, the abolitionist and liberals gradually gained strength in the Netherlands and were therefore able to put the abolition issue back on agenda in the 1850s.
5. Fifth, during the whole period the compensation of the planters remained the main discussion point, because of the planters' lobby in Amsterdam.

In the end, the Dutch Abolition of Slavery was established in 1863, because of finances from Java in Dutch East India and the decline of the enslaved populations in the overseas colonies, especially in Suriname.

With the abolition of slavery in 1863, the Dutch, like the British, also introduced like the United Kingdom an Apprenticeship system. This, they referred to as 'Staatstoezicht' or State Supervision. It is quite noteworthy, that, unlike the English and their broad trans-regional colonial policy, the Netherlands implemented such a system only in Suriname, not in the Dutch Antilles. This certainly had to do with the policy of the Netherlands to keep the plantation economy in Suriname as a viable development sector, especially because several groups in the motherland benefitted from it.

Without doubt, it can be stated that the Dutchmen copied a lot from the British with regard to Emancipation. The compensation, supervision, registration, contracting, mobility, material facilities, social services, military and civil services, education and religious obligations were all essentially similar to what was obtained under the British system. Like the British, the Dutch also made accounting and accountability, not through Special Magistrates, but District Commissioners, a critical basis of the operation of the post-slavery system. Using the Colonial Records, Slootweg (1987) was able to present several interesting figures about the decade of State Supervision in Suriname, such as the fact that during the ten years of supervision, on average 13 per cent of the freed population breached the colonial laws. In British Guyana, the percentage was higher: within two years, 22 per cent of all apprentices got punished, 3.7 per cent by flogging. In comparison, this was one of the main distinctions between Apprenticeship in British Guiana and State Supervision in Dutch Guiana (Suriname). Another important distinction was that in Suriname the freedmen under State Supervision, both praedial and non praedial, were paid either by wage or at a rate, and not only for extra work, as was usual in the British colonies, but also for regular work.

Bibliography

Bender, Thomas (ed.). 1992. *The Antislavery Debate: Capitalism and Abolitionism as a Problem in Historical Interpretation.* Berkeley/Los Angeles: University of California Press.

Blackburn, Robin. 1988. *The Overthrow of Colonial Slavery, 1776-1848.* London/New York: Verso, New Left Books.

Bolland, O. Nigel. 1981. 'Systems of Domination after Slavery: The Control of Land and Labor in the British West Indies after 1838.' *Comparative Studies in Society and History,* 23(4): 591-619. Retrieved 14 January 2021, from http://www.jstor.org/stable/178395

Burn, William L. 1970 (1937). *Emancipation and Apprenticeship in the British West Indies.* New York: Johnson Reprint Corp.

Carrington, Selwyn H. H. 2002. *The Sugar Industry and the Abolition of the Slave Trade, 1775-1810.* Gainesville: University Press of Florida.

Drescher, Seymour. 1996. 'The Long Goodbye. Dutch Capitalism and Antislavery in Comparative Perspective', in Gert Oostindie (ed.), *Fifty Years Later. Antislavery, Capitalism and Modernity in the Dutch Orbit.* Pittsburgh: University of Pittsburgh Press: 25-66.

Emmer, Pieter C. 1993. 'Between Slavery and Freedom. The Period of Apprenticeship in Suriname (Dutch Guiana), 1863-1873.', *Slavery and Abolition,* 14(1): 87-113.

Farley, Rowle. 1954. 'The Rise of the Peasantry in British Guiana.' *Social and Economic Studies,* 2(4): 87-103. Retrieved 19 January 2021, from http://www.jstor.org/stable/27850955

Koloniale Verslagen (Colonial Reports) 1863-1873.

Goss, Dave. May 2008. 'Apprenticeship & the Question of Labor Management in Jamaica.' (Paper 40th Annual Conference of Caribbean Historians in Paramaribo, Suriname).

Gowan Mc, Winston F. 1998. 'The Demerara Revolt, 1823', in Winston F. Mc Gowan, James G. Rose & David A. Granger (eds.), *Themes in African-Guyanese History.* Georgetown: Free Press: 107-40.

Green, William A. 1976. *British Slave Emancipation: The Sugar Colonies and the Great Experiment, 1830-1865.* Oxford: Clarendon Press.

_____. 1969. 'The Apprenticeship in British Guiana, 1834-1838.' *Caribbean Studies,* 9(2), 44-66. Retrieved 12 January 2021, from http://www.jstor.org/stable/25612128

Fergus, Claudius K. 2013. *Revolutionary Emancipation. Slavery and Abolitionism in the British West Indies.* Baton Rouge: Louisiana State University Press.

Foner, Eric. 1983. *Nothing but Freedom. Emancipation and its Legacy. The Walter Lynwood Fleming Lectures in Southern History.* Baton Rouge and London: Louisiana State University Press.

Helstone, Heinrich & Joop Vernooij. 2000. *Documentatie. Afschaffing van de slavernij in Suriname.* Paramaribo.

Heuman, Gad. 2006. 'The Historiography of Slavery and Abolition in the Anglophone Caribbean', in Jaunita De Baros, Audra Diptee & David V. Trotman (eds.), *Beyond Fragmentation. Perspectives on Caribbean History.* Princeton: Marcus Wiener Publishers: 93-109.

Hira, Sandew. 1984. *Van Priary tot en met De Kom. De geschiedenis van het verzet in Suriname, 1630-1940.* Rotterdam: Futile/Blok & Flohr.

Jagdew, Eric R. oktober 2014. 'Vrede te midden van oorlog in Suriname. Inheemsen, Europeanen, Marrons en vredesverdragen, 1667-1863.' (Proefschrift Doctor in de Geesteswetenschappen, Anton de Kom Universiteit van Suriname, Paramaribo-Suriname).

Josiah, Barbara P. 1997. 'After Emancipation: Aspects of Village Life in Guyana, 1869-1911.' *The Journal of Negro History,* 82(1): 105-21. Accessed 14 January 2021. doi:10.2307/2717498

Knight, Franklin W. 1997. 'The Disintegration of the Caribbean Slave Systems, 1772-1886', in Franklin W. Knight (ed.), *General History of the Caribbean, Volume III. The Slave Societies of the Caribbean.* Caribbean: UNESCO Publishing: 322-45.

Kuitenbrouwer, Maarten. 1996. 'The Dutch Case of Antislavery. Late Abolitions and Élitist Abolitionism', in Gert Oostindie (ed.), *Fifty Years Later. Antislavery, Capitalism and Modernity in the Dutch Orbit.* Pittsburgh: University of Pittsburgh Press: 67-88.

______. 1978. 'De Nederlandse afschaffing van de slavernij in vergelijkend perspectief', *Bijdragen en Mededelingen betreffende de Geschiedenis der Nederlanden,* 93: 69-100.

Latimer, J. 1964. 'The Apprenticeship System in the British West Indies.', *The Journal of Negro Education,* 33(1): 52-7. Accessed on 8 December 2020. doi:10.2307/2294514

Lenders, Maria. 1996. *Strijders voor het Lam. Leven en werk van Herrnhutter Broeders en -Zusters in Suriname, 1735-1900.* Leiden: KITLV.

Levy, Claude.1980. *Emancipation, Sugar, and Federalism: Barbados and the West Indies, 1833-1876.* Gainesville: University Presses of Florida.

Lier van, Rudolf. 1977 (1949). *Samenleving in een grensgebied. Een social-historische studie van Suriname.* Amsterdam: S. Emmering.

Moore, Brian L. 1987. *Race, Power and Social Segmentation in Colonial Society. Guyana after Slavery, 1838-1891.* New York: Routledge/ Gordon & Breach Science Publ.

Oostindie, Gert (ed.). 1996. *Fifty Years Later. Antislavery, Capitalism and Modernity in the Dutch Orbit.* Pittsburgh: University of Pittsburgh Press.

______. 1996. 'Same Old Song? Perspectives on Slavery and Slaves in Suriname and Curaçao.', in Gert Oostindie (ed.), *Fifty Years Later. Antislavery, Capitalism and Modernity in the Dutch Orbit.* Pittsburgh: University of Pittsburgh Press: 143-78.

Siwpersad, Jozef P. 1979. *De Nederlandse regering en de afschaffing van de Surinaamse slavernij (1833-1863).* Groningen/Castricum: Bouma's boekhuis/Bert Hagen.

______. 2009. *Gij zijt blank en wij zijn zwart. Gedragspatronen in een slaven-maatschappij (Suriname, negentiende eeuw).* 's Gravenshage: Nabestaanden.

Slootweg, E.J.G. 1987. 'Het Staatstoezicht in Suriname (1863-1873).' (Doctoraal scriptie Universiteit van Leiden, Leiden-Nederland).

Solow, Barbara L. & Stanley L. Engerman (eds.). 1987. *British Capitalism and Caribbean Slavery. The Legacy of Eric Williams.* Cambridge: Cambridge University Press.

Stipriaan van, Alex. 1996. 'Suriname and the Abolition of Slavery', in Gert Oostindie (ed.), *Fifty Years Later. Antislavery, Capitalism and Modernity in the Dutch Orbit.* Pittsburgh: University of Pittsburgh Press: 117-42.

Tyson, Thomas N., David Oldroyd & Richard K. Fleischman. 2005. 'Accounting, Coercion and Social Control during Apprenticeship. Converting Slave Workers to Wage Workers in the British West Indies, c. 1834-1838.', *The Accounting Historians Journal,* 32(2): 201-31. Retrieved 14 January 2021, from https://egrove.olemiss.edu/cgi/viewcontentcgi?article=1684&context=aah_journal

Part Two

Slavery's Legacy in the Caribbean

THREE

The Pamaka Road to Freedom
The Early History and Geography of the Pamaka Tribe in Suriname

J. MARTEN W. SCHALKWIJK

Introduction

The Pamaka tribe, in Suriname called the Paramakaners is one of the smaller Maroon tribes living in Suriname. In the Colonial annals this tribe is hardly mentioned and no peace treaty has ever been signed between them and the colonial government. The early history of the Pamaka is not very clear. In fact, there are several versions (theories) about the origin of the Pamaka. Wong (1938) and some oral traditions suggest that the ancestors left the plantations during the mid-eighteenth century. On the opposite side Benjamins (1916) and Lenoir (1974) proclaim that the Pamaka were split off from one of the other Maroon tribes around 1838. Hoogbergen (1985, 2015) and Reineman (1996) maintain that the Pamaka ancestors fled the plantations around 1830.

In this paper I present a logical version of the early Pamaka history from archival sources, original documents and existing literature. When using contemporary literature, I aim as much as possible to revisit their original sources. An important tool to make connections with the past is provided by the geographic moves of the Pamakas.

Some would call this the slave route of the Pamakas, but since they left the plantations and slavery behind them, I would rather call it the Pamaka road to freedom.

The geography of the Pamakas

Maroons in Suriname are descendants of enslaved people from Africa that were forced to work on plantations, but who successfully escaped slavery and formed new groups (tribes) in Suriname's hinterland. In general, there are six recognized Maroon tribes (Figure 3.1). The two

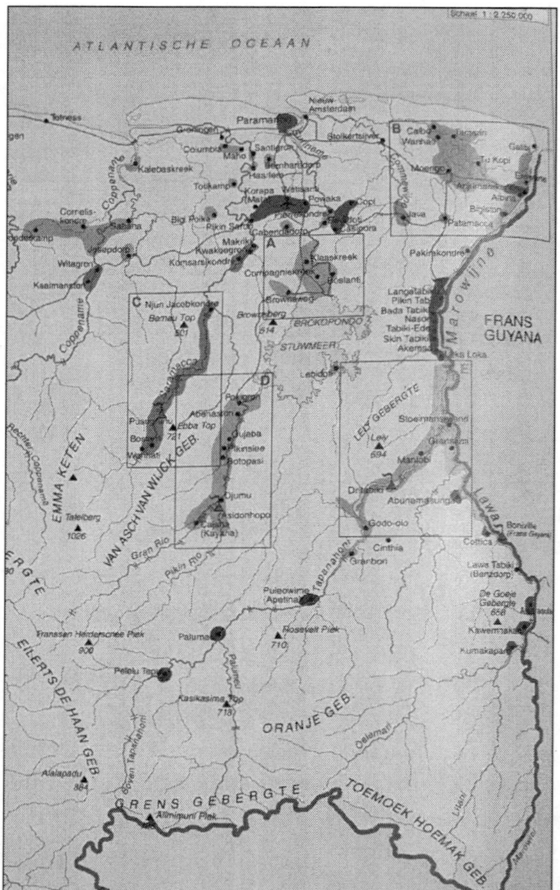

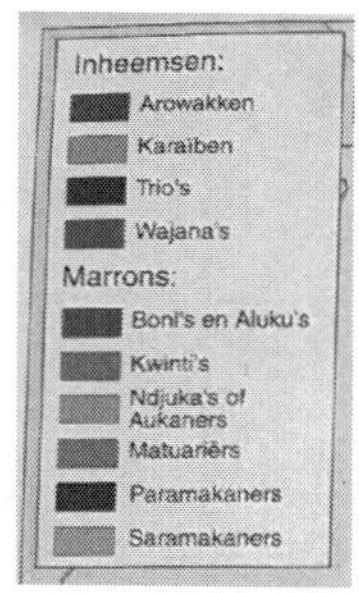

FIGURE 3.1: MAP OF THE TRIBAL AREAS IN CENTRAL AND SOUTH-PAMAKA TRIBAL EAST SURINAME (*Source:* Hebri Wereldatlas 2008)

largest ones are the Samaka (or Saramakaners) of the Suriname River and district Brokopondo, and the Djuka (Aukaners or Okanisi) of the Marowijne, Tapanahony, Cottica and Upper Commewijne river areas. Of the smaller tribes the Matawai (Matuariërs or Becoe- and Moesinga Negroes) live mainly along the Saramaka River, while the Kwinti settled along the Coppename River; the Aluku (or Boni) tribe live on the Lawa River, but most of their descendants are inhabitants of the French side, where they moved to in the past.[1]

The Pamaka tribe lives in the islands on the Marowijne River, but during the Internal War (1986-92) nearly half of the tribe moved to French Guyana for security reasons as the southern tribal area was located near one of the active war zones.[2] A distinct feature of the Pamaka tribe is that they mostly live on islands in the Marowijne River. Only in more recent times people have began to move to the mainland. As can be seen from the Pamaka area map (Figure 3.2), only Atemsa and Sebedoekondre are located on the mainland. In fact, Atemsa was also first established on an island, and known as the village Pinatjarimi, and the villagers originally came from Nason but due to an internal dispute some people moved away and established their own village. It turned out, however, that the island on which they had established the village was located in the French part of the river. According to the *granman* (the tribal chief) they would not be able to choose a village chief (*kapten*) if they remained on the French side, so around 1950 they moved to the Suriname mainland opposite the island (Ontwikkelingsplan Atemsa 2016).

The village of Sebedoekondre (also known as Krikimofo) was established around 1991 by people who moved from the village of Atemsa (Ontwikkelingsplan Sebedoekondre 2016). Snesikondre (lit. Chinese village) is also located on the mainland in the tribal area, but is a trading place (with Chinese shops) and intentioned as a regional government hub; thus, it is not a traditional tribal village. In recent times we have seen more mainland developments, espe-

[1] *Frans sei*, la Guyane.

[2] This war was started by the Jungle Commando under leadership of Ronny Brunswijk and mainly fought against the regular army, which was led by Desi Bouterse as commander.

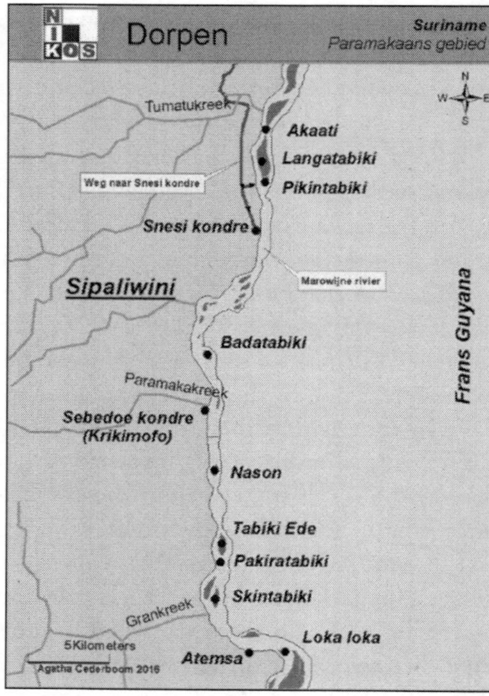

FIGURE 3.2: MAP OF THE MAIN AREA (*Source:* Nikos 2016).

cially of people who have moved from Langatabiki (but also from some other villages) to the mainland along the road from Moengo to Snesikondre. People also moved from the island of Loka Loka to the mainland across this island, mainly because the island is getting overcrowded. The small villages of Akaati and Pikintabiki are either uninhabited or have just a few inhabitants, with most people now living alongside the road to Snesikondre.

Plantation origin and linkage to clans

The historical and geographical origins of the Pamakas can be traced back to plantations in the islands on Cottica River, Upper Commewijne River and Tempatie Creek (Figure 3.3). E. Wong, District Commissioner of the Marowijne district (Eastern Suriname) did an in-depth study of the history and tribal composition of different Maroon tribes. He was commissioned in 1936 by the Governor of Suriname to undertake this study in the archives, in order to add to the knowledge that was available from oral sources and existing literature. The rationale for the study is provided in the opening sentence of his report: 'In order to decide on the correct governance attitude towards the Bushnegroes, an extensive and correct knowledge of their tribal organization and social organization is indispensable' (Wong 1938, 295).

Wong's report focused mainly on the two largest tribes, i.e. the Samaka and the Aukaner tribe. Only 2 pages (pp. 326-7) out of 68 are dedicated to the Pamakas, most probably because he found very little information on them in the colonial archives. In these two pages he mentions that the Pamakas are divided into three clans (*lo*'s). Wong did more extensive research in 1939 as District Commissioner in the Pamaka area itself and wrote another report.[3] He mentioned the same three *lo*'s, but provides extra information, including the tribal mother, i.e. where the original matrilineage of a *lo* starts. The *lo*'s according to Wong—we repeat what he wrote at the time—were:

1. **The Asaiti-Negroes** (about 350 persons), from plantation Hasard (or Hazard). They live in the villages: Asabia, Bada-Tabbetje, Nason or Amerikan, Pakira-Tabbetje and Bron Kassaba-Tabbetje. In the 1939 version he does not mention the villages of Asabia and Bron Kassaba-Tabbetje, which probably had been abandoned. The head of the *lo* at that time was David Koffie from Badatabbetje. The tribal mother was Amba (or Aminba), who fled around 1830 from plantation Hazard. Asabi Asani and her sister Dienki accompanied her, as well as Abeni and her sister Sanna; and later Jaba. These ladies formed different *bee's* or *bere's* (sub-clans, families) of the Asaiti. The current population from Skintabiki mentioned that they are descendants from Sanna, although some of her children also settled in Badatabbetje and Bonidoro (which is now abandoned).[4]

[3] Nationaal Archief Suriname - Gouverneur van Suriname 1846-1957: inv. nr. 9927-9930, Res. No. 591: 26 February 1940, tweede bijlage: verslag van Wong. Brief: 5 januari 1940.

[4] About Bonidoro see S. de Groot.

2. **The Anthroshi-Negroes** (about 250 persons) from plantation Handtros or Entros (as Wong wrote in 1939). They live in Langa-Tabbetje. The tribal mother Ninne (Ma Asa) fled from the plantation around 1830. Apensa, who in 1901 became the first officially recognized grand chief (*granman*) of the Pamaka by the government, was the first child born in the jungle (i.e. not on the plantation but in freedom). When Wong visited Langatabbetje, Aboenawroko was the granman, while Kamille was the captain of the *lo* and village.
3. **The Molo-Negroes** (about 150 persons), from plantation Molhoop (in 1939 Wong changed this to plantation Mazon), live in Loka Loka. Around 1830 the tribal mothers Sa Doifi (Awake) and Adjoeba fled the plantation. Abena, a daughter of Sa Doifi, became the second wife of granman Apensa and moved to Langatabbetje. When Wong visited Langatabbetje about 30 Molo-Negroes lived there and they had an own Molo captain in that village (Willem Apensa, also called Asijèrè). The *lo* captain was captain Asaidih of Loka Loka.

In the description by Wong, it is interesting that he mentions that the tribal mothers all fled the plantations around 1830, to which we will return. John Lenoir (1974), an American anthropologist, spent two years with the Pamakas, collecting information for his dissertation. He mainly used oral traditions and stories as sources. In his description, the Antoisie group fled the plantations as early as 1780s and later linked up with the two other groups. Reineman (1996), who did archival research on the origins of the Pamaka and read most published work and documents, however, questions the reliability of Lenoir's time line. Most authors and documents point towards marronage by the Pamaka groups around 1830, which seems to fit with archival and verifiable sources.[5]

In his dissertation, Lenoir (1974) mentioned the same three *lo*'s same as Wong, i.e. the Antoisies from plantation Hantros, the Asaities from plantation Hazard, and the Molos whose origin was unclear, but possibly from plantation Molhoop. These

[5] These sources are mentioned by Reineman 1996.

were the three original groups of Maroons who came together and formed the Pamaka tribe. After emancipation in 1863 and in fact after the Pamakas had settled along the Marowijne River, three other groups of emancipated Africans from the plantations joined the Pamaka. According to Lenoir, they formed three other *lo*'s.

4. **The Bakabusi**. The *lo* mother was a woman from a *bakabusi* settlement near Paramaribo, but was brought to the Marowijne by a Djuka suitor (Aukaner).[6] The intended marriage was forbidden by the man's family and she could not stay in the village. On the way back to Paramaribo, she stopped in Langatabbetje where she married an Antoisie man. Due to a dispute over land they moved to the centre of the island and established the village of Akatie (Lenoir 1974, 28-9).
5. **The Wata-Weliki**. The Wata-Weliki moved from Nason and established the village Atemsa and the village of Tabiki-Ede. From Atemsa some people later relocated to Sebedoekondre. Aboeka was one of the leaders who helped the Wata-Weliki flee from the plantations.[7] Polimé (1995) mentioned that some of the Wata-Weliki also lived in Skintabiki.
6. **The Wajiampibo**. The other two groups were *baka-fii* (after freedom people, i.e. after emancipation) but claimed kinship with Paramaccans. The Wajiampibo located near Langatabbetje and the Wata-Weliki near Nason. The older Pamaka *lo*'s did not accept the kinship claim and wanted to dominate the newcomers. 'These situations resulted in the new groups forming their own separate settlements under the *lo* names of their former plantations' (Lenoir 1974, 29). Nowadays, not much is heard of

[6] *Bakabusi* people were Maroons who fled the plantations but stayed in their vicinity. One famous and large *Bakabusi* group were the Brooskampers, who lived between the Surnaus Creek and the Commewijne River (Hoogbergen 2009).

[7] Lenoir (1974) does not provide more information about the Wajiampibos and the Wata-Weliks and neither do other written sources. Wong does not even mention these groups and probably was not aware of their existence. We retrieved some information during our field research and interviews with Pamaka village captains in 2016.

the Wajiampibo and thus it seems as if they have been absorbed by the other *lo*'s.[8]

The plantation map of around 1840 (Figure 3.3) shows the location of the plantations Molhoop, Hazard and Wajampibo. The plantation Handtros or Entros could not be found in the almanacs and maps of Suriname, and neither was there any reference to the plantation Mazon.[9] According to Hoogbergen (2015), Antoosi was the local name for the plantation Arendsrust, which is also shown in Figure 3.3.[10] Hoogbergen (2015) stated that there were four Pamaka *lo*'s, i.e. the Antoosi, Molo, Asaiti and Wata-Weliki, but he based this on Polimé (1995).[11] In his article, he focused on the Pamakas during the period of marronage (*lowéten*) and by using archival sources he made an attempt to connect them with the plantations. He also used the work of Reineman (1996), to whom he had given his archival material on the Pamakas, and who dug further into the archives. In her reconstruction she found many enslaved people among the early Pamaka groups from Arendsrust, but also from other plantations. One of the first leaders—also in the oral tradition—was Papa Doffin (also Da Dofin or Tata Doffin, but according to the slave registers his name was Dauphijn, from plantation Hooyland). In

[8] In an interview with one of the older captains of Langatabiki, I asked about the Wajampibos, but he was not aware of any recent activities, nor could he remember any Wajampibo captain.

[9] One can verify this in the database of all plantations that were ever operational. The website www.surinameplantages.com contains 1220 names of plantations and related grounds in Suriname, but none with the name Hantros (Wong 1938) or Entros (Wong 1940) or Mazos (Wong 1940). The website clearly has made use of several maps and almanacs and can be considered as very extensive. The almanac of 1841 listed all the local names (*negernamen*) of the plantations, but a scan of these names did not match with Hantros, Entros or Mazon either.

[10] The website above mentioned 'Di Losi' as local name for Arendsrust, but Hoogbergen stated it as 'Antoosi'.

[11] Polimé was part of a consultancy group that wrote a regional development plan for the Pamaka area and had thus visited the Pamakas. I could not find the full document, but got a part of it.

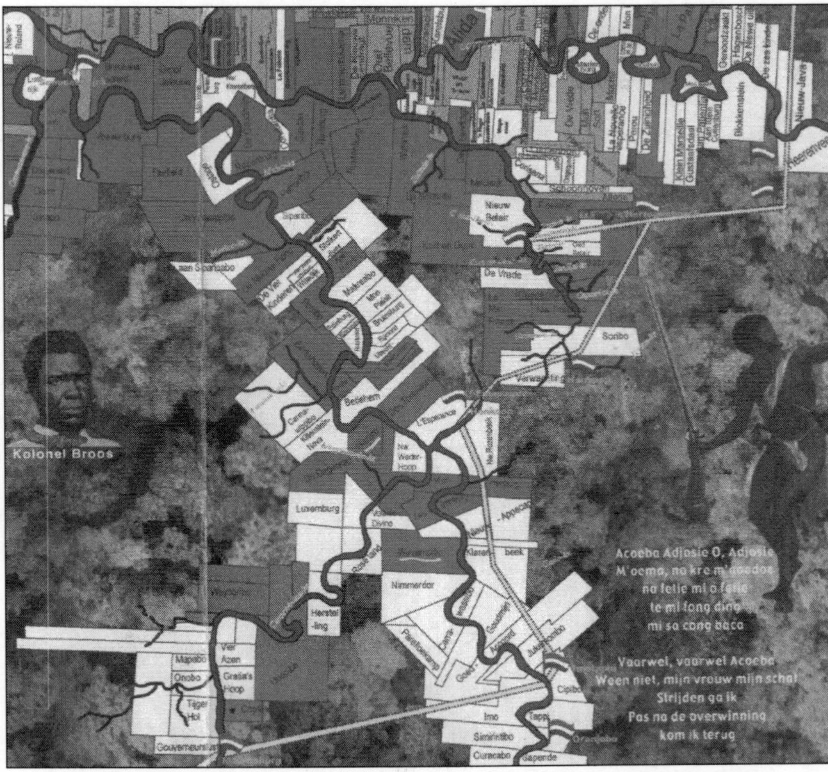

FIGURE 3.3: SOME OF THE PLANTATIONS FROM WHICH THE ENSLAVED PEOPLE ORIGINATED, WHO LATER FORMED THE PAMAKA TRIBE (*Source:* Afaka International, 2004).

The map in Figure 3.3 is based upon the situation of plantations around 1840. Blue areas are sugar plantations, red areas are coffee plantations, brown are timber plantations, while white areas are abandoned plantations. The map shows the Cordon Defense Line (in white with Dutch flags at the points of the military posts) which was put in place by the end of the eighteenth century to defend the plantations from attacks by Maroons. The map also shows some Maroon leaders. Four plantations of origin are marked with yellow, i.e. from South to North: Wayampibo (Tempatie Creek), Hazard (Upper Commewijne River), Arendsrust (Upper Commewijne River), and Molhoop (Cottica River).

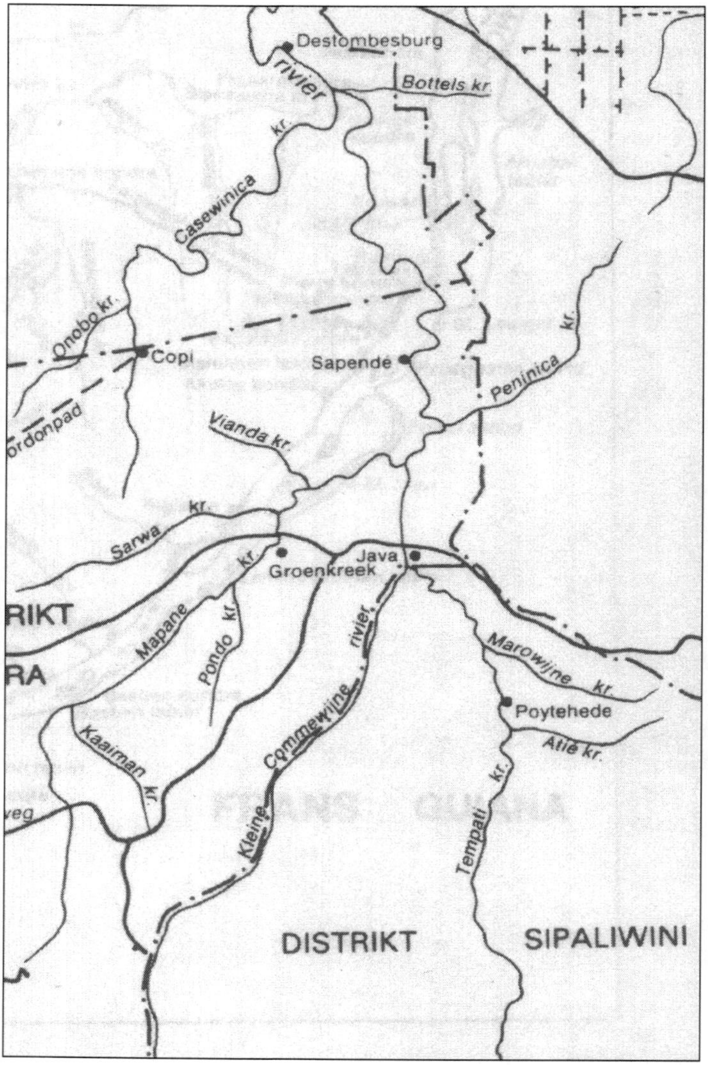

FIGURE 3.4: MAP OF THE UPPER COMMEWIJNE AND TEMPATIE CREEK AREA (*Source:* E.J.E. Wekker 1986).

The plantation Destombesburg (across from plantation Hazard) provides a good orientation point in this map. The Maroons under leadership of Doffin were located in the Peninica Creek area. Doffin often visited Destombes-burg.

different stories it is said that he travelled with Afo Abena (Ma Asa) and ten-year-old Kwaku Apensa, who is often mentioned as the first maroon child born in freedom. Archival research seems to trace the *Antoisie-lo* back to a Maroon by the name of Maandag (from plantation Meulwijk), who became head of a village in the vicinity of the Penninica Creek. Maandag was born in Africa and trained as a carpenter, but he fled the plantation when they took away his wife from him.[12] He probably provided shelter to Doffin and his family, although in the oral tradition it also says that Da Anansi and Da Bigiman (both were former enslaved persons from Arendsrust) took them in. In any case, by 1829 Da Doffin had his own village four hours from the military post Oranjebo (the most southern military post with a Dutch flag, on the map shown in Figure 3.3).[13] In 1830 a captured Maroon said that there were nine men and four women in Doffin's village, whose names he gave; they came from plantation Hooyland, Destombesburg, Arendsrust, Penoribo, Beekvliet and Concordia. Among the names of the women, we did not find any of the clan mothers.[14]

During this period several patrols were sent from the plantations and the government to find and eradicate the Maroon villages in the neighbourhood of the plantations. Reineman (1996) and Hoogbergen (2015) detail several such patrols in the period 1829-37. In September 1830 Maandag visited the village of Doffin around the same time a patrol raided the village and wounded Maandag, who was able to escape, but two other Maroons were killed and three were taken prisoner. This meant that the remaining people had to

[12] Reineman (1996) provides this information and called this group the Penninica Maroons. In 1829 Maandag was already living 'many years' in the jungle.

[13] We do not know how long this village existed, but probably not more than five years. His group at the time consisted of 15 persons. The village of Maandag was in the same area.

[14] The four women in the village were: Julia (Plantation Arendsrust), Europa (Arendsrust), Pori, Polly or Paulowna (Arendsrust) and Calista or Clarista (Concordia). Polly and Calista were captured in 1830.

Europa was captured in 1837 when she was 32 years (Reineman, 1996).

establish another village somewhere else. Unfortunately, Maandag was captured in July 1831 when he visited a plantation and was later executed.[15] Doffin took the leadership of Maandag. In November 1831, a military patrol destroyed Doffin's old village, but he had already moved away. In December 1831, the military destroyed his new and larger village, killing one person and capturing another.[16] We learn that the Maroons did not own any guns, only two persons had a spear, one had a bow and arrow, and all the others carried machetes. Jantke was a well-known Maroon hunter in those days, who led many patrols. Because of the attacks Doffin gradually moved his villages further away from the plantations. At the same time, Doffin also visited friends at some plantations in secret and thus kept up with the news. In October 1835, during another military raid, two villages of Doffin were discovered and destroyed, along with all food and crops. Julie of Destombesburg was captured during this raid and confessed to his captors that Doffin was the leader of both villages, who together counted about 30 people.[17] He also disclosed that there were many slaves from Arendsrust living in the jungle, who did not live in the villages, but befriended them. In 1837 during another raid of villages, under Doffin's leadership, three Maroons were captured. At that time Doffin was the head of three villages of

[15] These details can be found in the reports made by the patrols and interrogations that followed and which Reineman (1996) has consulted. Profiet (see note 16) stated that Doffin took the leadership after Maandag was captured.

[16] From the interrogation of the captured Maroon Profiet, we learn that there were 38 adults in the village (of whom 14 fled from Arendsrust, 5 from Destombesburg, 4 from Siparibo, 3 from Concordia, 1 from Kortenduur and 1 from Hooyland), and probably also several children. Again, we do not recognize any of the names of the Pamaka clan mothers. Profiet was 30 years old and a former basja of plantation Destombesburg; he fled the plantation 7 months before he was captured. He stayed in the shrubs behind a plantation when he was spotted by Doffin, who persuaded him to join the groep (Reineman, 1996).

[17] Among the names that he—and another captured Maroon—provided, we now see some persons that later appear in Pamaka history, notably Frans Kwaku (a later leader) and Nero (who seized the leadership by force).

about 50 persons (30 males and 20 females).[18] After 1837 not much can be traced in the archives, which could indicate that Doffin and his group of Maroons probably had moved towards the Tempatie Creek or reached the Nassau Mountains. This seemed to be the case, because one of the captured Maroons stated in 1837 that Doffin had crossed to the Marowijne River.

The oral tradition dates the *Asaiti-lo* back to the time when Da Anansi and his wife Afo Amba fled from the plantation Hazard, around 1830. They left together with Da Abita and Da Bigiman. From the beginning they seem to have established villages in the Upper Tempatie Creek area. There is, however, also a story about the Maroon Kwami from the plantation Concordia, who linked up with the Maroons Mey and Castor, who had established a village Mapane, where several former slaves from plantation Hazard lived. Kwami later fled, because some other Maroons wanted to kill him; he went back to the plantation area, but was captured and was forced to guide a patrol under Maroon hunter Jantke, but Kwami escaped by jumping in the water. Later another patrol captured a number of Maroons from Mapane, who were paddling in the Tempatie River. There seems to have been a linkage between these groups. The story goes that Da Anansi and Da Bigiman had met Da Doffin early on and at some point, had lived in the same village, but later split up.[19] Thus the forefathers and mothers of the *Antoisie-lo* and the *Asaiti-lo* had met before and later linked up again.

Not much is known about the early history of the *Mollo-lo*. They probably made their way towards the South and linked up with the other groups when they all roamed the Upper Tempatie Creek area.

[18] Most Maroons on the list, which several captured Maroons provided, originated from Arendsrust and Destombesburg.

[19] Morssink (1932-5) calculated—based on the age of a child that was mentioned and who was baptized in 1897 at age 50—that this meeting (when Apensa was about ten years old) must have happened around 1848. Morssink's calculation was based on a story that was told by captain Amerikan from the *Asaiti-lo*. We know, however, that Apensa was born in 1823 and thus would have been 25 years old if the meeting happened in 1848. By that time Apensa himself said that they had moved to the Paramaka Creek.

Reineman (1996) communicates that the archival resources about the Penninica Maroons (i.e. the *Antoisie-lo* and possibly also the *Asaiti-lo*) run dry around 1844. So most probably these Maroons had moved further down south and were not seen as a menace to the plantations any more. Reineman found some other Maroon groups, who may have linked up with the Pamaka. There was a group of a Maroon with the name of October, who created a settlement in an island on the Cottica River, but later moved towards the South. In 1835 this village was attacked by a patrol and several members of the group were enlisted in Doffin's village in 1837. In the late 1840s, two groups formed in the Upper Commewijne River and Tempatie River area. In the late 1840s, a lone Okanisi (Aukaner) man by the name of Kwamina (also known as Waidudu) had a wife, Constantia, from the plantation Waicoribo. There were many slaves from the plantations Wayampibo and Waicoribo in his camp. Not far from Waidudu, another man, Pikien Kwaku, probably from Waicoribo, build another camp. In 1849 and 1850 military patrols were sent out to capture the runaway slaves from both plantations and some were caught. Around that time, Waidudu and others killed a free guide and his daughter and this caused major problems. Waidudu was killed by a patrol, some persons were captured, while Pikien Kwaku and others fled to the Tempatie area, more to the South, and probably linked up with the Pamakas around 1850.

Maps and Almanacs

Most of the marronage that led to the formation of the Pamakas, took place around 1830, so we will trace the main plantations that have been associated with the different *lo*'s up to this point. In different maps and almanacs of Suriname we can find information about the plantations mentioned above.

Arendsrust. The map of De Lavaux[20] of 1737 shows the plantation

[20] Alexander de Lavaux made a crude map of Suriname while he was in the army (Bijlsma 1921). The map (published in 1737) is the first one with all the plantations (436 at the time) and has important information about the location of every plantation, its acreage and its owner(s). In 1752 his

Arentrust of 1,218 acres (about 500 hectare), which at that point belonged to Franc de Loges. Bijlsma (1921/22) made an inventory of plantations between 1713 and 1742 from the notary archives. He listed Arentrust and found documentation dating back to 1725.[21] The almanac of 1793 by Charles Brouwn was the first almanac with a list of plantations. Arendrust is listed as a sugar plantation owned by a Dutch (investment) fund of R. Braamcamp. In the almanac of 1796 the name was spelled 'Ahrendrust'. The report of the militia commander (*burgerkapitein*) in the region of Arendrust listed the number of slaves on this plantation in 1790 as 45. The map of Moseberg (1801) mentions the plantation with its acreage. In 1818 the plantation still produced sugar, but there was a new owner, i.e. the fund under the direction of J.J. Poncelet and Son. The almanac of 1825 provides the same information about Arendsrust, but now Gerritsen was the Director of the plantation and one of its administrators; we will see that he was the main reason why many slaves left the plantation. By 1827 the plantation area had been expanded from 1,218 acres to 2,218 acres and thus more slaves were needed. The almanac of 1838 gives the name of P. van Leeuwen Jr. as the new Director; it also informs us that there were now 214 slaves.

Hazard. The plantation Hazard did not exist when De Lavaux made his map in 1737, but it is shown in the updated version of 1752.[22] At that point it was spelled 'Hasard' and was owned by the heirs of F.N. Tuimelaar and measured 500 acres (200 hectare). The almanac of 1793 listed it as a coffee plantation, while ownership changed to a Dutch fund of S. van Nooten Janszoon. The almanac of 1796 states that Hazard was a sugar plantation of 1,500 acres (600 hectare), while the plantation Bergen op Zoom (500 acres) was now attached to Hazard and belonged to the same owner. In 1790 there were 76 slaves. Moseberg (1801) lists the plantation with its acreage. In 1818 Hazard was still a sugar-producing plantation, but ownership had changed to the fund under the Director C. Frymersum and Son.

publisher, Hendrick de Leth, extended the map with some new information.

[21] Bijlsma (1921-2) did not describe each plantation, but just mentioned if there was a file in the notary archives.

[22] See footnote 20.

The almanac of 1830 still provides the same ownership and a size of 2,000 acres. The almanac of 1838 mentioned the Dutch fund of Widow J.S. van de Poll as the new owners, while the size had somewhat decreased to 1,800 acres with 103 slaves working in this sugar plantation.

Molhoop. The plantation Mollenhoop was mapped by De Lavaux in 1737 and owned by J. Mol. The acreage was given as 351 acres (140 hectare). Mol also owned the land adjacent to Mollenhoop, and he owned another plantation nearby. In the map of 1752, Mollenhope was owned by the heirs of J. Mol. The almanac of 1793 listed Molhoop as a coffee and cotton producing plantation, which was owned by five different people, including L. Brederode. The almanac of 1796 mentions that the size of the plantation was 696 acres (278 hectare), so it had probably merged with a neighbouring plantation (most probably De Gekroonde Pauw). Moseberg (1801) lists the plantation with its expanded acreage. In 1818 the plantation produced coffee, but ownership changed to the fund under the supervision of Van den Broeke & J.J. Poncelet and Son. In 1825 E.G. Veldwijk was listed as the owner. In 1830 the plantations De Oude Bijenkorf (370 acres) and De Gekroonde Pauw (450 acres) were joined with Molhoop (492 acres), so the total size after this merger became 1312 acres. The product listed was still coffee, but according to the almanac of 1838 this changed to sugar as a new crop, while there were 305 slaves. Ownership remained the same, but the change in produce and size meant a major change for the slave population and the working conditions and could have triggered marronage.

Wayampibo. According to the map of De Lavaux (1737), the plantation Wyampoba was owned by G. de Vree. In the map of 1752 the name is spelled 'Wayampibo', while ownership was transferred to the heirs of H.W. Bransse. No acreage was listed in either year. Bijlsma (1921/22) found notary information of 1727. The almanac of 1793 lists Wajampibe as a sugar plantation owned by C.V. and D.A. Brantzen and van Engelen. The almanac of 1796 gives a size of 2,000 acres (800 hectare). There were 62 slaves in 1790. Moseberg

(1801) mentions the plantation, but without acreage. In 1818, the ownership of Wayampibo had changed to G. Titsingh and Son. According to the almanac of 1825 ownership of the plantation had once more changed hands to J. de Vries, who was also the director and administrator. By 1830 the owner probably had died, because his heirs are listed as owners, with J.F. Betten as the Director. In 1838 there were 128 slaves listed in this sugar plantation.

Reasons for marronage

Most marronage in Suriname took place at the height of the plantation period in the mid-eighteenth century, which was also the height of economic exploitation (Schalkwijk 2011). After the slave trade was abolished in 1807, treatment of slaves in Suriname in general seemed to improve. In 1817, slave regulations were extended and in 1828 slaves were finally recognized by law as persons and not any longer as mere goods. Nevertheless, there still were many individual cases of maltreatment and injustice. We saw that Maandag fled plantation Meulwijk, because they took his wife from him. Many Maroons, when captured, complained that they had been unfairly beaten or maltreated and therefore left the plantation. Others left because the work was too strenuous. Sometimes, Maroons who had fled earlier left their wife and children behind at the plantation and later went back to fetch them. Most Maroon villages initially had more males than females, so sometimes the Maroons raided plantations to get women but women here did not always volunteer to go along.

Teenstra (1842, 154-5) describes a situation in 1829 when Negroes from plantation Siparipabo refused to be taken to the neighbouring plantation Arendsrust, because its Director, B.A. Gerritsen, was a harsh master. Fourteen of the slaves from Siparibo even went to the capital city to complain about their transfer and this director. They described him as a brutal and unfair man who ill-treated his slaves. He had even killed a runaway slave, had cut off his genitals and had thrown them into the river. The 14 slaves were seeking justice, but instead received injustice by the colonial authorities, who punished their audacity; they were severely flogged, branded and chained for two years. Such was still the inequality—also in the courts—in those days. Reineman (1996) found in the archives that a special military patrol was sent out in September 1831 because many slaves from plantation Arendsrust had fled, which probably was a collective protest against the harsh treatment by the Director.

All four plantations mentioned earlier became sugar estates. In the sugar plantations, more often, the regime was tougher for the slaves than other plantations. At mechanized sugar estates the slaves also had to work at night, and often in shifts of 36 hours without sleep, so that sugarcane juice could be processed (Teenstra 1842, 23). Sugar plantations were also larger in size than the others and thus social life and solidarity at the plantation were of a different nature than at smaller estates.

In the eighteenth century, marronage sometimes occurred on a large scale when the enslaved people from entire plantations rebelled and fled. After the formation of the main Maroon tribes in Suriname (notably the Aukaner and Saramaka, with whom peace treaties were executed in 1760), large-scale marronage did not happen and the marronage pattern changed to a more individual or small group scale. Many slaves who fled the plantation often stayed in the vicinity and received their food still from the plantation. These were called *schuylders,* or people who were in hiding. Often these *schuylders* were picked up by Maroons who were also circling the plantations, where they still had connections or where they tried to lure slaves to choose freedom. Once a *schuylder* joined a group who had formed and established a village, especially when the village was at a good distance from the plantation area, he/she became a Maroon. Maroons were far less dependent on the plantation than *schuylders* and gradually formed tight social groups, which later became kinship groups. Initially the plantation from which the Maroon originated was a point of identification, because they already knew each other and had experienced mutual solidarity and trust at that location. Often, the core of a Maroon group was formed by people from the same plantation—or from which the clan mother came—and we see that the name of many clans are also derived from this core plantation. The pattern outlined above is also evident for the Pamaka groups.

Reconstruction of the trek of the Pamakas

The Maroons from the four core plantations first formed villages in the upper Commewijne River area (around 1820 to 1830) and later moved toward the Tempatie Creek area (around 1830 to 1840), where they lived for several years. From that area they tracked over the Nassau Mountains and settled in the Paramaka Creek (possibly around 1840). They probably stayed in the Paramaka Creek for several decades and in fact their name is associated with this creek. Residence at the Paramaka Creek was temporary, because after emancipation, they moved to several islands in the Marowijne River (around 1870). This was not their final move, however, since later about half of the tribe moved to French Guyane, which was mainly caused by the Internal War (1986-92), although some had moved even earlier. About a quarter of the tribe nowadays resides in the urban areas in and around Paramaribo, which is due to better access to the capital, and more employment and educational opportunities. Thus, only one quarter of the tribe still reside in the tribal area.

The situation sketched above seems the most probable sequence and timeline. Nevertheless, there are some conflicting accounts that we need to address. Wong (1938) states that the Pamaka tribe was formed in the mid-eighteenth century around the same time as the Aukaners. Lenoir (1974) used Wong as one of his sources, but also Benjamins (1916), who suggested a much later date, i.e. in his view Pamakas had split off from one of the larger Maroon tribes in 1838.[23] Lenoir wrote that '(…) the Paramaccans avoided military confrontations with either Djuka or the plantation forces. Perhaps this explains why the Paramacca Maroons have been largely overlooked by historians and anthropologist, and why there is so little

[23] Benjamins (1916), whose article Lenoir describes as an 'authoritative history', did not investigate the Pamakas at all in his article. He just wrote a very short paragraph about them and suggested that since there was no peace treaty with the Pamakas in 1838 (while this did exist with the Samakas, Djukas and Matawais), they probably had split off from one of those tribes after 1838. So, Benjamins' assessment was not authoritative at all but mere speculation.

agreement as to their origin' (1974, 18). In the earlier sections of this paper we saw, however, that even if the Maroons did not seek confrontations, the military patrols still would hunt them down, and thus they would be 'found' in the colonial documents. The Pamakas could not have escaped 'discovery' for nearly a hundred years by the colonial authorities and thus it is very unlikely that the Pamakas were formed before the 1800s.

Morton Kahn (1931) visited the Djuka (Aukaner) tribe along the Marowijne River thrice in the period between 1927 and 1930. He also met some Pamaka people during his travels on this river. During one such visit he also met with 'Captain Koffay' of the Pamakas, '(…) who claims to be some eighty years of age (…)'. This captain said that he 'is the grandson of the original women slaves who escaped and aided in founding the tribe'. He met Koffay in the Pamaka village of Seeton Ponta on the French side of the Marowijne River (p. 109). This captain almost sure has to be David Koffie, who died in October 1939. We know this from Wong (1940), who wrote about the appointment of new captains for the Pamakas. He informed the Governor that it was difficult to appoint a new captain for the *Asaiti-lo,* since David Koffie was still the main captain of years old this *lo.*

For many years he had not been living in the village of Badatabbetje, but in a village opposite Herminadorp on the French side (which must have been Seeton Ponta).[24] Koffie told Kahn that he knew his grandmother who had escaped from a plantation. This means that if Koffie was about 80 years old in 1930 he was born around 1850. If his grandmother was around 40 years old when he

[24] Wong (1940) writes that Koffie's sister Adolfina and her children had also moved (most probably to the French side). The colonial government, however, wanted captains to live in their village. Koffie himself had appointed his sister's son Alexander (also known as Eglisi) as his successor, who still lived in the tribal area. Wong did not support this choice, because the village of Baddatabbetje was hardly populated and did not need a captain. The lo did not need a captain in Wong's opinion, because the lo was quite small, so neither did the other lo's need a lo-captain (lebi djakti) and just a village captain would do.

was born, this must have been around 1810. If she fled the plantation when she was a young woman of 15 to 20 years, this must have been around 1825 to 1830, which corroborates with the periodization given before. But if his grandmother was 50 years old when he was born and was about 10 years when she escaped, then the date of the marronage is about 20 years earlier, but not more than that.[25] It is a pity that David Koffie did not provide the name of his grandmother (or rather that Kahn did not write it down). The name is also not listed in the family tree which Wong drew of the *Asaiti-lo*. In Wong's family tree, the mother of David Koffie was Abeni, who had fled the plantation Hazard together with her sister Sanna, with the clan mother Amba, Asabi Asani and her Sister Dienki. It is not clear if they all fled the plantation at the same time as Amba, because she is the clan mother. Koffie's grandmother (if from mother's side) thus probably did not flee the plantation at the same time as her daughter, otherwise her name would surely appear as a clan mother. It is possible that she fled later and joined the group, but it is also possible that Koffie referred to his grandmother from father's side or to an uncle's mother (given the matriarchal family system). In the family trees that were drawn up for the Asaiti, it appeared that Koffie was from a different *bee* (family) as Amba, i.e. the *bee* that moved to Badatabbetje.

It is mentioned in various accounts that Kwaku Apensa (the granman), who died in 1923 at the age of 101 years, was the first child born in the jungle in the Tempatie Creek area.[26] This actually means that when he was born in 1823, his mother (Ma Asa also known as Ninne, the clan mother of the *Antoosi-lo*) therefore already had fled the plantation area, which puts the time of early marron-

[25] Women at that time begot children when they were still quite young and thus the first scenario seems more likely.

[26] The Moravian missionary Freytag wrote in 1926 that Apensa was born in the Tempatie Creek and that he was an adolescent when they moved from there to the Paramaka Creek. '*t Is nu bijna honderd jaar geleden, dat hij aan de Tempati geboren werd als zoon van een gevluchten slaaf. Hij was een opgroeiende jongen, toen zijn stam naar Paramakka toog*' (Reineman 1996). This information Freytag must have got from Apensa himself.

FIGURE 3.5: DAVID KOFFIE AROUND 1930 AT AN AGE OF OVER 80 YEARS.

Note: Kahn (1931) does not mention who is in the photo, but this is the only photo of a Pamaka. Kahn spoke at length with Koffie, which makes it more likely that this is his picture.

age of this clan of the Pamakas as around 1810 to 1820.[27] Kwaku was an adolescent when he moved from the Tempatie Creek to the Paramaka Creek, which suggests that if he was around 15 years old at that time and born in 1823, the group moved to the Paramaka Creek around 1838.

Koffie's recollection of his grandmother's narrative is one of the very few authentic, first hand stories about the early Pamaka, and thus worth telling.

[27] We assume that Ma Asa fled as a teenager or young woman and soon after got her first child in the jungle (*in het bos*). If she fled as a girl and only had her first child after ten years than the period of marronage shifts to around 1810 but not much earlier. It also indicates that the Pamakas did not linger long in the plantation area on the Upper Commewijne River, but probably moved earlier to the Tempatie Creek.

He can remember his grandmother telling of the terrible privations of the early days when they first escaped into the jungle, how starvation nearly overtook them on a number of occasions, how they wandered for forty-seven days aimlessly in the high bush, and then happened upon the putrid remains of a tapir which had been killed by a jaguar and which food, after they chased the vultures away, was what saved them from starvation (Kahn 1931, 110-11).

There is also a gap in the exact history around the time that the Pamaka clans crossed from the Tempatie Creek area over the Nassau Mountains to the Paramaka Creek. Lenoir tells us that the Pamakas fled from the Tempatie Creek area after residing there for about ten years. 'This time they fled from the Djuka Maroons, who found the Paramacca settlement, and it was presumed, were preparing to turn the unauthorized Maroons over to the military for a ransom' (1974, 24).[28] According to Lenoir's version '(…) the period on the Paramacca Creek, ca. 1810-1876, was marked by a gradual movement of camps downstream toward the Marowijne River (…)'. In the Paramaka Creek they first built villages upstream on higher ground, but later they moved towards the mouth of the Creek. If the clan leaders and mothers of the Pamaka, however, fled the plantations around 1830, they could not have crossed the Nassau Mountains in 1810, but probably did so in the 1840s or even 1850s. But if they fled earlier, around 1810 to 1820, which seems to have been the case for the *Antoisie-lo*, than they reached the Paramaka Creek in the 1830s. Actually, the story of granman Apensa puts the date that they crossed the Nassau Mountains around 1835.

An interesting source to get a sense of dates is provided by government surveyor W.L. Loth, who led an expedition from August to October 1878 to trace a path from the Tempatie Creek to the Suriname River. He went by steamboat from Paramaribo to plantation Hazard in the upper Commewijne River. From there they travelled to the Tempatie Creek but stopped at the Maroon village of Matappi, headed by chief Mijnzak. When they reached the Tempatie

[28] The Djuka Maroons were free people, based on the Peace Treaty of 1760, and renewed in 1809. The Pamaka Maroons were still 'unauthorized', i.e. there was no peace treaty with them.

Creek they stopped at another Maroon village of Loka and later an abandoned military post Maagdenburg. They continued until the Atie Creek (see Figure 3.4) and travelling by canoe about a day further they arrived at an abandoned Maroon village Foto (= city).[29] Only two persons still lived there, one of them was a 'Paramaka Negro'. Loth wanted to recruit some Maroons, but they needed permission from chief Mijnzak first, which they obtained. At that time Governor Van Sypesteyn was interested in Loth's expedition and visited him in the Tempatie Creek. He stayed two days there and many Maroons gathered there and organized a dance in the evening. The Maroons had been reluctant to assist Loth to visit the Upper Tempatie Creek area, because they thought that he wanted to discover the path the Pamaka Maroons had taken. Remember that it was only 1878, just five years after the period of State Supervision had ended and not even 20 years after the last military patrols were hunting runaway slaves.[30] The Maroons later told Loth that because the Governor assured them about his intentions, they opened up about the Pamakas:

It is through this Creek that in 'later' times most of the runaway slaves reached the Marowijne River, where they settled at the foot of the Nassau Mountains. Those Maroons who fled 'later' have become known as Paramaka Negroes.

They made clear that they first lived in the Paramaka Creek, before they '(…) two years ago transferred their homes to the banks of the Marowijne River (…)'. The Maroons showed Loth the path that the Pamakas had taken:

Here and there remnants of trees that were used to make canoes (*korjalen*) to continue their flight were still visible. The Paramaka man who accompa-

[29] This village was about three hours south of the Sokoti Creek (Loth 1879). Loth does not tell us to which tribe the Maroons who lived in the villages belonged, but they were not Pamaka, because there was only one Pamaka man among them. The Atie Creek is on the map in Figure 3.4.

[30] Emancipation of slaves took place on 1 July 1863, but there was a period of 10 years of State Supervision (*Staatstoezicht*) to prevent the slaves from abandoning the plantations in large numbers.

nied us knew of nearly every tree that was cut who made that specific canoe and what hardship and misery the runaways had to bear.

From this account we gain several insights. First, there were several Maroon villages, but only one Pamaka Maroon man; the other Maroons, however, showed solidarity and did not 'betray' him. Second, there was a military outpost in the Tempatie Creek, which was not there in the 1840s, thus indicating that the military had expanded their operational territory to capture escaped slaves, and most probably added 'heat' to the Pamaka to leave the area. Third, the Pamaka man knew all the trees and canoe makers by name, which indicates that the move of the Pamaka from the Tempatie Creek area to the Paramaka Creek had happened only recently. This corroborates that they had left the Tempatie Creek area not around 1810 but probably much later, because the Pamaka man could not otherwise have remembered who had made the canoes, while the remnants of the trees would not have been visible anymore. Fourth, by this account the Pamakas moved from the Paramaka Creek to the Marowijne River in 1876. Fifth, the story talks about Maroons who had fled 'later' most probably meaning that they did not belong to the first groups of Maroons (such as the Djukas), but to more recent groups.

Interestingly, Cateau van Roosevelt published a map of Suriname in 1879 (Figure 3.6), but his field work for the map was done earlier.[31] In his report Loth wrote that he had consulted Cateau van Roosevelt, who had given him part of his (then unpublished) map. We see many interesting features on the map. The village Foto is on this map and probably had not as yet been abandoned when Cateau van Roosevelt visited that area. It is described on the map as an Aukaner village, but most probably was established by the Pamakas and could have been the first *Antoisie-lo* village in that area. There are no drawings of Maroon villages along the Marowijne River, only in the Paramaka

[31] The curriculum of Johan François Adriaan Cateau van Roosevelt can be found in Benjamins & Snelleman (1917). The previous map of Suriname, before his map, dates back to 1801, but because of the gold industry a new map was needed. He performed his field work from 1861 to 1879.

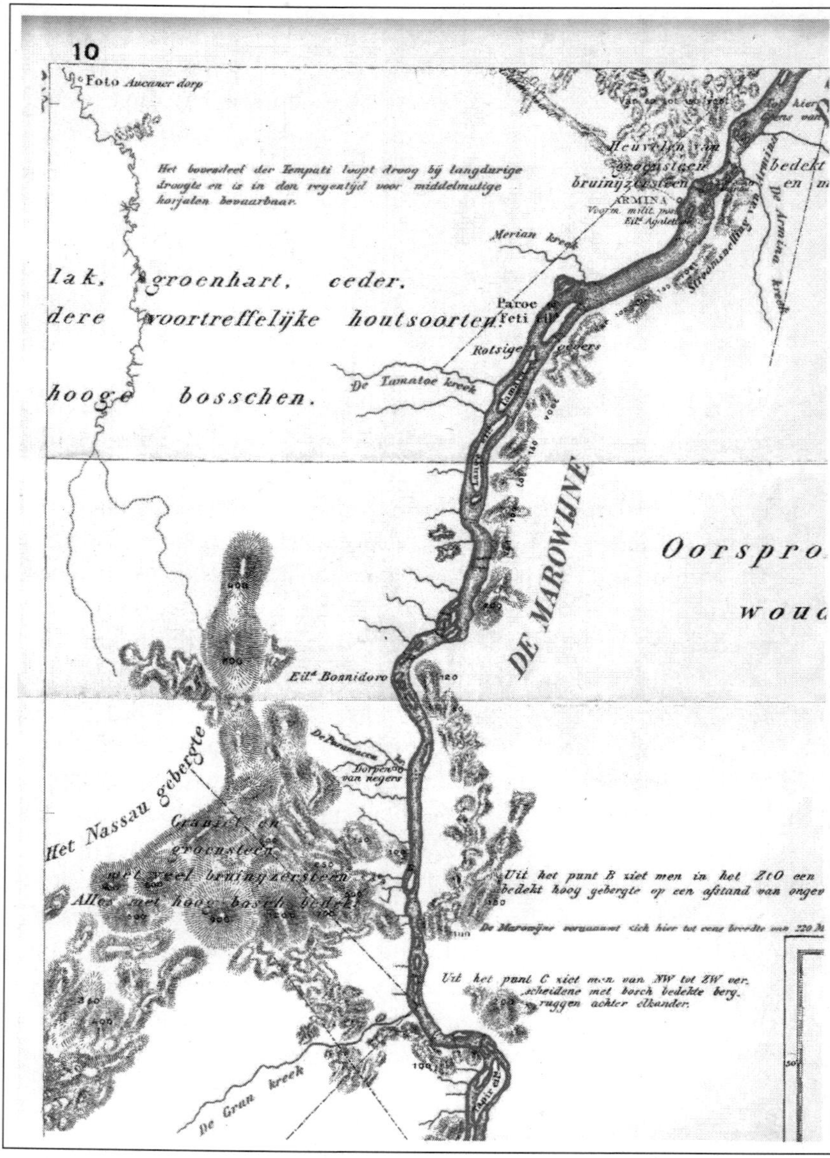

FIGURE 3.6: MAP OF CATEAU VAN ROOSEVELT, PUBLISHED IN 1879
(*Source:* Wikipedia.org/wiki/Johannes_Cateau_van_Rosevelt).

Creek; but these are near the mouth of the Paramaka Creek. This most probably means that when Cateau van Roosevelt visited the Marowijne in 1861, he did not observe any Maroon villages along that stretch of the Marowijne River.[32] Thus the Pamaka had not yet settled there, although they clearly had reached the mouth of the Paramaka Creek.

From Paramaka Creek to Marowijne River

It seems most likely that the Pamaka clans reached the Paramaka Creek around 1835 and probably stayed in that creek until after emancipation (1863). The account that the Pamaka man told surveyor Loth was that they actually moved to the Marowijne River in 1876. Because there were several groups that later joined to form the Pamaka tribe, it is possible that one group reached somewhat later than the other group. It is also possible that there were some advance groups to check out the area.

The postholder (*posthouder*) to the Djuka, F. Schachtrupp, was the first colonial bureaucrat to report about the Pamaka.[33] He observed some of them working for the Djuka and for several months he investigated who they were. Wong (1938, 327) quotes the following details from Schachtrupp's journal of 4 June 1830:

> Today I found out who the Negroes were whom I mentioned in my journal of 18 October: they are runaways (wegloopers) who were found by the rebels, who gave them a place to live. They number, as I have heard, 8 men and

[32] Cateau van Roosevelt's cartographic work on the Marowijne River was done in the period 1861 when he was member of the French-Dutch Commission to establish the border between Suriname and French Guyane and travelled the whole Marowijne and Lawa River (Benjamins & Snelleman 1917).

[33] The postholder was a special envoy of the Colonial State who lived among one of the pacified tribes. In the beginning these civil servants were recruited from ex-military, who had to make sure that the articles in the peace treaty with the tribe where they were stationed, were followed or implemented, while they also issued travel passports. The postholder reported what was happening in the territory he was assigned to. Sometimes he had an assistant (*bijlegger*).

1 woman; the Aukaners call these Negroes Paramakkaners. As I have heard there is a much larger group of these negroes in their old village, because they want to wait and see if the Aukaners are going to take them from the rebels and hand them over to the White people; if not they will move to the Marowijne River. This old village, where they live, they call Paramakka, and a few rebels have visited them there already, but the Aukaners do not know this.

According to Schachtrupp, they probably lived in French Guyana, where they had met the 'rebels' (i.e. the Poligudu). By 'rebels' he meant the Black Guides, a group of hired slaves, who had formed a special black unit (*Zwarte Jagers* or *Redimusu*) to hunt runaway slaves and protect the *Cordonpad* (the Colonial Defense line surrounding the plantations).[34] In 1805 a group of the Maroons went on a mutiny and killed 30 soldiers from the military posts Imotapie and Oranjebo on the Upper Commewijne River (see Figure 3.3). They were supported by 30 slaves from neighbouring plantations and left on foot to the military post Armina. There they also killed the White soldiers, while other Black Guides joined them. With 80 other men they joined the Boni tribe, who were fighting the Dutch colonial army. Later they received permission from the Aukaners to settle at Poligudu (De Groot 1970). So this group of 'rebels' were also called the *Poligudu Nengre*. When Schachtrupp found out who the Pamakas were, he demanded from the granman of the Djuka (*Aukaners*) that he hand them over to the Colonial Government. But granman Trobie told him that he had nothing to do with them, since the Poligudus found them. This indicates that the Poligudu were allowed to live with the Djukas, but were kept at some distance by them.

Reineman (1996) suggests that the group from 1830 probably was not related to the Pamaka tribe, but as I indicated, the Pamakas probably were testing the waters and had sent some advance group to check out what the intentions of the Djuka were. This is supported by the fact that Schachtrupp's report mentions that there was

[34] Leden van het korps werkten voor vijf jaar en kregen pas daarna hun vrijbrief.

a larger group in the old village. Furthermore, the connection with the Poligudu seems to have lasted and thus was not incidental.

In 1850 another postholder, F.W. Hostman, reported that there were Paramaka Negroes living in the Gran Creek (see Figure 3.6). He also mentioned that the Poligudu had good relationships with the Pamakas. The Djuka formally were not involved with the Pamakas, but Hostman suspected that in secret they also had a good relationship with them (Reineman 1996). Again, this is quite possible, because the Pamakas had already crossed the Nassau Mountains and although they had not as yet settled on the Marowijne River, some of them may have moved toward the Gran Creek. This area became part of the tribal area of the Pamakas, so it actually makes sense that some of them went there.

Postholder August Kappler reported in 1857 that the Pamakas were living in the Paramaka Creek—a few hours land inward from the Marowijne River—before 1836. They first lived on high ground, which was very fertile, and due to this location, a good hideout for escape. Later their villages were closer to the banks of the Marowijne River (in Reineman 1996).[35] Kappler provided more information to G. Duykinck, a member of the governing board of the colony (*raadcommissaris*), who wrote a report for the Governor in January 1872, based on this information. According to the report the Pamakas were cutting timber for the Djukas in the Tempatie Creek, while they also sold food to the Djukas. But the Djukas seemed to 'supervise' them and pressure them to work for them.

We know that in the 1860s the Pamakas were still in the Paramaka Creek, because a French priest, Pere Krämer, spend two months with them. Granman Aboenawroko remembered this visit which was in Bebi-holo, half a day by boat into the Paramaka Creek.[36] This thus

[35] F. Schachtrupp (1824-40), F.W. Hostman (1840) and A. Kappler (1841-78) were all postholders at some point, who stayed with the Djuka tribe or reported about the Djukas (Kappler actually lived in Albina) and thus had to travel the Marowijne River frequently.

[36] Aboenawroko told this to the priest Morssink on 5 March 1932. The fact about Krämer's visit was noted by August Kappler, but Morssink clearly did check this with Aboenawroko, who confirmed his visit.

supports the information on the map by Cateau van Roosevelt and the story that the Pamaka man told surveyor Loth.

It was most probably that during the period in the Paramaka Creek that there was a traumatic leadership drama within the tribe. The Pamaka man who met surveyor Loth gave this account:

> … later two ferocious men, Amani and Nero, joined them; how these men took control over them by treacherously killing their elders; how those cruel men sought to hurt the Djuka by ambushing captains and other chiefs of the Djuka, who were passing by in boats in the Wane Creek, which connects the Marowijne River with the Coermotibo Creek and the Cottica River, by shooting them, until one day they themselves, while they were in their camp in a Creek which connects with the Tempatie Creek, were attacked by two Aukaners, named Anoké and Azwakie, and decapitated.

It most probably was Kappler who convinced Frans Kwaku—the leader of the Pamaka at that point—to visit Paramaribo in 1871, because Duykinck wrote in his report: 'Finally, after many efforts to dispel their fear, it was possible to persuade them last year to go to the city.' There is a very short mention of this visit in the Colonial Report of 1872:

> A tribe of the Paramacca-Negroes, of the Marowijne River, who before had no contact with the urban area of this colony, which was caused by fear, have changed their mind and have sent their chief with entourage to Paramaribo in late 1871.[37]

There is clear evidence that Frans Kwaku and his delegation met the Governor and Duykinck gives us a short account of what transpired during that meeting:

> Their chief, accompanied by some ten tribesmen, went there (to Paramaribo) and had the honor to be received by Your Excellency, at which occasion you (the Governor) explained what their duties were and told them about their unfounded fear that they were taxable (*cijnsbaar*) by the Bushnegroes (i.e.

[37] 'Eene stam der Paramacca-negers, gevestigd aan de Marowijne, die vroeger geene gemeenschap onderhield met het bebouwde gedeelte dezer kolonie, hetgeen aan vrees moest worden toegeschreven, is daarvan teruggekomen en zond in het laatst van 1871 zijnen hoofdman met gevolg naar Paramaribo.' (Koloniaal Verslag van 1872, 543).

the Djukas). It is to be expected that the impression of this visit, will be such that they will have more relationship with the urban part of the colony, which surely will lead to the civilization and development of these Negroes.

Captain Amekan (or Amerikan) told ranger Febis that Frans Kwaku (Amerikan's father) was officially installed as granman by the Governor.[38] According to Scholtens (1994), this was not the case, if so, Wong would surely have mentioned this. No documentation was found in the archives of an official installation either. Nevertheless, this visit by Frans Kwaku was a major step by the Pamakas to connect with the larger Surinamese society.

When Frans Kwaku visited Paramaribo, the Pamaka tribe most probably were still living in the Paramaka Creek, otherwise Kappler (and Duykinck) would have mentioned that they had moved to the Marowijne. It is also probable that the tribe had just built their first village near the Marowijne River at the mouth of the Paramaka Creek. This village was called Amoesa and from here every Pamaka clan moved further to new villages along the Marowijne River (Lenoir 1974).

Conclusion

In conclusion we come back to the three suggested versions of the origin of the Pamaka. It seems very unlikely that the initial leaders of the Pamaka fled the plantations during the eighteenth century [which Wong (1938) suggested]. It is simply not true that the Pamakas split off around 1838 from one of the main Maroon tribes (as suggested by Benjamins 1916). The linkage of the different clans with the plantations around 1830, as in the research done by Hoogbergen (2015) and Reineman (1996), is not completely convincing either, because the link could not be made with names and/or for all clans. Still this was the best attempt so far.

Given all the facts and circumstances this reconstruction of the early history is as follows. Most probably the different groups, who

[38] Febis spoke with captain Amerikan in April 1924 and send his report to father Morssink, who wrote it in his manuscript 'Boschnegeriana' (1934). Information from Reineman (1996).

later formed the Pamaka, left the plantations between 1810 and 1830. They formed some villages in the Peninica Creek area, but later moved to the Tempatie Creek area, where they lived for several years. From that area they trekked over the Nassau Mountains and settled in the Paramaka Creek (around 1835), one of the main villages being Bebi-holo. They stayed in the Paramaka Creek for several decades, but eventually shifted closer towards the mouth of this creek. They build a village, Amoesa, close to the Marowijne River, from where they moved to different villages along the Marowijne River in the 1870s, most probably in 1876.

Different clans, however, may have moved at different times, so there probably is some spread when they crossed the Nassau Mountains, while some people probably migrated back and forth. The same is true for the period in which they reached the Marowijne River.

In this attempt to tell the story of the first period of the Pamaka Maroons I was able to draw on some oral stories of members of the group, although often quoted by others. I did not address more speculative assumptions that the Pamaka are somehow connected in history to the Boni (Aluku) and the Kwinti tribes, which is an interesting line to pursue, but which is difficult to support by evidence, since I did not find any in the archives.

In their early history, the Pamakas crossed paths with the Aukaners on several occasions, since they were active in the same general area. Their relationship seemed to be one of caution and distrust. The Aukaners were a large group, whose freedom was officially recognized by the Colonial State through the Peace Treaty of 1760. The Pamakas were a small group of recent Maroonage and not covered by any peace treaty. On the one hand, the Aukaners had an obligation to return all run-away slaves, while on the other hand, they had a tendency to tolerate such groups, but supervised their activities to make sure they were no threat to them or to the Colonial State. The meeting between granman Kwaku and the Governor indicates the nature of the relationship between the Pamakas and Aukaners. The assurance by the Governor in 1871 that the Aukaners had no supervisory rights over the Pamakas, most probably gave them enough self-confidence to move to the Marowijne River shortly afterwards.

Bibliography

Benjamins, H.D. 1916. 'Politieke contracten met de Boschnegers in Suriname.' *Bijdragen tot de Taal-, Land- en Volkenkunde van Nederlandsch*-Indië: 371-411.

Benjamins, H.D. & Snelleman, J.F. 1917. *Encyclopedie van Nederlandsch West Indië.* Den Haag: Martinus Nijhoff/E.J. Brill.

Bijlsma, R. 1921. Alexander de Lavaux en zijne generale kaart van Suriname van 1737. West Indische Gids 2: 397-406.

_____. 1921-2. 'Surinaamsche plantage-inventarissen uit het tijdperk 1713-1742.', *West Indische Gids* 3: 325-32.

Brouwn, Charles. 1793. *Surinaamsche Staatkundige Almanach voor den jaare 1793.* Paramaribo: W.P. Wilkens.

_____. 1796. *Surinaamsche Staatkundige Almanach voor den jaare 1796.* Paramaribo: W.P. Wilkens.

Bruijning, C.F.A., J. Voorhoeve & W. Gordijn. 1977. *Encyclopedie van Suriname.* Amsterdam: Elsevier.

Hoogbergen, Wim S.M. 2015. 'Les Pamaaka dans les Lowéten', in J. Moomou, *Sociétés marrones des Amériques, mémoires, patrimoines, identités et histoire du XVIIe au XXe siècles.* Paris: Ibis Rouge.

_____. 1985. *De Boni-oorlogen, 1757-1860: Marronage en guerilla in Oost-Suriname.* Den Haag: Stichting Nieuwe West-Indische Gids en Centrum voor Caraïbische Studies.

_____. 2009. *Het kamp van Broos en Kaliko. De geschiedenis van een Afro-Surinaamse familie.* Paramaribo: VACO.

Groot de, Silvia W. 1970. 'Rebellie der Zwarte Jagers.' *De Gids*: 133 (9).

Jagdew, Eric R. 2014. 'Vrede te midden van oorlog in Suriname. Inheemsen, Europeanen, Marrons en vredesverdragen, 1667-1863' (Proefschrift, Anton de Kom Universiteit van Suriname).

Kahn, Morton C. 1931. *Djuka: The Bush Negros of Dutch Guiana.* New York: The Viking Press.

Koloniaal Verslag van 1879. *Verslag van eene expeditie tot het traceren van een weg van de Tempatiekreek naar de rivier Suriname, Zitting 1879-1880, no. 17.*

Lenoir, John D. 1974. The Paramacca Maroons: A Study in Religious Acculturation. Michigan: University Microfilms, A Xerox Company.

Maatschappij Tot Nut van 't Algemeen, Departement Paramaribo. 1825. *Surinaamsche Almanak voor het jaar 1825.* Amsterdam: Gebroeders van Cleef/ C.G. Sulpke.

Maatschappij Tot Nut van 't Algemeen, Departement Paramaribo. 1827.

Surinaamsche Almanak voor het jaar 1827. Amsterdam: Gebroeders van Cleef/ C.G. Sulpke.

Maatschappij Tot Nut van 't Algemeen, Departement Paramaribo. 1830. *Surinaamsche Almanak voor het jaar 1830*. Amsterdam: C.G. Sulpke.

Maatschappij Tot Nut van 't Algemeen, Departement Paramaribo. 1838. *Surinaamsche Almanak voor het jaar 1838*. Amsterdam: C.G. Sulpke.

Morssink, F. 1932-'35. *Boschnegeriana (Silvae-nigritiana): Eenige gegevens omtrent geschiedenis en missioneering onzer Surinaamsche Boschnegers*. Paramaribo.

NGO Instituut voor Kaderontwikkeling en Onderzoek in Suriname. 2016. *Pamaka Ontwikkelingsplan 2016-2020*. Paramaribo: NIKOS.

NGO Instituut voor Kaderontwikkeling en Onderzoek in Suriname. 2016. *Ontwikkelingsplan Atemsa 2016-2019*. Paramaribo: NIKOS.

NGO Instituut voor Kaderontwikkeling en Onderzoek in Suriname. 2016. *Ontwikkelingsplan Badatabiki 2016-2019*. Paramaribo: NIKOS.

NGO Instituut voor Kaderontwikkeling en Onderzoek in Suriname. 2016. *Ontwikkelingsplan Langatabiki 2016-2019*. Paramaribo: NIKOS.

NGO Instituut voor Kaderontwikkeling en Onderzoek in Suriname. 2016. *Ontwikkelingsplan Loka Loka 2016-2019*. Paramaribo: NIKOS.

NGO Instituut voor Kaderontwikkeling en Onderzoek in Suriname. 2016. *Ontwikkelingsplan Nason 2016-2019*. Paramaribo: NIKOS.

NGO Instituut voor Kaderontwikkeling en Onderzoek in Suriname. 2016. *Ontwikkelingsplan Pakiratabiki 2016-2019*. Paramaribo: NIKOS.

NGO Instituut voor Kaderontwikkeling en Onderzoek in Suriname. 2016. *Ontwikkelingsplan Sebedoekondre 2016-2019*. Paramaribo: NIKOS.

NGO Instituut voor Kaderontwikkeling en Onderzoek in Suriname. 2016. *Ontwikkelingsplan Skintabiki 2016-2019*. Paramaribo: NIKOS.

NGO Instituut voor Kaderontwikkeling en Onderzoek in Suriname. 2016. *Ontwikkelingsplan Tabiki-ede 2016-2019*. Paramaribo: NIKOS.

Polimé, T. 1995. *Streekontwikkelingsplan Paramakkaans stamgebied*. Paramaribo.

Price, Richard & Sally Price. 2003. *Les Marrons*. Châteauneuf-le-Rouge: Vents d'ailleurs/ Ici & Ailleurs.

Price, Richard. 1973. Maroon societies: Rebel Slave Communities in the Americas. Garden City/ New York: Anchor Books.

Reineman, M. 1996. '*In het spoor van de Paramaka*.' (Afstudeeronderzoek Universiteit Utrecht).

Schalkwijk, J. Marten W. 2011. The Colonial State in the Caribbean. Structural analysis and changing elite networks in Suriname 1650-1920. Den Haag: Amrit, NiNsee-reeks.

Scholtens, Bernardus. 1994. *Bosnegers en overheid in Suriname: de ontwikkeling van de politiekeverhouding 1651-1992*. Paramaribo: Minov.

Steinberg, H.G. 1933. *Ons Suriname: de zending der Evangelische Broedergemeente in Nederlandsch Guyana*. 's-Gravenhage: Algemeene Boekhandel voor Inwendige en Uitwendige Zending.

Surinaamsche Staatkundige Almanak voor den jaare 1818. Paramaribo: Gepriviligeerde Gouvernements Drukkerij.

Teenstra, Marten D. 1842. *De negerslaven in de kolonie Suriname*. Dordrecht: H. Lagerweij.

Wong, E. 1938. *Hoofdenverkiezing, stamverdeeling en stamverspreiding der Boschnegers van Suriname in de 18e en 19e eeuw*. Rapport uitgebracht aan Z.E. den Gouverneur van Suriname, ter voldoening aan de Resolutie van Z.E. den Minister van Staat, Minister van Koloniën d.d. 1 Juli 1936, 7e afdeeling No. 20, Paramaribo.

_____. 1940. *Betreffende organisatie binnen den stam der Paramaccaners*. Nationaal Archief Suriname, Gouverneur van Suriname 1846-1957 nr. 9923-9926, folio nr. 591. Paramaribo.

Maps

Barron, Gerrit. 2004. *Plantagekaart van het 'Rijke' Suriname, ca. 1840*. Paramaribo: Afaka International.

De Lavaux, A. *Algemeene kaart van de Colonie of Provintie van Suriname* (c. 1770). Amsterdam: Universiteitsbibliotheek.

_____. *Algemene kaart van Suriname 1737-1757*. www.rijksmuseum.nl/nl/collectie/NG-478.

Hebri Wereldatlas. 2008. *Suriname Wereldland*. Uitgeverij Hebri BV.

Van Roosevelt, Cateau J.F.A. & J.F.A.E. van Lansberge. 2004. *Kaart van Suriname. Naar de opmetingen gedaan in de jaren 1860-1879*. Amsterdam: Buijten & Schipperheijn Recreatief.

Wekker, E.J.E. 1986. *Ken uw Land II. Lijst van aardrijkskundige namen in Suriname*. Paramaribo: Warimbo (herziene uitgave).

Archival sources

Note: These archival sources were all checked for entries on Pamaka (Paramaka, Paramacca) in the period 1850 through 1920 (if available).

Nationaal Archief Suriname: Gouverneurs van Suriname, 1846-1957.

Nationaal Archief Suriname: Gouvernementssecretarie, 1829-1954.

Nationaal Archief Suriname en www.statengeneraaldigitaal.nl: Koloniale Verslagen Suriname 1860-1920.

FOUR

Sugar Strikes
Confronting Plantation Legacies in the 1930s British Guiana

NICOLE BURROWES

Introduction

The project of empire relied on overlapping dispossessions of land, body and labour. The plantation complex in the Caribbean was a critical node for European empires. Its very development was fuelled by racialized logics that were reasserted and rearranged over time. Caribbean peoples fought against these systems of reason that were cemented by the labour regimes of the plantation.

In this chapter, I shall briefly explore three processes that became fundamental to plantation development: Indigenous erasure, enslavement, and indenture. I will argue how the logic attached to these dispossession projects still persisted in the 1930s British Guiana. However, the affected communities pushed back through a labour movement. Finally, I shall discuss the possibilities and limitations of this movement, and discuss dispossession in the Caribbean and beyond.

Affected communities in British Guiana fought back in the most unlikely of times—in 1935—during a period of high unemployment, the upheaval of the Great Depression and in the aftermath of environmental crisis.[1] Specifically, African- and Indian-Guianese youth, women and men working on sugar estates led a movement that challenged the plantation system, attendant racial logics and colonialism itself. Through strikes, cultural processions and acts of sabotage, they advocated for themselves, their loved ones and their communities. In the wake of the centennial celebrations of emancipation in 1934, they contested the conditions on the plantation by utilizing the spectre of slavery and exposing the continued logic of indenture, despite its formal end in 1917.

This movement did not lead to the overthrow of a system that had been oppressive and exploitative from its inception. Workers' efforts impacted concrete conditions, salaries and unsettled a variety of planter narratives and operations. They fought against the legacies of enslavement, indenture and colonial beliefs about their lives and value through their actions. But, as we will see, other colonial narratives remained firmly in place. Through a discussion of this movement, and the larger entanglements created by these systems, we can begin to understand the legacies of the plantation complex and the politics of racialized dispossession.

Modernity, Entanglement and Indigenous Erasure

Caribbeanists have long argued that the Caribbean is central to the development of capitalism and modernity, a modernity born in the plantation and racialized labour regimes. Caribbean historian and feminist Melanie Newton (2013) points out that this formulation, particularly powerful in the Anglophone Caribbean, has its dangers because it obscures Indigenous dispossession and unwittingly adopts the colonial logic of Indigenous erasure. Other scholars have argued that Indigenous erasure itself was a 'fiction' of possession (Lowe 2015). Newton notes that 'Caribbean history is defined by aboriginal absence, and the plantation marks the Caribbean's entry into modernity' (2013, 109). In response to this thinking, she pushes

[1] British Guiana is the colonial name of the country, renamed Guyana after independence in 1966.

FIGURE 4.1: CANE CUTTERS AT WORK

Source: Report of an Inquiry into the Sugar Industry in British Guiana. CO/946/4 National Archives, London.

us to think about 'original geography' and to conceptualize the Caribbean as indigenous space (2013, 121).

Highlighting the centrality of the plantation and its connection to modernity does not have the same erosive tendency in other parts of the Caribbean. For example, in the Spanish-speaking Caribbean, particularly in Puerto Rico and the Dominican Republic, there is an emphasis on Indigenous heritage. As one leading Puerto Rican scholar of indigeneity, Jalil Sued-Badillo (2011, 103), wrote, 'Taino world has been an intrinsic part of Caribbean historic memory and modern national identities—if not biologically, then certainly culturally and spiritually.' However, this identification with the Indigenous, at least in the case of the Dominican Republic, came with an attendant symbolic and violent erasure of African roots based in a deep politics of denial, anti-blackness and anti-Haitianism. There is something different about the Spanish Caribbean where sometimes people cling to their Indigenous heritage, to the point of sometimes erasing their African heritage.

These contradictory positions on the role of Indigenous peoples in Caribbean history, point to the distinctive historical experiences and trajectories that developed in different geographies of the

Caribbean. This history has high stakes. We must recognize that the Caribbean is the epitome of points of entanglement that exist because of empire and the plantation complex. How did these entanglements operate on the ground? In Guyana, the response to this question is drawn from a multi-faceted legacy.

Europeans depended heavily on Indigenous peoples for the initial development of the plantation system in what is today Guyana. As Brackette Williams (2001) and others have pointed out, they served as critical guides for explorers. European settlers initially tried to enslave Indigenous people, but couldn't because of their familiarity with the territory: they kept escaping. Ironically, they would later serve as both trackers and refuge communities for fugitive enslaved Africans. However, European dominance on the coast in the interest of developing plantations meant a systematic dispossession of Indigenous lands.

On Dispossession of Land, Body and Labour

The renewed debate about dispossession, particularly in the United States of America, has primarily focused on the issue of land. However, historian Robin Kelley (2017) argues that the discussion of settler colonialism in the Americas should consider African history. Kelley maintains that if we examine the history of South Africa, for example, we understand that dispossession is not only about land, but also about labour. The development of the plantation complex in British Guiana was fundamentally about dispossession of land from Indigenous people, of bodies and labour from Africa through the captive trade in human beings and enslavement, and labourers from around the world through indenture.

The Dutch were the first to establish sugar plantations during the 1630s. During the seventeenth century, they brought enslaved African people to work on cotton, coffee, and sugar plantations, and to subdue a particularly harsh landscape. Even under Dutch rule, British enterprise in what became known as Demerara sugar was rapidly increasing. If we look at a small 50-year window of the Transatlantic slave trade between the years 1776 and 1825, over 80,000 enslaved Africans disembarked in the territory that became

British Guiana to quench the insatiable labour needs (Emory University, 2013).[2] Slave rebellions and abolitionist movements across the British Empire would lead to emancipation in 1834 and the end of the apprenticeship system in 1838. But the desire for a controllable labour force would lead to the extensive employment of indenture as a strategy.

As Madhavi Kale (1998, 5) explained in her work *Fragments of Empire: Capital, Slavery, and Indian Indentured Labor Migration in the British Caribbean*, the turn to indentured labour was an imperial labour reallocation strategy. Imperialism brought people from far-flung lands to labour on plantations. Tapping into the networks of empire, over time merchants brought indentured labourers from all over the world, including South Asia; the West Indies; the Portuguese Atlantic islands of Madeira, Azores, and Cape Verde; other parts of Africa, China, and Malta (Garner 2007, 50).

British Guiana would become home to the largest number of Indian indentured labour brought to the Americas during the nineteenth century (Jayawardena 1963, 5). Between 1838 and 1917, 429,623 Indians came to the Caribbean as labourers; 55 per cent or 238,909 settled in British Guiana, while 33.5 per cent went to Trinidad (Look Lai 1993). Two-thirds of those who came remained in the country beyond their contract period (Jayawardena 1963, 14). Desperate to maintain their labour force, plantation owners offered land grants to ex-indentured people and the colonial government also relaxed the prohibitive land laws that stifled the African village movements in the post-emancipation period. Both measures helped to stimulate Indian movement away from estates and into villages once their circumstances allowed (Peake & Trotz 1999, 44). However, the indenture system continued until its official end in 1917 (Rodney 1981, 53-4).

Yet, in British Guiana, the development of the plantation would

[2] See: Emory University (2013). *Estimates Database. Voyages: The transatlantic slave trade database.* Retrieved from: http://slavevoyages.org/assessment/estimates. In 1814, the British Empire obtained the territory from the Dutch, and in 1831, it united the colonies of Demerara-Essequibo and Berbice into one British Guiana.

become bound to the logic of Indigenous erasure. Amerindians were pushed further and further into the interior, away from the coast and largely excluded from coastal plantation economies. In addition to physical erasure through dispossession of land, symbolic erasure occurred through the census where Amerindian communities were not counted, or extremely undercounted. Census takers admitted this in 1931 when they wrote,

> Following the precedent of the previous Censuses it was decided that the enumeration of the Aboriginal Indians living in their primitive state in the remote parts of the Colony, would prove an expensive and difficult undertaking, and productive of results of but little economic value (Government, 1932, note K).

Given the taxonomic nature of the British colonial project to not be counted was to not exist. Given that Indigenous labour did not provide the mainstay for the plantation economies on the coast, it was not considered cost-effective to make the effort to truly include them in the census.[3]

This erasure was also political. For example, during the 1930s, a former government official in British Guiana described the lack of relationship between the indigenous population and the life of the colony. Amerindians, he wrote, 'take no part in the agricultural, political or commercial life of the Colony, the more remote parts of which they inhabit (…). To this day the aborigines are not, in strictness, citizens of British Guiana' (Clementi 1937, 373-5). Elites widely shared such views about Indigenous subjects.

By the 1930s, Indigenous peoples were positioned as outsiders, non-citizens and non-entities. Politically, Black and Brown peoples

[3] Shona Jackson's book (2012) examines the ways in which a creole identity based on African and Indian labour became a postcolonial identity of belonging and indigeneity that displaced and dispossessed Amerindians. Although she is focused on the 1950s and beyond, she makes the point that Marxist formulations about 'working people' as well as ideas about creolization in Guyana and the larger Caribbean have been problematic because these ideas marginalized and excluded Indigenous people and by extension continued colonial practice. She also uses settler language to describe African and Indian arrival.

in Guyana were considered subjects of the British empire, positioned in this way because of the need for their labour. A series of decisions made in 1927, and a fear of a small but growing electorate of coloured people, resulted in British Guiana becoming a Crown colony in 1928. This decision would not only serve to disintegrate the fragile property-based representation that included a sliver of (mostly) African and Indian representation, but made the colony even more susceptible to the power of sugar interests.

1930s Labour Rebellions in British Guiana

The largest and most important employer in the colony was the sugar industry. Like other places and industries in the Caribbean during the 1930s, that industry was rocked by labour unrest in 1933, 1934, 1935 and 1938.[4] The largest of these encounters in British Guiana took place in 1935, in rebellions that spread across the coast of the colony from August through October and beyond. A combination of factors, including a rising racial consciousness among people of African and Indian descent, the spread of socialist ideas, the economic effects of the Great Depression, a cohort of insurgents born in the combat of World War I, and outrage over the beginnings of World War II—in the heart of Africa—provided the logs for the fires that literally spread from plantation to plantation.[5] People who were literally at the edge of the empire drew on the spectre of slavery, confronted the logic of indenture and engaged in struggle together in a colonial situation that positioned them against each other. In this chapter, I will give two examples from this struggle: one from a group of labourers at Plantation Farm and the other based on the life of one individual, Joseph Pembleton, who worked on Plantation Lusignan.

[4] Labour unrest occurred throughout the Caribbean during the 1930s including in Suriname, St. Kitts, St. Vincent, St. Lucia, Cuba, Trinidad, Jamaica, Belize, Puerto Rico, and Martinique.

[5] See Byfield (2015, 25) for a discussion of the need to re-periodize World War II beginning with Italy's invasion of Ethiopia in 1935.

Collective Representation at Plantation Farm

At Plantation Farm, protesters reminded plantation owners that slavery was over and that their lives and livelihoods should reflect this fact. In his testimony about the events of 1935, plantation manager Henry Regany Barnwell argued that those who caused the disturbances on the plantation where he worked were outside agitators.[6] This was a familiar claim, one that even those on the commission tasked to investigate the unrest, found incredulous. Plantation managers would repeat this claim often: their workers did not rebel, they were happy and peaceful, and the trouble was caused by outside agitators entering their plantations and stirring up trouble. For them, it was not contradictory that the Sugar Planters Association did not recognize unions and union leaders weren't allowed to host meetings on the plantations. According to plantation staff testimony, these faceless agitators appeared on all the plantations involved in the unrest and forced everyone to stop working.

In October of 1935, when the uprisings that were spreading across the coast overran his plantation, Barnwell claimed that the agitators were Blacks, and outsiders. He discussed how the police officers brought in to deal with these issues on private estates tried in vain to stop the crowds from marching and taking over the streets. In one instance, marchers went through two villages, Arcadia and Mocha, before reaching the next plantation, Diamond. This march in particular was a dramatic spectacle; the protestors commandeered hostages (plantation staff) to march with them, they broke through police lines and took the march off the plantation to the streets and villages, all the while drawing in supporters as they moved through with their red flags, cutlasses, and sticks. Barnwell's testimony was laced with stereotypes about violent Black people who forced docile East Indians not to work. However, throughout his testimony, a more complex story would unfold eventually.

When Barnwell met with them after a number of confronta-

[6] The governor established a commission to explore the causes of the rebellions and make recommendations. These testimonies hail from the evidence collected for the commission.

tions, the various workers had chosen representatives from among their ranks to communicate their demands. Rebecca Peters, who was described as 'an old granny' discussed the hardship associated with weeding and cleaning trenches, a job done by a mainly female labour force. Jerome Pierre came forward to represent the cane-cutters. Eleazar Barlow spoke for 'the black forking gang'. Harry Ram represented the creole gang, which on this plantation was the youngest and mostly East Indian. Soobrian Singh represented the Black and East Indian shovel men. Abdool Azez represented the punt loaders. Ramcharitar, represented the boy gang. Randolph Lynch represented the task gang weeders. Sookra spoke for the mule boys. Ganga Charran spoke for the cross-mule boys who were responsible for pulling the mules in and out. These protestors were young and old, mostly males with one female speaker, Blacks and East Indian.

At some point, when Barnwell confronted the people to tell them that their demands were 'impossible', they started to yell at him, 'Slavery done long time (...)' (Government 1935, 152). This assertion tapped into a deep concern that reared its head over and over again throughout this struggle. Just the year before, there were a string of celebrations for the centenary of emancipation throughout the colony. The same year, union organizers challenged the British policy towards the Italian invasion of Ethiopia pushing policymakers to take a stand against a type of re-enslavement happening on the continent. And during the rebellion, they would again evoke the language of slavery to confront their situation, highlighting the ways that their conditions were based in a legacy that had yet to be eradicated. To assert that slavery was over was to intimate that its conditions still existed. To argue that this should not be the case, workers were upending plantation logic.

Joseph Pembleton and Life at Lusignan Plantation

Workers also challenged the continued logic of indenture. Joseph Pembleton was one of few resident estate workers who testified before the commission set up to investigate the disturbances of 1935. British Guiana had three classes of sugar estate workers: resident labourers, village labourers and pasture labourers. Resident labourers lived on plantation grounds and were majority East Indian. Village labourers lived in independent settlements near the estates and were majority African. And, pasture labourers rented land and erected their own housing on estate grounds (Government 1936, 12-13). Commissioners had tremendous difficulty obtaining testimonies from resident labourers in particular because they were afraid of retaliation (Government 1936, 16). Resident labourers who participated in the strikes were defying both employer and landlord. Through Pembleton's testimony, we learn first-hand about the experiences of resident workers, what it meant for them to take a stand, and the ways in which indenture logic operated on multiple levels.

Pembleton lived with his wife and mother in what he described as 'a dirt house' with two rooms on Plantation Lusignan, one of the more modern estates. Lusignan had newer-style single-family housing for residents, a crèche for children, and an artesian well, and was one of three estates in the country to have a railway. Reportedly, before the railway, many workers travelled by foot, five and a half miles each way to work. The estate also paid sea defence, water rates, irrigation, and drainage costs for all residents (Government 1935, 100).

Despite these improvements, life at Plantation Lusignan was a daily reminder of residents' lack of autonomy. Pembleton's testimony demonstrated the precarious nature of existence for resident estate workers. If a resident received a directive that he did not obey, often there were consequences. For example, if the driver gave an order to clean the front or back of his house, '[i]f it is not done, our money is stopped.' His pay would be docked for disobeying orders whether he showed up to work in the fields or not.

Pembleton testified, he had already been evicted from his home and fired for participating in the strikes. He worked in the cane cutting gang. On the day the strikes began, they had been cutting cane as usual. They started by cutting the dam bed first, but then the overseer came and told them what the overall price would be. 'Many times', Pembleton stated, 'the price does not suit us but as we are on the work we have to continue to finish the work.' He described the stakes for not working: 'As we are living on the estate and they compel us [,] if we don't work they would put us off the estate, we

FIGURE 4.2: CONSTRUCTION OF A ROAD OR DIGGING A CANAL BY INDENTURED LABOURERS IN BRITISH GUIANA
Source: Views of British Guiana; album. Early 1900s. Schomburg Center, NY.

work on the bed that day but did not work the whole day because we were disgusted over the price.' He described several moments where 'everybody was determined to go away'. However, during what Pembleton described as 'the time of the strike', the workers stopped working when they were given an unsatisfactory price. Pembleton stated that prior to striking, workers asked for higher wages: 'Every day we used to complain to the overseer and also to the manager, but they said they can't give more.' Finally, he and others refused to keep working. After the strike began, the driver went to him and asked directly whether he was going to take on more work. He replied, '[n] o, not if they don't give me more money because I can't give away my labour' (Government 1935, 724).

After the strikes ended, Pembleton, who had lived on Plantation Lusignan for six years, was summoned to the manager's office. There, the acting manager, listed as Belgrave, told him he had 14 days to vacate the premises. According to Pembleton, Belgrave demanded, '[w]ell Pembleton, 14 days after to-day I want the house.' Pembleton accepted the order but later returned to ask why. The acting manager responded, giving him unsolicited advice: 'Pembleton, we have no reasons, but the conditions of the estate does not suit you (…) the more you get the more you want and Mr. McKenzie give me authority to serve you notice' (Government 1935, 728).

During his tenure at Lusignan, Pembleton had developed a small garden and created fortifications to protect his home. He testified, 'I bought boards and board it and fence the place for my convenience. I fetch dirt to build a gallery high so that the water should not go inside.' He cited these renovations of his home because he felt that they compounded the injustice of his eviction. Pembleton also sustained an injury during his time on the plantation while combatting a fire. His story about the fire sheds light on the experience of resident workers:

> The building catch fire one night and they rang the bell, and it is the rule that you must go and assist to put out the fire. I went to assist in putting out the fire and on the Sunday, I got pain (Government 1935, 728).

After the fire, he could no longer do certain plantation jobs. He was convinced that due to his injuries, plantation staff unfairly barred him from receiving provision or rice lands, one of the expectations of the moral economy of resident labour life. Pembleton's story exposed the hazardous nature of sugar estate work and life's uncertainties during this time period. There was no disability or insurance payments for those who were injured on the job—they simply meant that the person injured would endure a lower quality of life and losses of income, sometimes for the remainder of his or her existence.

Pembleton's story further revealed that resident labourers were expected to do what they were told. If the bell rang, they were expected to put out fires. If other workers were on strike, they were expected to go and take on their work. Sometimes residents were subject to arbitrary decisions that affected not only their livelihoods, but their homes and ability to feed themselves. Prevailing estate staff wisdom saw resident labour as the group of workers tied to the estate and beholden to do whatever was asked of them irrespective of whether or how much they were paid. One manager described it unabashedly as a throwback from the indenture system (Government 1935, 66). Even the legal framework at play here, the very law that governed these employees at this moment, was the Employers and Servants Ordinance of 1853 which had archaic provisions governing labour relations bound in the indenture system, including , for example, the right to evict workers from their estate homes for absenteeism with only three days' notice.

By participating in the rebellions, resident labourers fundamentally questioned the heart of these arrangements. While soliciting testimony, one examiner, a Sugar Producers' Association member, also displayed indenture logic when he asked Pembleton about his statements:

> You have made reference more than once [saying] 'we are compelled to work for the estate'. Do you agree that if you work on the estate, and you get a free home and hospital free, you should work for the estate when you are well enough to do so? (Government 1935, 734).

Pembleton adamantly replied, 'I agree to work for the estate at any time provided the price paid me is reasonable.' As a resident labourer, Pembleton belonged to the class of workers that plantation staff admitted was a legacy of the indenture system. When Pembleton argued that he would only work when he agreed to the level of pay, (when he said, 'I can't give away my labour,') and when he participated in the strikes, he was upending plantation logic based in the system of indenture (Government 1935, 734).

Conclusion

In the year 1935, African- and Indian-Guianese workers challenged the plantation complex together. Despite differences in positionality, histories, cultures and experiences they worked to challenge a regime that dehumanized them. The subject of this chapter was demand for wage increases and shorter hours. They pushed not only for rights, representation and the modern benefits of 'free labour', but they also pushed for something deeper.

They demanded that their humanity be recognized, and they

pushed back against racial logics ensconced in enslavement and indenture. They reminded plantation owners that slavery had ended. They exposed the logic from indenture that continued to inform behaviour and practice. Dignity and anti-racism punctuated their demands. They had a desire for autonomy. What they ultimately received was a modernized version of colonial government, but they challenged the whole system telling those who controlled it, 'you do not define our existence'.

Yet, there was an invisible assumption that permeated the whole foundation of their struggle that delimited before it was even birthed. It was a line formed before these actors were born, but it was a line that informed their very existence on the plantation. It is the colonial logic of erasure that existed and undergirded their labour. This reasoning informed the original colonial dispossession of land, labour and bodies. It is the story of those peoples who had been pushed to the interior and made non-citizens in a land that they had named and taken care of centuries before Europeans set foot on their shores. In the 1930s, those peoples had been made invisible. They were invisible too in the worker struggle that I highlight. But their invisibility was structured there.

Their invisibility in that moment is based on colonial sources, but they were not invisible in the lived reality of that moment. If we understand the terms and terrain of the struggle that colonial records have left to us, it means that ultimately, the very terms of the struggle had already been set. The 1935 struggle challenged the terms of the debate about life in the colony in a multiplicity of ways. Other terms were left untouched, unexamined and unchallenged. A fuller more robust freedom did not emerge from this struggle, not just for these workers because of how their demands were later reframed, but even in the content of their own framing.

Many have argued that this is precisely why African and Indian peoples in present-day Guyana—despite the troubled and tortured ways in which their ancestors ended up there—are the beneficiaries of (and now embody) the settler colonial project (Jackson 2012). These invisibilities are how scholars and politicians of African and Indian descent could actually claim indigeneity on the basis of colonial dispossession of the labour and bodies of their ancestors. I reject both of these claims that Black and Indian peoples are settler colonists in the British Guiana context, and the claim to indigeneity by these same peoples. It is the postcolonial Caribbean state that has continued the settler colonial project. And the colonial dispossession of land, labour and body remain entangled. They are and have always been predicated on each other. Hindsight allows us to see what remained hidden in the 1930s. Colonial plantation logic 'erased' Indigenous peoples. But just as sugar workers of the 1930s exposed the plantation legacies of both the systems of enslavement and indenture and frontally challenged them, our job today is to uncover and challenge the multiple racial logics that continue to threaten our pursuit of full freedom in the Americas today.

Bibliography

Byfield, Judith. 2015. 'Producing for the War' in J. Byfield, C. Brown, T. Parson & A. Sikainga (eds.), *Africa and World War II.* New York: Cambridge University Press: 24-42.

Clementi, Cecil. 1937. *A constitutional history of British Guiana.* London, United Kingdom: Macmillan and Company.

Garner, Steve. 2007. *Guyana, 1838-1985: Ethnicity, class and gender.* Kingston, Jamaica: Ian Randle Publishers.

Government of British Guiana. 1932. *Report on the results of the census of the population, 1931.* Georgetown, British Guiana: The Argosy Company.

______. 1935. *Labour Disputes Commission, 1935, evidence of witnesses.* The National Archives of the United Kingdom: CO 111/739/2.

______. 1936. *Report of the commissioners appointed to enquire into and report on the labour disputes in Demerara and Berbice during the months of September and October, 1935.* Georgetown, British Guiana: The Argosy Company. The National Archives of the United Kingdom: CO 111/739/1.

Jackson, Shona. 2012. *Creole indigeneity: Between myth and nation in the Caribbean.* Minneapolis, MN: University of Minnesota Press.

Jayawardena, Chandra. 1963. *Conflict and solidarity in a Guianese plantation.* London, United Kingdom: University of London Athlone Press.

Kale, Madhvi. 1998. *Fragments of empire: Capital, slavery, and Indian indentured labor migration to the British Caribbean.* Philadelphia: University of Pennsylvania Press.

Kelley, Robin D.G. 2017. 'The rest of us: Rethinking settler and native.' *American Quarterly.* 69(2): 267-76.

Look Lai, Walton. 1993. *Indentured labor, Caribbean sugar: Chinese and Indian migrants to the British West Indies, 1838-1918*. Baltimore, MD: Johns Hopkins University Press.

Lowe, Lisa. 2015. *The Intimacies of Four Continents*. Durham, NC: Duke University Press.

Mbembe, Achille. 2015. *On the postcolony*. Johannesburg: University of Wits Press.

Newton, Melanie J. 2013. 'Returns to a native land: Indigeneity and decolonization in the Anglophone Caribbean.' *Small Axe: A Caribbean Journal of Criticism.* 17(2): 108-22.

Peake, Linda and D.A. Trotz. 1999. *Gender, ethnicity and place: Women and identities in Guyana.* London: Routledge Press.

Rodney, Walter. 1981. *A history of Guyanese working people, 1881-1905.* Baltimore, MD: Johns Hopkins University Press.

Shepherd, Verene. 2002. *Maharani's misery: Narratives of a passage from India to the Caribbean.* Kingston, Jamaica: University of the West Indies Press.

Sued-Badillo, Jalil. 2011. 'From Taino to Africans in the Caribbean: Labor, migration and resistance', in S. Palmié and F.A. Scarano (eds.), *The Caribbean: A history of the region and its peoples*. Chicago, IL: The University of Chicago Press: 97-113.

Williams, Brackette. 2001. 'Ideology and the formation of Anglo-European hegemony', in C. Barrow, and R.E. Rheddock (eds.), *Caribbean sociology: Introductory readings.* Kingston, Jamaica: Ian Randle Publishers: 270-86.

FIVE

Afro-Surinamese, 1863-1963
Integration in Suriname after the Abolition of Slavery

CHAN CHOENNI

Introduction

In 1863 Suriname was a Dutch colony with a small population not exceeding 60,000 inhabitants and very sparsely populated. Beside the population from African backgrounds, the rest of the population consisted of around 2,000 Whites and Jews, as well as Indigenous

I thank Dr. Barryl Biekman and Dr. Roline Redmond for their advice and comment. Both are female Afro-Surinamese academics and they commented on sensitive issues such as racism, 'opo yu kloro' and prejudices about laziness. I have a Hindustani background and was born in Paramaribo. I grew up in a predominantly Afro-Surinamese neighbourhood and was educated by Afro-Surinamese teachers. My paternal grandfather adopted the Afro-Surinamese cultural leader Eugéne Drenthe in the 1920s and my family befriended Afro-Surinamers. Furthermore, I was employed between 1985 and 1991 as a researcher at the National Bureau against Racism (LBR) in The Netherlands. Although, I consider myself a relative insider among the Afro-Surinamese group and I am a dark-skinned person, the racism the Afro-Surinamese endured can only be fully grasped by the Afro-Surinamese themselves.

(Amerindians) and Chinese. Suriname had a plantation economy producing primarily staple products such as sugar, cacao, coffee and cotton. Almost half of the population resided in the capital, Paramaribo, while the other half lived in the so-called districts in the countryside but mostly on the plantations. The Whites, Jews and the Coloured (the mixed group) resided in the capital Paramaribo. On the eve of the abolition of slavery only a minority—less than 5,000—of the Afro-Surinamers lived in Paramaribo. The overwhelming majority, namely 85 per cent (approximately 30,000) lived in the countryside in the districts.

Hence, Paramaribo was then not a 'Black' city, but became gradually so after the abolishment of slavery and in particularly in the twentieth century after the continuous migrations from the districts. Most of them in 1863 freed (formerly enslaved) persons had to serve in an '*Staatstoezicht*' (Apprenticeship) of 10 years between 1863 and 1873. After 1873, Afro-Surinamers started to move from the districts to Paramaribo. This urbanization process of Afro-Surinamers was boosted in the beginning of the twentieth century with the emergence of the mining industries, in particular gold, balata and later, bauxite. While residing in Paramaribo, many men travelled by boat to the interior (jungle) of Suriname for work on temporary basis or on short term. Afro-Surinamers left agriculture, in particular after the 'witch broom' disease of cacao plants had almost disrupted the cacao industry on the eve of the twentieth century. At the same time, Suriname experienced a huge Asian immigration (of Hindustanis and Javanese) after 1873. In 1963, the overwhelming majority of Afro-Surinamers lived in Paramaribo and they were the largest ethnic group in the capital.

TABLE 5.1: THE ENSLAVED POPULATION OF SURINAME IN 1862/1863

	Paramaribo	*Districts*	*Total*
Men	1,784 (41%)	15,378 (48%)	17,162 (47%)
Women	2,537 (59%)	16,785 (52%)	19,322 (53%)
TOTAL	4,321	32,163	36,484

Source: Van Stipriaan 1991, 311.

This research focuses on how and to what extent the Afro-Surinamese group became part of the Surinamese society during 1863-1963. I will describe this integration process of the Afro-Surinamese group on three dimensions— political, the cultural and the social-economic. The Afro-Surinamese group acquired political hegemony in 1963 and became the successor of the colonial power. In the cultural field, the Afro-Surinamese group became relatively successful; in music, arts and sports they excelled, but still their authentic religion—Winti—and to a certain extent their language —Sranang—was marginalized. In the social-economic domain, the Afro-Surinamese group was less successful in the period 1863-1963, while they were still the largest ethnic group in Suriname. During this period a small middle class emerged, but the largest group remained in the lower class and even an underclass emerged.

I designate this development as Integration Afro-Surinamese style in contrast to the Integration Hindustani Style (Choenni 2016). Tentatively, I shall detect the factors related to slavery and its aftermath, in particular the negative consequences in explaining the Afro-Surinamese Integration style. The interaction between structural factors and group factors, such as cultural and psychological factors were crucial. For example, racism and discrimination in the period 1863-1963 combined with White and light-skinned privilege and also aesthetic notions about black skin and assumed negative 'negro traits' often internalized by Afro-Surinamers lead to social-economic marginalization (Helman 1978, 62; Hoetink 1962, 202).

Research Design

In this section I will describe this integration process of the Afro-Surinamese group on the political, the cultural and the social-economic dimensions, known as the Triad of Integration, during the period 1863 to 1963. Historical documents in the archives, literature and oral history are the main sources. In particular, interviewing informants and some focus groups about sensitive themes have been an important part of the fieldwork carried out in Suriname as well as in The Netherlands. It's important to note and should be mentioned here that engaging informants in discussions regarding sensitive topics like experiences with skin colour discrimination, challenges with curly hair texture, poverty and the marginalized role of the fathers was particularly challenging. Because I am not an Afro-Surinamer but was born and raised in an Afro-Surinamese neighbourhood (Abra Broki) in Paramaribo, I have acquired, to some extent, acceptance and respect as a researcher by the Afro-Surinamese community.

For the fieldwork I also mobilized a number of Afro-Surinamese interviewees. All of this notwithstanding, it is difficult to gather information about sensitive themes. Another complication is that in historical documents Afro-Surinamers are ~~not~~ frequently perceived and portrayed negatively and stereotyped with traits such as being lazy ('lui'), unreliable ('*onbetrouwbaar*'), prodigal ('*verkwistend*') and emotionally strenuous (Van Lier 1971, 178-9). Not only historians and planters, but also some Governors like J.C. Kielstra (1933-44) used such qualifications. Kielstra even perceived the Afro-Surinamers as indolent and a 'lost group for agriculture' (Hoefte 2018).

What makes this research even more complex, is the distinction between Afro-Surinamers, predominantly dark-skinned (referred to as '*Volkscreolen*') and the mixed people ('*Gekleurden*') mostly light-skinned, who were lumped together as the Creole group until the beginning of the twenty-first century. I have excluded the mixed group and also the 'Maroons' because the latter had a rather different history and economic development during the 100 years after the abolishment of slavery. Accordingly, I have used the definition of Afro-Surinamers for the non-mixed predominantly dark-skinned people referred to then as '*Volkscreolen*'. The demarcation between the Afro-Surinamers and the coloured/mixed group is not absolute but more fluid.

According to the historian Neslo (2016), one-third of the free population before slavery was Black and two-third was coloured. My estimate is that two-third of the Creole group belonged to these Afro-Surinamese group and one-third to the coloured group, mostly Mulatto's. In due course the coloured group increased through intermixing. Intermixing was the result of primarily White men having children with Afro-Surinamese women, and sometimes even rape was involved. On the other hand, Afro-Surinamese mixed with light skinned persons acquired what was perceived as better physical features and better chances for their children. This so-called '*Opo yu kloru*' (improve your skin colour) orientation was based on the somatic norm image that white was beautiful and dark was ugly (see also: Hoetink 1967). Continuous intermixing meant in consequence a relative decrease of the Afro-Surinamers population.[1]

The coloured group belonged mostly to the middle class. During the period 1863 to 1963 black skin colour and so-called African traits were not perceived as conducive for reaching middle class status. Meanwhile, intermixing facilitated upward mobility in the Surinamese society. Hence, racism and discrimination constituted a key factor in the social-economic integration of the Afro-Surinamers during 1863 to 1963. However, because the distinction between the Afro-Surinamer and the coloured was not always made we cannot obtain a clear picture of the Afro-Surinamese group in the social-economic statistics. As a rule of thumb, though, the social economic position of the Afro-Surinamers was weaker than that mentioned for the total group of the Creoles; hence, the statistics about the Creoles/Creole group must be interpreted accordingly.

Stagnated Population Growth

The annual decline of 3 per cent of the Afro-Surinamese population preceding the abolition of slavery was a reason for the White planters to plead for immigration (Emmer 2007). The stagnated growth of the Afro-Surinamese population is striking. After the end of slavery child mortality was high among the Afro-Surinamese because the living conditions in Paramaribo in particular were bad: healthcare for the majority of the Surinamese population and the largest ethnic group was insufficient during the nineteenth century. However, as

[1] The descendants of mix couples are counted as belonging to the mixed group. The effect was visible in the censuses of 2003/2004: 87.302 Afro-Surinamers and 61.524 Coloured (Mixed group) and in 2012: respectively 88.856 and 72.340 (Menke & Sno 2016, 116).

a term of their contract, immigrants were guaranteed healthcare by the government. While the Afro-Surinamers were the overwhelming majority of around 40 per cent in 1920s, the influx of Asian immigrants and in particular the increase of the Hindustani group and related social economic competition, changed the course of Suriname's history.

TABLE 5.2: AFRO-SURINAMESE AND MIXED POPULATION (CREOLES), 1862-1963

Year	*Creoles (AS + mixed)*	*% Suriname Population*	*Total Population*
1862	50,984	96	52,963
1900	51,944	72	72.144
1915	51,602	60	85,536
1922	44,288	47	93,762
1935	54,336	42	129,672
1945	66,086	42	156,783
1950	71,678	40	178,078
1958	95,042	40	237,291
1963	113,929	39	289,282

Source: Colonial Report 1901-2, 1915; Lamur 1973: 141-2. Bijlage; Hoefte 2013: 30.

A remarkable aspect in the Afro-Surinamese population has been the overrepresentation of women. On the eve of the abolition of slavery, Afro-Surinamese women were overrepresented; in particular in Paramaribo (59 per cent versus 41 per cent). The overrepresentation of women continued during 1863-1963. The rate was on 100 women 88,9 men in 1862/1863; 89,2 in 1922 and a decrease to 85,5 in 1930, due to emigration of Afro-Surinamese men to Curacao. In 1940, the rate was 89,9 and 89,6 in 1946. In 1957, through high birth rate the balance was better with a rate of 90,5 and in 1963 a further improvement of the gender balance with a rate of 95,2 was achieved (Lamur 1973, 178-9).

Urbanization of the Afro-Surinamers after the abolishment of slavery was deliberately opposed by consecutive Surinamese governments. Nevertheless, the Afro-Surinamese community of Paramaribo increased, because those settled in Paramaribo took care of them and many Afro-Surinamers ended up living in rundown neighbourhoods in so-called '*pras'oso's*' (hovels/barracks). They survived by 'hustling', often under unhygienic circumstances, and became part of the growing lower class and even underclass. It was not until the 1950s that a ten-year plan was developed to provide for public housing. Only a small group of the lower middleclass could haves benefitted from this provision; most of the lower class and underclass remained impoverished. They depended on their families, friends and other acquaintances for food, and on government provisions ('*bedeling*') and support from religious organizations.

Periodization: Six Phases

The integration process of Afro-Surinamese between 1863 and 1963 demonstrates certain patterns that can be distinguished in six chronological phases related to structural developments in the Surinamese society:

- Phase 1: Peasantry, Cultural Ambivalence and Powerlessness, 1873-99.
- Phase 2: Urbanization, Cultural Aloofness and Political Exclusion, 1900-20.
- Phase 3: Impoverishment, Emigration and Political Repression, 1921-39.
- Phase 4: Economic Boom, Americanization and Political Awakening, 1940-5.
- Phase 5: Social-Economic Progress, Cultural Consciousness and Rising Fraternity Politics, 1946-57.
- Phase 6: Social-Economic Support, Cultural Self-Respect and Political Hegemony, 1958-63

This study ends in 1963 when the charismatic Afro-Surinamese Leader, J.A. Pengel became Prime Minster of Suriname and gave a boost to the Afro-Surinamese identity.

Integration Afro-Surinamese Style

The *de facto* emancipation of the Afro-Surinamese group after the abolition of slavery began at a very slow pace. It acquired an upswing, but at an unequal pace with respect to three important life domains after the Second World War. After hundred years the Afro-Surinamese group gained political power and became politically successful as the successor of the colonial power. In the cultural field they were relatively successful; in music (and in sports) they excelled. However, their traditionally authentic religion ('*Winti*') and to a certain extent their language ('*Sranan Tongo*') were, and are still, not fully accepted. In the social-economic domain the Afro-Surinamese group became less successful. Besides a small middle class, a lower class (the majority), and even an underclass, developed. I designate this as the Integration African Style in contrast with the Integration Hindustani Style (Choenni 2011).

Several factors after the abolition of slavery had been a determining factor for the acquired position of the Afro-Surinamers. One of the most important factors was the intense racism towards the Afro-Surinamese group that, even long after the abolition of slavery. Although over time the prejudices and racist images decreased gradually, still after hundred years—in 1963—the opportunities of many were determined by racial prejudices. In particular, there was the lingering predominance of the myth of the Curse of Ham, which, as depicted in the Holy Bible, posited Blacks as destined to be the servants of Whites, who were still considered superior in management and leadership. Racism and discrimination in the period 1863 to 1963 combined with White and light-skinned privilege and aesthetic notions about Black and 'negro traits', strengthened the somatic norm imaging framework and worked towards the development of the Afro-Surinamese Integration Style.

Negative Consequences

Tentatively, I have detected many negative consequences of the brutal slavery in Suriname that have had a huge impact on the integration of the Afro-Surinamese group during 1863 and 1963. This means they impacted how this group performed during the hundred years in the three aforementioned domains of life.

I emphasize, though, that these consequences did not have the same impact on every individual of the Afro-Surinamese group; hence, much individuality and variegation remain. Also, in two parts of Suriname the negative impact of the aforementioned debilitating influences were minimal, namely, among the Afro-Surinamese in the districts of Para and Coronie where almost everybody was black; for long time close communities existed in these regions. In Para, many families purchased land, while in Coronie many families acquired land as compensation of wages from the planters who left the district. Another development was that some small groups succeeded due to specific circumstances and personal factors or attributes in achieving middle class status, particularly since the 1940s. For example, some embraced patriarchal relationships and, often also, a monogamous lifestyle, inclusive of legal marriage. Furthermore, some among the lower-class group were less affected by the negative consequences, while those belonged to underclass were the most affected.

I emphasize also that I only focus on the period of 1863-1963, because after 1963 the so-called emancipation process and modernization among the Afro-Surinamese group intensified significantly. For example, the influence of modern communication media, such as television and the rise of (international) black power and black is beautiful movement emerged after 1963 and became very important in the emancipation struggle of the Afro-Surinamese group. Additionally, ethnic rivalry and later ethnic polarization between the Afro-Surinamese Party (NPS) and the Hindustani Party (VHP) erupted towards the end of the 1960s. I reiterate that the present effort is not intended to stereotype and stigmatize the Afro-Surinamers group, but to understand specific developments and explicate them. Moreover, these are always going to be preliminary findings about sensitive issues, which have to be addressed when writing history. Slavery was based on racism and the myth of Cham (Ham in the biblical text), legitimating the superiority of Whites against Blacks, with the latter as 'a serving race'. Such a notion could not have disappeared overnight with the abolition of slavery. Moreover, such a notion would have determined the relationships between the Afro-

Surinamers and others, in particular the Whites and were passed over through generations, albeit to a lesser extent.

More than ninety years after the abolition of slavery (around 1953) the rising charismatic Afro-Surinamese leader Jopie Pengel was referred as 'an ape' and in particular the coloured élite who felt endangered in their powerbase used racist notions to disqualify Afro-Surinamese for high holding office. Despite this, the reality of the equality of all human beings irrespective of skin colour gained ground slowly between 1863 and 1963 and became self-evident later. Because the enslaved people were considered 'property' they were dehumanized: they were simply not treated as human beings. What is more, many enslaved people and their descendants internalized related negative notions about themselves after the abolition of slavery. This is often referred to as mental slavery.

Somatic norm imaging to the effect that black skin colour is ugly and curly hair and black African features are not beautiful resulted in many among the African-descended attempting to erase or alter these phenotypical features. 'Opo yu kloru' led, on the hand, to trying to have relationships and mating with whites or coloured people. Given the level of skin colour discrimination, this was not only about aesthetics but equally about accessing better opportunities and advancing one's status in Surinamese society. On the other hand, many were using all kinds of means to become as 'beautiful as the whites': aesthetical norms tend to become passionate, fashionable and socio-psychological. White-dominated somatic norm imaging has had a negative impact of the ethnic identity of the Afro-Surinamers (Biekman 2018). Basically, time and money were spent on efforts to meet a beauty ideal, when, more ideally, they could have been diverted towards economic progress.

Internalizing notions of inferiority and the Curse of Cham also resulted in aversion and a false sense of pride when it came to doing servile jobs and manual jobs, and, just as well, the development of notions such as 'Afro-Surinamers are less fitted for agricultural task'. In 1930s a counter movement spearheaded by A.L. Waaldijk against these notions experimented with Afro-Surinamese families and founded the agriculture settlement Creola (Van Traa 1946, 107; Gobardhan 2001, 208). While the Afro-Surinamese ancestors have been victims of oppression and assumed inferiority during the period 1863 to 1963, many still behaved like victims and used this victimization as an excuse for their passive behaviour and dependence on others like families or the State.

Cultural Heritage

The capture of Africans and their forced transportation and enslavement in Suriname meant also the blocking of the transfer of the African cultural heritage. Although, some aspects of the African culture were preserved and fused with local customs and circumstances into an Afro-Surinamese culture like the Winti religion, still it was a cut off from their cultural roots.[2] Furthermore, the African culture was assumed as inferior and primitive and not conducive to agricultural production and economic progress. Thus, the preservation of African culture was obstructed and opposed by the Government, the coloured elite and the religious organizations.

Many Afro-Surinamers had to become Christians. Furthermore, often they felt ashamed of their authentic culture. But Winti and also other African cultural practices were still practised often covertly. Ambivalent behaviour but also creativity and improvization prevailed during 1863-1963 in the Afro-Surinamese group (Jap-A-Joe 1993; Binderhagel 2014). However, pride on their ancestral culture in Suriname was not predominant. Moreover, their cultural heritage was degraded. An inferiority complex among some Afro-Surinamers existed during 1863-1963. Besides, the image of Black Africa was bad and it was then portrayed as wild, uncivilized and underdeveloped.

One remnant of the African culture combined with restrictions of slavery was the establishment of matrifocal family patterns. After slavery most Afro-Suriname women continued to be the head of households, while fathers were to these household families, almost marginal. There was also the so-called visiting relationship (*'hori'*) and promiscuity prevailed. A household with a single female head

[2] *Winti* is a belief system in supernatural powers primarily based on the authentic African culture, i.e. folklore (Wooding 1972; Stephen 1985).

per se is not necessarily problematic. But in a society where in the state structure patriarchal norms dominated and also among other ethnic groups and legal marriage was the norm, the female headed household was in a weaker position. When, in the aftermath of the abolition of slavery, it became possible to marry legally, with this option also being promoted by the churches (the Moravian Evangelican Brother mission and the Roman Catholic mission), the majority of the Afro-Surinamers did not opt for this solution. The so-called '*ferbontu*', a kind of living together temporarily of man and woman, was predominant.

Moreover, many Afro-Surinamese women were overburdened with being mother and father at the same time. For the most part, they had also to earn the family income, while relying on their mothers or other women to take care for their children. The over-representation of Afro-Surinamese women in Paramaribo is to be considered. Many Afro-Surinamese men worked in the interior or far from Paramaribo. They spent weeks, sometimes months, away from their families. Hence, many Afro-Surinamese women in Paramaribo often had to survive with children, but without their male partner. Meanwhile, the fierce competition with the other groups, in particular the hard-working Hindustanis male resulted in the transfer of many skilled jobs into the latter's hands. Accordingly, many Afro-Surinamese men did not succeed in securing a regular income.

Survival Culture

The alternating economic downfall and boom in Suriname between 1863 and 1903 had a huge impact on the Afro-Surinamese. Suriname also relied heavily on imports and exports, and the transportation of goods through ships docking in Paramaribo was also a source of income. Afro-Surinamese porters, chargers, laundresses and even prostitutes earned an income. But this was also an irregular income, often insecure, often affected by delays in the arrivals of ships. Suriname had a small and vulnerable economy and the lower class and underclass living in Paramaribo, mostly Afro-Surinamers, were its victims. Many had to live in some kind of survival mode. They were always looking for informal jobs to earn some more money, sometimes through illegal or criminal activities, the so-called hustle ('*hossel*') activities (Buschkens 1973). But a mentality of depending gratuitously on others also developed. Among Afro-Suriname helping each other and sharing and caring was normal.

During slavery there were already '*pikin nyan*' persons: free persons who did not have the papers to prove that they were free. In some instances, their owners had died, or they had become handicapped or disabled, and their owners did want to take care for them. These persons were tolerated in Paramaribo and helped (Neslo 2016). After slavery many of them would hustle; and, in particular, some young Afro-Surinamese men in Paramaribo copied their behaviour. They were free and did not have an address and often lived temporarily with family members. They became part of the urban underclass. In the Afro-Surinamese group the family members who achieved middle class status had an obligation to help others: for example, when someone had a business or a shop, he or she had to assist the needy. Often, such shopkeepers or business owners could not behave business-like, and many lost their business in the competition against the Chinese and Hindustani.

Although after the abolition of slavery the Apprenticeship of 10 years was also implemented to constitute stable households and nurture the Afro-Surinamese to deal with money, many continued to have problems with budgeting (Waaldijk 1948). They now earned money and had to take care of themselves with this income. It turned out most of them spent their money directly; that is to say, without developing habits of saving or delayed gratification. Moreover, many used their wages for conspicuous consumption. It is understandable that they purchased (expensive) shoes, because, generally, the enslaved had not been allowed to wear shoes. However, this attitude of conspicuous consumption continued through time and also among the next generations. Although, saving was promoted and the attitude to create or buy property, many remained focussed on the short time.[3] Perhaps they were afraid of what the future would bring, because during slavery their future was insecure. The notion that one

[3] A saving system named '*kasmoni*' (cash money) developed among Creole women, who saved money regularly at a woman banker. Periodically,

should enjoy life, because you do not know what tomorrow would bring was very much a part of the Afro-Surinamese community.

Another consequence of the brutal slavery in Suriname was the continuation of use of force to discipline others. The tradition of 'I will whip you' ('*ik ga je zwepen*') was very predominant in educating their children, but force was also used both in and outside the schools. The authoritarian way of rule from slavery was transferred in Afro-Surinamese community (Hoefte 2013). Furthermore, communication within families but also in the school was straightforward and commanding. In particular, the Afro-Surinamese mothers, often overloaded and overburdened, did not have much time to communicate and explain, but threatened their children with physical force to get things done.

Last but not the least in Suriname an aversion against agriculture and agricultural jobs developed among many, the so-called agricultural trauma. As already stated, in Para and Coronie. Afro-Surinamese continued to work in agriculture, but most Afro-Surinamers from Paramaribo considered them as backward persons and they were often ridiculed. These jobs were left for the Asians, for example, Hindustanis and Javanese. Many Afro-Surinamers left their land or sold it quite cheaply to them. Even a kind of false shame developed among Afro-Surinamese against manual labour and, accordingly, a preference for white collar jobs. In a very fertile and sparsely populated country it was an anomaly that many Afro-Surinamers lived in the rundown and poor neighbourhoods of Paramaribo on subsistence level, while there was enough land available to cultivate in the districts. There were also some indirect consequences of slavery like the aforementioned mental slavery and also so-called self-excluding mechanisms. These were attitudes like distrusting others, confrontational and militant attitudes, the development of inferiority complexes, and also underestimating their own skills and potencies.

---

for example, every month one of the participants received the total amount of the savings minus the costs for the banker (Bijnaar 2002).

Conclusion

We have disentangled the complex interrelationship between the negative consequences of the brutal slavery in Suriname resulting in the attitude, lifestyle and behaviour of most Afro-Surinamers between 1863 and 1963. During that period an Afro-Surinamese ethos developed a set of ideas and attitudes associated with a particular group of people. The Afro-Surinamers reacted to the structural factors such the opportunities, government policies, and (institutional) racism and discrimination, and developed survival modes. Perseverance, mutual help and support, humour and a relaxing but often militant lifestyle became components of this ethos. Tied to these remnants of the African cultural heritage and problematic ethnic identity developed in interaction with the structural factors. These are sensitive issues that should be further analysed.

However, it is fascinating that despite the exceptionally brutal slavery and inadequate facilities like bad housing and insufficient healthcare the Afro-Surinamese group has been able to survive. Mutual aid, support and solidarity, and in particular the determination of Afro-Surinamese women played a prominent role in this survival. Furthermore, with a culture full of humour and liveliness a resilient and spiritual ethnic group arose in Suriname. But we must keep in mind that the cruel slavery system placed the free enslaved persons and their descendants in a disadvantage position. This dramatic history left many traces that had a huge impact on integration of the next generations, for example, the Afro-Surinamese integration style in Suriname between 1863 and 1963.

Bibliography

Biekman, Barryl. 2018. *Uitsluitingsmechanismen; Blaka tara en afrofobie.* Volendam: LM Publishers.

Bijnaar, Aspha. 2002. *Kasmoni; spaarzame levensgenieters in Suriname en Nederland.* Amsterdam: Universiteit van Amsterdam.

Binderhagel, Headly R. 2014. *Woordbreuksyndroom: een psycho-neuro-endocriene benadering van fyofyo programmering.* Tilburg: Tilburg University, Prisma print.

Breeveld, Hans. 2000. *Jopie Pengel 1916-1970. Leven en werk van een Surinaamse politicus.* (Proefschrift in de Maatschappij Wetenschappen, AdeKUS, Paramaribo-Suriname).

Buschkens, Willem F.L. 1973. *Het Familiesysteem der Volkscreolen van Paramaribo* (Proefschrift in de Sociale Wetenschappen Leiden Universiteit, Leiden-Nederland).

Choenni, Chan E.S. 2016a. *Hindostaanse contractarbeiders 1873-1920.* Volendam: LM Publishers.

———. 2011. Integration Hindostani Style. Amsterdam: Vrije Universiteit. www.indiawijzer.nl.

Egger, Jerome L. (ed.). 2013. *Ontwaakt en Ontwikkelt U: Creolen na de afschaffing van de slavernij, 1863-1940.* Paramaribo: IMWO/NiNsee.

Emmer, Pieter C. 1993. 'Between Slavery and Freedom. The Period of Apprenticeship in Suriname (Dutch Guiana), 1863-1873', in: *Slavery and Abolition.* 14(1): 87-113.

———. 2007. *De Nederlandse Slavenhandel 1500-1850.* Amsterdam: De Arbeiderspers.

Gobardhan-Rambocus, L. 2001. *Onderwijs als sleutel tot maatschappelijke vooruitgang. Een taal- en onderwijsgeschiedenis van Suriname,* 1651-1975. Zutphen: Walburg Pers.

Heilbron, Waldo. 1982. *Kleine boeren in de schaduw van de plantage.* Rotterdam: Erasmus Universiteit.

Helman, Albert. (ed.) 1977. *Cultureel mozaïek van Suriname. Bijdrage tot onderling begrip.* Zutphen: De Walburg Pers.

———. 1978. *Facetten van de Surinaamse samenleving.* Zutphen: De Walburg Pers.

Helstone, Heinrich E., O. ten Hove & W. Hoogbergen. 2009. *Surinaamse Emancipatie 1863. Coronie.* Amsterdam: Rozenberg Publishers.

Hira, Sandew. 2009. *Decolonizing the mind.* Den Haag: Amrit.

Hoefte, Rosemarijn. 2013. *Suriname in the long twentieth century.* New York: Palgrave, Macmillan.

———. 2018. *The Last Convulsions of Colonialism: The Suriname Experiment in the 1930s,* Amsterdam: University of Amsterdam.

Hoetink, Harry. 1962. *De Gespleten Samenleving in het Caribisch Gebied.* Assen: Van Gorcum.

Hove ten, Okke, H.E. Helstone & W. Hoogbergen. 2003. *Surinaamse Emancipatie 1863. Familienamen en plantages.* Amsterdam: Bronnen voor de Studie van Suriname.

Jap-A-Joe, Harold. 1993. *Tussen kruis en kalebas: acculturatie va het christendom onder gedoopte slaven in Suriname.* Paramaribo: Theologisch Seminarum der EBGS.

Lamur, H.E. 1973. *The Demographic Evolution of Surinam*, Den Haag: Martinus Nijhoff.

———. (2001). 'The evolution of afro-Surinamese National Movements (1955-1995)', in *Transforming Anthropology,* 10(1): 17-27.

Lier, R. van. 1971. *Samenleving in een grensgebied.* Zutphen: Walburg Pers.

Menke, Jack (ed.). 2016. *Mozaïek van het Surinaamse volk.* Paramaribo: ABS/ISGR.

Menke, Jack & Iwan Sno. 2016. *Ras en etniciteit in volkstellingen in Suriname,* in: Menke, Jack. (ed.) *Mozaïek van het Surinaamse volk.* Paramaribo: ABS/ISGR.

Neslo, Ellen B.A. 2016. *Een ongekende elite. De opkomst van een gekleurde elite in koloniaal Suriname 1800-1863.* De Bilt: HaEs producties.

Ramsoedh, Hans. 1990. *Suriname 1933-1944: Koloniale politiek en beleid onder gouverneur Kielstra.* Delft: Eburon.

Stephen, Henri J.M. 1985. *Winti. Afro-Surinaamse religie en magische rituelen in Suriname en Nederland.* Amsterdam: Karnak.

Stipriaan van, Alex. 1991. *Surinaams contrast, roofbouw en overleven in een Caribische plantage- economie.* 1750-1863. Amsterdam: Vrije Universiteit.

Traa, A. van. 1946. *Suriname 1900-1940.* Deventer: Van Hoeve.

Waaldijk, A.L. 1948. 'De Creolenbevolking van Suriname', *Verslag van de Commissie tot bestudering van Staatkundige hervormingen,* 's-Gravenhage: Staatsdrukkerij.

Wekker, Gloria. 1994. *Ik ben een gouden munt, Subjectiviteit en seksualiteit van Creoolse volksklasse vrouwen in Paramaribo.* Amsterdam: Vita.

Willemsen, Glenn. 1980. *Koloniale politiek en transformatieprocessen in een plantage-economie, Suriname 1873-1940,* Amsterdam: Drukkerij Kaal BV.

Wooding, C. J. 1972. *Winti: een Afro-Amerikaanse Godsdienst in Suriname. Een Cultureel-Historische Analyse van de Religieuze Verschijnselen in de Para.* Meppel: Krips Repro.

Part Three

French and Jewish Entities and Experience

SIX

Emergence of the Attached Workers Phenomenon in Martinique from 1848 to 1880

MARIE-ROSE NOÉMIE

Introduction

When the day had gone by without any incident or misfortune, the evening arrived, smiling tenderly. From as far as I could see M'man Tine, my grandmother, coming in, at the end of the wide path that led the negroes into the cane fields of the plantation and bringing them back, I rushed to meet her.

Joseph Zobel (2009, 1) wrote this in *La rue Cases-Nègres.*

This novel, which narrates the author's childhood in the 1930s in Martinique, stresses that the reality of the plantation labour and 'Negro huts' living put in place during the slavery period remained at least until the twentieth century on the island. This is surprising enough, for one might have thought that the abolition of slavery would put an end to the work on the plantations and the life on the lands of the ones that are no longer the masters.

This essay intends to understand the advent and subsequent evolution of the attached workers phenomenon in the post-abolitionist period on the island of Martinique. What is referred to as attached work is not merely the fact of a recently freed person, in the wake of the abolition of slavery, committed to doing the work he was previously performing under slavery. This activity would be perceived as related to one or a particular plantation for a lengthy period of time, as an infringement of the newly granted right to work freely. But this worker was also deemed attached because this phrase entails the return for the newly freed to the 'Negro huts' left vacant after slavery: they were allowed to live in the huts and have a garden, for food crops and livestock.

This essay will focus on understanding how the system of attached work survived the abolition of slavery in Martinique, and indeed why it can be argued that the attached workers phenomenon epitomizes the paradoxical context of mutations and continuities that arose after the abolition of slavery? Following the abolition of slavery, the phenomenon of attached workers was maintained through a set of specific contracts, which were renewed in an effort to reach a new equilibrium between 1852 and 1880, through the evolution of the legally-enforced labour organization. However, it seems that the balance sought was only struck in the 1880s, with the first documented occurrences of the phenomenon of *gens casés* (hut-bound people), the most widely known example of the attached workers phenomenon.

Contract Terms after Abolition of Slavery

It appears that in 1848, after the abolition of slavery, some of the former slaves remained in the houses of yore through the said contracts. These contracts maintained some conditions similar to those of the slavery period after its abolition while providing for certain evolutions: they seem to bridge the gap between the two periods. Among the body of aforementioned contracts, it is interesting to analyse further the contract of association, since sources attest that it included the granting of a hut on plantation lands, in addition to organizing rural work on plantations. Through this contract, we will attempt to understand the characteristics of the permanence of the attached work phenomenon in the immediate post-abolition period.

On the one hand, it can be argued that the contract of association partly continued the previous period, not only because it provided for identical work, performed under similar conditions; but more specifically because it had the particularity of arranging the return of huts and gardens to the workers. Indeed, it is correct to state that this type of contract restored, for the newly freed people, work on plantation lands, from 1848 onwards. To further illustrate this point, let us analyse a text published in the *Official Journal of Martinique* regarding this contract, which organized the work on plantation lands for the newly freed, with modalities which recall the previous period. For example, Article 7 of the text states that: 'The working day will be nine o'clock, it will start at sunrise and end at sunset. This time span will be cut by rest intervals in accordance with the customs of the plantations'.[1]

Consequently, the working hours were not significantly shortened, and the breaks promised by the contract were linked to the employer's goodwill. We can therefore wonder if there was any material change to the physical arduousness of the work assumed. Moreover, the distribution of the workers was also identical, since the article further specifies that: 'There will be two classes among the workers; the first category or large workshop will consist of farmers from 16 to 50 years old. The second category or small workshop will consist of those aged 10 to 16 and 50 to 70.'[2]

This distribution is homogeneous with the one that was in force during the slavery period. In addition to these elements of homogeneity, the actual originality of this contract when compared to others of the period, since it is not the only one to allow a remuneration-earning activity on plantations, was to reinstate the 'Negro huts'. Indeed, Article 6 of the above-mentioned text states that workers: 'shall retain the enjoyment of the huts they inhabit and the gardens they cultivate for themselves on the plantations'.[3]

This extract, by its use of the verb retain seems to hint at the fact that the very workers who were formerly slaves on the planta-

[1] Journal officiel de la Martinique, Volume XXXI. N°55, Mercredi 5 Juillet 1848, Parti non officielle. Url: http://gallica.bnf.fr/ark:/12148/bpt6k56032781.item

[2] Ibid.

[3] Ibid.

tions were the ones who were to associate themselves on these same plantations: this contract thus perpetuated, for the former slaves concerned, characteristics of their slave life on the same premises.

On the other hand, it is not possible to claim unquestionably that this contract enabled, in the post-slavery era, a servile existence. Because even though the work was the same, the organization similar, and the huts-system continued, the power of employers was framed and circumscribed by the law and workers were granted effective rights. Indeed, the first gain of this situation, which constituted a fundamental disruption with the previous period, was the remuneration, fixed by Article 9 of a publication in the *Official Journal of Martinique* on the contract of association:

> The products of any kind of the property will be divided into three equal portions, one for the owner, the other for expenses with no open recourse or claim against the workers if the expenses exceed this amount and the third for the workers, or, net of expenses, the net proceeds shall be divided into two equal portions, one for the owner, and the other for the workers.[4]

Furthermore, the contract of association did not only enact the requirement of remuneration; it also established the right to claim advances from the employers, as indicated in Article 11 of the same document: 'every worker will be able to claim a weekly sum of two francs from his share as advances'.[5]

Finally, in addition to the right to a remuneration, this new contractual arrangement provided remedies that limited the action of the employers and was supposed to guarantee the rights of the workers. These were provided for in Article 13 of the text quoted above, in the following terms:

> The workers shall elect a five-member council from among their members, whose duties shall be to settle all the difficulties that may arise between them; to preside over the distribution of workers' due and to mediate between the workers and the owner or administrator.[6]

[4] Ibid.
[5] Ibid.
[6] Ibid.

There was, in this contract, the establishment of intermediaries responsible for the mediation of disputes. It is possible to find this group, also known as '*prud'homme*', in notes concerning the cantonal juries. The latter were set up at the same time as the decree of abolition on 27 April 1848 and had jurisdiction over so-called in civil matters and in criminal matters. In civil matters, it was provided that:

> the jury will reconcile, if possible, ex officio, or on the voluntary presentation of the parties, or on notice of appearance, without costs, any dispute over the fulfillment of the commitments, or between the owners and managers, master workers, workers, or servants, whether between heads of industry, manufacturers, or merchants, and clerks, counter-masters, workmen, or apprentices.[7]

We can infer that these representatives were able to bring disputes internal to the plantation to the administration: the state thus intervened in the plantation matters to guarantee both rights and duties. These representatives also intervened in the case of a dismissal. Indeed, according to this contract: 'the dismissed worker [...] may [...] harvest or have people harvest crops from his private garden, within a period of time to be determined by the Council of Commissioners'.[8]

To conclude, the contract of association brought important novelties into the employment relationship on the plantation: the salary, the early workers' rights, and the defense of these rights backed by the power of the State.

The Working of the Contract System

In its attempt to reconcile the owners' expectations, which did not differ from the previous period regarding plantation work, and the rights acquired with the abolition of slavery, the 'contract of associa-

[7] ANOM: Généralités: Carton 119, Dossier 1061, Gouvernement Provisoire, Décret de Formation et composition des jurys cantonaux, Fait à Paris en Conseil de Gouvernement, le 27 avril 1848.

[8] Journal officiel de la Martinique, Volume XXXI. N°55, Mercredi 5 Juillet 1848, Parti non officielle. Url : http://gallica.bnf.fr/ark:/12148/bpt6k56032781.item

tion appears to have produced mixed results. Indeed, if it did help to maintain a labouring population on the plantations, this population quickly decreased, because of growing discontent linked to the working conditions it provided for.

The main criticism of this contract is best formulated by French abolitionist and politician Victor Schoelcher, in his book *The Truth to the Workers and Farmers of Martinique*. In this text, the author contends that:

> We must not be deluded about this, the freedmen will hardly accept an association in which they would have to wait, during a whole year, the uncertain realization of the fruit of their hardships; they want to feel that they are free by receiving a salary for their work. This is the first manifestation of their need for independence. It is therefore a question of reconciling the advantages of an actual salary with the benefits of the association. For that, it is enough to give them each day a minimum of pay, from the gross product (Schoelcher 1849, 408).

The remuneration approach implemented by this contract benefitted employers, who were spared the treasury conundrum of paying off their various charges without themselves being paid first, or without knowing that they will be paid at all, but was perceived as detrimental to the workers. Consequently, it was not surprising that, as early as 1850, salary-providing contracts have replaced the association contract in some places in Martinique.[9] As a result, after the abolition of slavery, a new equilibrium was in the making to satisfy the demands of colonial agriculture, along with the imperatives of the new post-slavery period. However, these two goals were difficult to reconcile, and the association contractual framework was by then struggling to reach a satisfactory balance for both employers and workers.

In the immediate after-abolition phase, the administration in place, in tune with the perceived importance of making the agricultural economy thrive, and in an effort to maintain the relative financial and social soundness of the colony, sets as an overarching

[9] ANOM: Généralités: Carton 79, Dossier 650, Martinique Gouvernement Générale, lettre du l'amiral Gouverneur au Ministre datant du 17 décembre 1850.

objective, to have a workforce permanently present on agricultural plantations. From that moment on, the administration would try to influence the rural professionals by legal means, and to bring them back to working on plantations. To achieve this goal, it was necessary to ensure a new balance that reconciles the demands of the newly freed workers and the needs of the agricultural employers: efforts in this direction were deployed until the 1880s.

In this context, the 1849 report of the Colonial Commission on the Repression of Vagrancy offers valuable insights. This report announced that: 'every worker or farmer working alone or by day and every individual attached to domesticity has the obligation to hold a livret'; but at the same time, it dispensed from the livret: 'any laborer or worker attached on a regular basis to a workshop or plantation, that includes associates, committed laborers, colons partiaires or farmers'. All possible classes of workers were included in these first definitions: some, regular, tied to the ground or to the plantation, were exempted from carrying a livret; the others, irregular, in isolation and subject to the livret.[10] The latter was an administrative document stating:

> the surname, forenames, nicknames, age, place of birth, residence and occupation of the bearer as well as his description, his affiliation and his registration number. The livret will be signed by the Mayor or by one of his deputies and the bearer, or mention will be made that he does not know how to sign.[11]

It can be concluded that the administration imposed, for agricultural workers, either the use of the livret, or the regular attachment to a plantation. If one analyses the contracts that are considered as attachment under this report, they would be 'associates, committed laborers, colons partiaires or farmers'.[12] This is important because a

[10] ANOM: Généralité: Carton 145, Dossier 1226, Commission Coloniale, Répression du Vagabondage, Rapport au nom de la Sous-Commission de la Police du Travail et Projet de la loi ou de décret, sans date.

[11] ANOM: Série Géographique Martinique: Carton 79, Dossier 652, Gouvernement de la Martinique, Fort-de-France le 9 Octobre 1852 par ampliation A. Vaillant.

[12] Ibid.

decree of the private council of 1852 further elaborated on this list of contracts by stating that: 'the workers [that are] attached to the plantations by virtue of a commitment of one year at least, either as colons partiaires or as associates, or with a salary, are exempt from the livret'.[13]

Consequently, contrary to the enumeration of the report of the Colonial Commission which placed at the same level four contracts, this decree of the private council singled out a category of contract, the commitment, which would be declined in the three others: the association, the colonage partiaire and perhaps the fermage. In addition to these contracts, another category was emerging: work for salary, which would also be a form of commitment. This reinforces the idea that one cannot speak of salary in the context of the contracts of association and colonage partiaire: the workers involved received a remuneration, and no actual salary. As shown, in the immediate aftermath of abolition, the attached work concerned only the newly freed (and the people freed during the era of slavery). But in its amendments, too, the administration appears to have foreseen the resistance of the rural population. In response, it also extended the new provisions to immigrants, so that plantation owners could have a complementary or alternative source of labour. That is why it was stated in the draft decree of 1852 that the latter:

> regulates the work commitments and determines the reciprocal obligations of the workers and of those who employ them, are indistinctly applicable to the contracts of hire of immigrant workers to those laborers and workers belonging to the colonial population.[14]

As a consequence, the new legal framework of rural labour in Martinique was deeply modified in the immediate post-abolition period: it generalized two categories, commitment and livret, promotes three new contracts (association, colonage partiaire and salary) and opened the job market to immigration. To study these contracts

[13] ANOM: Généralités: Carton 79, Dossier 652, note du Gouverneur Vaillant datant du 9 Octobre 1852.

[14] ANOM: Généralités: Carton 145, Dossier 1226, Décret sur les Immigrations et les Engagements de Travail dans les colonies, Rapport au Prince Président de la République Française, p. 3.

in an exhaustive way, it is critical to analyse the provision that makes them specific: the granting of a hut and a garden. This analysis will target the three contracts that allow the granting of these benefits, that is to say the three contracts of commitment: the association, the colonage partiaire and the salary.

Colonage Partiaire

The modalities of the benefit of the hut and the garden within the context of the contract of association has been detailed above. Thus, it is arguable that the other two contracts, since they also include the notion of commitment, itself included in that of attachment, shares its characteristics. This idea is supported by the definition of colonage partiaire published in the *Official Journal of Martinique* in April 1848. This publication is essential because it gives a definition from M. Colson, 'President of the central committee for the organization of work'.[15] For him, the colonage partiaire can be summed up as follows: 'The colonage partiaire is the one where you give a piece of land to clear to a worker, if it is a negro who needs advances, you give them to him, and at the end of the harvest, you pay yourself and give him his share'.

There appears to be a strong resemblance between the colonage partiaire and the association. To go further, it is possible to study the terms of this contract as detailed in the plantation Saint-Jacques in 1850,[16] to understand the obligations of workers. Indeed, in this contract it was stipulated that only 'families or companies composed, at least 6 workers valid from 14 to 60'[17] were admitted to colonage partiaire. These workers must grow cane within a predefined period of time. At the end of the harvest, after processing the cane into sugar, workers receive a 'gross third'.[18]

[15] Journal officiel de la Martinique, Volume XXXI. N°48, Samedi 10 Juin 1848. Url : http://gallica.bnf.fr/ark:/12148/bpt6k5603272j/f1.item

[16] ANOM: Série Géographique Martinique Carton 125, Dossier 1121, Gouvernement de la Martinique, Extrait des Procès-Verbaux, document daté du 4 avril 1850.

[17] Ibid.

[18] Ibid.

The deferred and third-party payment would therefore also have been practiced in this contract: here again, it seems that this is not a salary *per se*, but a more complex remuneration system. Also, the study of this contract allows us to understand what was meant by the idea of attachment: a worker was deemed attached when he legally limits his ability to sell his work capacity to several plantations and dedicates themself to only one. This attachment was not an attachment to the workshop, but rather to the plantation and culture. The possible choices of workers in rural areas was as follows: either they attach themselves and give their labour to a single plantation for a lengthy period, which enables them to enjoy a hut and a garden, or they chose to hold a livret and retain the autonomy of their work.

The Livret

To take stock of the search for this new balance and in order to understand the developments that occurred from 1852 to 1880, it is instructive to recall the actual differences between the livret and the commitment. Against the background of such an analysis, one can then attempt to assess the results obtained in relation to the objectives, and to venture reasons for the instability of the model put in place at the time. Indeed, it will be useful to remember that the purpose of the definition of two categories imposed on rural workers was not really that they choose between two equivalent forms of work. The livret, which has already shown its unpopularity in the period of slavery (for the freedmen) was not an alternative deemed equivalent to the commitment by the very administration which pronounced its reintroduction. Moreover, it was because this form was so strongly rejected that the administration enacts it, in order to direct the workers towards the commitment. Thus, the decree of 13 February 1852, which organized the work in the colonies, and which gave a legal basis to the commitments made by the local population was clearly intended to 'push the agricultural population to commitments of more than one year, a profitable commitment to the regularity of work'.[19]

[19] ANOM: Série Géographique Martinique Carton 79, Dossier 652,

This position is also clearly assumed in the minutes of the Colonial Commission of 1849 which states that:

> if it is true that the obligation to submit to the livret is considered in some colonies as a sign and a remnant of the old servitude, as a sort of conveyance to return to it, it is also good to impose this sign of disfavor on those who would be reluctant to regular work and commitment. It is exploiting a prejudice, a prevention, for the benefit of sound ideas about work.[20]

Given our awareness of this fact, the failure of this policy is even more striking: while the livret was supported for its unpopularity by the local administration, people did not turn massively towards the option of commitment. Actually, it was announced by the Governor of Martinique that as on 31 December 1852 the workers were divided as follows: 39684 livrets and 9193 committed.[21] Worse, this trend further accentuated and as on 31 December 1853, there were in the category of rural workers 26221 people white the livret and 10345, and 9193 the commitment. It is this assessment that motivates the research of the following period, mobilized further by the attempts to amend the legal context in order to, if not make the commitment more attractive, at least to question its separation from the livret. These changes were rationalized in a report made to the Governor in 1855 which stated that: 'it had become indispensable to coordinate them, to cut off the provisions whose opportunity had ceased, to make the modifications and additions required by experience'.[22]

Martinique direction de l'Intérieur, Extrait des Procès-Verbaux, Fort-de-France, le 9 octobre 1852, Rapport à Monsieur le Gouverneur en Conseil Privé.

[20] Procès-Verbaux de la Commission Colonial Institué par décret du Président de la République du 22 novembre 1849, Paris, Imprimerie Nationale, Première Partie, p. 148. Url: https://books.google.fr/books?id=ubMJtAEACAAJ&printsec=frontcover&hl=fr&source=gbs_ge_summary_r&cad=0#v=onepage&q&f=false

[21] ANOM: Généralités: Carton 145, Dossier 1229: Gouvernement de la Martinique, lettre du Gouverneur de la Martinique au Ministre daté du 12 Janvier 1853.

[22] ANOM: Série Géographique Martinique Carton 79, Dossier 652, Présentation d'un arrêté d'ensemble sur la police du travail et l'immigration,

Following this report, a new order was promulgated in 1855, the provisions of which seem designed with a certain sense of realism. It combines the commitment provisions and the livret, and provides in its Article 33 of Title II, Work for Others, the 1st Chapter, that:

'The commitment results from:

1. Agreements passed in accordance with the provisions of the Decree of 13 February 1852 in respect of work commitments;
2. By an employee having received advances from his employer as wages, duly recorded on the livret;
3. By the fact of an employee being established on a rural plantation on the condition of giving his work, either to wages, or in any other way, and subject to the concession of a hut or a garden, the whole to be found on the livret.'[23]

It is likely that this law sought to introduce the commitment each time the worker asked to enjoy a benefit offered by the employers: advances on payment, and the granting of a hut and a garden, even if the worker had chosen to hold a livret earlier on. Moreover, the livret became the guarantor of the benefits received, and compelled workers and owners alike to respect the situation depicted on a livret that follows any granting of a favour on the part of the agricultural employers. But this order also created attached workers without these workers' proper consent. So, we have the institution of not freely consented attached worker.

This fact is noticed by Victor Schoelcher (1872, 16) in his book on The Gueydon order in Martinique and the Husson order in Guadeloupe. Indeed, 'Whoever borrows from his committer becomes by the very fact, without judgment of any kind, his liege man, his serf; he loses the free disposition of himself until repayment.'

Consequently, from this order on, two kinds of attached workers existed. The first were those with a commitment freely signed as explained. The second was more complex. It applied to the workers

---

le 8 Septembre 1855, Rapport à Monsieur le Gouverner en Conseil Privé.

[23] Comte de Gueydon, Arrêté sur le travail et l'immigration à la Martinique, fait le 10 septembre 1855, p. 10. Url : http://gallica.bnf.fr/ark:/12148/bpt6k5487418d/f4.image

who chose the livret and created within this category two kinds of attached workers, those who chose to be housed on the plantation and those who had to repay their salary advance.

Developments after 1880

If it seems decisive to pick up the history of this evolution in the 1880s, this is so because sources attest in these years for the first time of a new phenomenon, the *gens casés*. We would like to grasp the articulation of this reality in relation to the contracts of the previous period. Indeed, this paper left the previous period in its attempt to strike a new equilibrium for attachment, which it had first attempted to find by imposing two categories, commitment and livret, and then by expanding the commitment to certain situations specific to the livret.

Yet, during the investigation following the 1900s, M. Liottier, Director of Galion Exploitation, a farming company, provides a definition of the *gens casés* that raises further interrogation. According to him:

> During the time of immigration there were on the property a core of immigrants workers living on the property; when the immigration was ended, the huts occupied by these immigrants were empty and some nomadic workers benefited from the housing of former immigrants. They attached themselves to the property.[24]

This statement is important in many ways. First, it clearly claims that, in fact, the original population of the phenomenon of *gens casés* was the immigrant population. If the fact of being *casé* was limited to working on a plantation and being housed on it, as this statement seems to announce, the assertion of M. Liottier requires some developments. Indeed, the commitment, which mainly targeted the colonial populations, offered the workers the opportunity to live in the huts of the plantation. Therefore, the first occupants of the huts could not have be the immigrants solely. It is certain that the

[24] ANOM: Série Martinique: Carton 179, Dossier 1649, M. Liottier, Directeur de l'exploitation du Galion et de l'exploitation du François, Note sur les évènements de la Martinique, fait à Fort-de-France le 23 Mars 1900.

draft decree of 1852 on the engagement opened this possibility of commitment to the immigrant workers, probably to prepare for the defections of the colonial population in reaction to the regulatory changes.

Does this mean that the dwindling of the number of committed workers was of such a nature that only immigrants remained? Would it be accurate to speak of a return of Creole populations after the end of legal immigration in 1884, rather than a complete arrival on that date? This seems unlikely, however, since in 1852, the date of the opening of the commitment to immigrants, the number of engaged Creoles was already of 9193,[25] and this phenomenon was growing in 1853. What is more, the registers of plantations, like those of Pécoul in Basse-Pointe, mentioned people present since the abolition. By studying the lists of the names of the workers on this plantation, it can be seen that there were workers who were born on it and were still housed there in 1883.[26] It is consequently possible to assume that these workers went through the previously mentioned contracts.

Thus, the distinction made between the phenomenon reported by M. Liottier and the workers present on plantations from 1848 to 1880 can only be done at the level of the working conditions provided in the context of the *gens casés*. The phenomenon is then new regarding the arrangements of the work, rather than aspects of the hut, the garden, or the population itself.

It is possible to identify actual differences between the *gens casés* contracts and the previous ones. First, it is certain that at the time of the *gens casés*, the work included in the contract was protean, whereas it seems to involve only the work in plantation in previous periods. Thus, we can see on the lists of workers on plantation La Montagne in 1886, some *gens casés* constrained to non-purely agricultural tasks.[27] The nature of the contract therefore seems to be changing

[25] ANOM: Généralités: Carton 145, Dossier 1229: Gouvernement de la Martinique, lettre du Gouverneur de la Martinique au Ministre daté du 12 Janvier 1853.

[26] Archives de Pierrefitte: 376AP/58: Papiers Pécoul Martinique, Procuration, instruction, inventaire général 1832-99.

[27] Archives de Pierrefitte: 376AP/53 – 376AP/54: État des lieux évalua-

further. For, in addition, the payment system appeared to have evolved during the period of the contracts of engagement, since the *gens casés* received a salary,[28] not a remuneration after processing the fruit of their labour (as was the case in many of the earlier contracts).

This practice, which was a major complaint of the rural workers since 1848, was therefore ceded by the employers. It is undeniable that the contract of the *gens casés* emerged in a situation where the bosses tried to keep their workers on the plantations. The workers living on the plantations constituted a stake that was of utmost importance for the bosses, because they needed a continuous workforce on the plantations. In 1871, there already appeared to be a desire to keep the workers on the plantations. During a debate on the conservation of the livret regime, one interlocutor asserted that: 'fieldwork [...] requires more or less diligent care and demand at every moment, the eye or the arms of the farmer, lodging for most of the time on the property he cultivates.'[29]

This need was confirmed after the establishment of the phenomenon of the *gens casés* by M. Liottier's remarks, who declares himself: 'happy to have a workshop at hand, instead of waiting every morning, their late arrival sometimes, because they slept very far, we wanted to promote this movement'.[30] Consequently, this system marked a new balance in the Martinican rural world, supported by a contract that better reconciled the interests of the plantation owners with those of the workers.

Yet, there are noticeable similarities between the situation of *gens casés*, as it manifested itself after 1880, and the contracts of commitment defined after 1848. First, it is beyond question that the

---

tion des Troupeaux et Inventaire d tous les effets appartenant à Messieurs les Propriétaires de l'Habitation La Montagne 1886, État nominatif des Noirs employés et logeant dur l'Habitation la Montagne.

[28] Ibid.

[29] Archives Nationales Section Outre-Mer, Carton 91, Dossier 767, Martinique année 1871, extrait des Procès-Verbaux, Session Ordinaire, Séance du 21 Décembre, Présidence de M.F. Godissard.

[30] ANOM: Série Martinique: Carton 179, Dossier 1649, M. Liottier, Directeur de l'exploitation du Galion et de l'exploitation du François, Note sur les évènements de la Martinique, fait à Fort-de-France le 23 Mars 1900.

work on the plantation dimension remains: there was a continuity of the activity carried out, which did not change significantly between 1848 and the 1880s. Similarly, as recalled above, the granting of a hut and a garden remained a constant feature of the attached work since inception in 1848. Then, it should be recalled that the working conditions remained as painful as in the previous periods. It can be seen from the records of the Pécoul plantation that there were workers in the fields from the age of 10 to the age of 70.[31]

Finally, the social rights acquired since the days of the abolition in the various contracts of commitment are found in the *gens casés* contracts. As an example, M. Liottier stated that the workers and their families received 'free medical care, whatever the illness',[32] rights already guaranteed in the contract of association. Moreover, there were elderly people among the *gens casés*: it was therefore already a particularity, not only at the end of the abolition, but also in the contract of association. This contract stipulated that the elderly could live on the plantations and were supported by the plantation without providing work in return.

This continuity of treatment also appeared valid for the disabled and for the sick. For instance, in 1895, on plantation La Montagne, a blind man resided in a hut without a garden but is paid 10F per month.[33] This phenomenon also existed on a Basse-Pointe plantation where a disabled worker is referenced.[34] It seems that this treatment

[31] Archives de Pierrefitte: 376AP/53 – 376AP/54: 1886. Inventaire des constructions états des troupeaux avec leurs estimations et de tous les efforts appartenant à l'Habitation de Messieurs les Héritiers Pécoul à la Basse-Pointe, Martinique, Liste nominative des travailleurs Créoles logeant sur l'habitation Pécoul Casse-Pointe année 1896.

[32] ANOM: Série Martinique: Carton 179, Dossier 1649, M. Liottier, Directeur de l'exploitation du Galion et de l'exploitation du François, Note sur les évènements de la Martinique, fait à Fort-de-France le 23 Mars 1900.

[33] Archives de Pierrefitte: 376AP/53 – 376AP/54: État des lieux évaluation des Troupeaux et Inventaire d tous les effets appartenant à Messieurs les Propriétaires de l'Habitation La Montagne 1886, État nominatif des Noirs employés et logeant dur l'Habitation la Montagne.

[34] Archives de Pierrefitte: 376AP/53 – 376AP/54: La Montagne et Basse Pointe Inventaire 1886-1897, Habitation Pécoul, Basse-Pointe à

was a direct legacy of Article 8 of the contract of association, which provided that:

> The sick workers will be treated at the expense of society. The elderly and the disabled workers will each be cared for by their families. Those who will be without families, where their parents will be disabled, unable to work, will remain the responsibility of society. However, the workers may, when the Republic has opened hospices, place at the expense of the colony the old and the infirm.
>
> The infants will be cared for and raised in a room of the house, at the expense of the parents, until the age of six, by means of the withholding on their part of the product, which will be determined by the council of the commissioners. Children who are orphans, or whose parents are disabled, unable to work, will remain dependent on the society until the age of ten years.[35]

As a result, it can be contended that the contract of *gens casés* was similar to previous contracts, such as the contract of association, not only in the work that it provided, but also in its conditions that it offered.

In conclusion, this presentation set out to study the specific reality of work and workers attached to plantations, parallel to the residency of the workers on the plantations, since the end of slavery and until the emergence of the *gens casés*, one of the most famous manifestations of among the Creole population in Martinique. If we can hold *gens casés* as a system inherited from those who followed from abolition, and from the slavery era itself, it is because the analysis of the contracts immediately put into place after 1848 uncovers actual similarities between the contracts of attachment from the post-abolition period, and the contract of *gens casés*. The nature of the work, as well as its conditions to a certain extent, the housing provided and the social benefits, remained very similar between the two periods. And although it proves complicated to precisely identify

---

Messieurs les Héritiers Pécoul, Nom des travailleurs créole casés sur la propriété au 31 Aout 1894.

[35] Journal officiel de la Martinique, Volume XXXI. N°55, Mercredi 5 Juillet 1848, Parti non officielle. Url: http://gallica.bnf.fr/ark:/12148/bpt6k56032781.item

all the contracts enforced on the plantations in each period, and all the provisions envisaged by each contract (given that these changed from one plantation to the other), the contracts that we were able to study are informative as to this idea of genealogy between them.

What we know about this genealogy is that it starts with contracts of attachment such as the contract of association, promulgated at the end of slavery. Quickly, the administration, which understood the acute need for a stable workforce on agricultural lands, intended to extend the contracts of attachment by leaving two options to rural agriculture workers: the livret and the commitment. Since the livret had already shown its limitations during the slavery period, the actual purpose of the administration was to push the workers towards the commitment. But faced with the problems inherent to the commitment, this control of the rural work was a failure. In the years following 1855, the administration therefore focused on imposing the commitment by regulatory changes.

However, it seems that it was above all the vested interests of the land owners, who embarked on a bidding war to attract workers, that motivated the evolution of the contracts in order for them to be more in agreement with the demands of the workers. Therefore, it appears that the phenomenon of *gens casés* can be read as the equilibrium provisionally found between the dynamics of the antagonistic interests of the owners on the one hand, who wanted a permanent workforce on the plantations at less cost, and workers on the other hand, who demanded less financial precariousness and more social rights. As such, it can be concluded that the dynamics of the evolution of the attached workers phenomenon is to be found in the continuity of the plantation needs, which bolstered a continuity in the work activity and housing situations, while the abolition of slavery opened up a series of disruptions beneficial to the workers after 1848.

Bibliography

Comte de Gueydon, Arrêté sur le travail et l'immigration à la Martinique, fait le 10 *Septembre 1855,* p. 10. Url: http://gallica.bnf.fr/ark:/12148/bpt6k548741 8d/f4.image

Zobel, Joseph. 2009. *La Rue Cases-Nègres.* Paris: Présence Africaine.

Schoelcher, Victor. 1849. *La vérité aux ouvriers et aux cultivateurs de La Martinique* (…). Paris: Pagnerre Éditeur.

_____. 1872. *L'arrêté Gueydon* à la Martinique et l'arrêté Husson à la *Guadeloupe.* Paris: Armand Le Chevalier Éditeur.

Procès-Verbaux de la Commission Colonial Institué par décret du Président de la *République du 22 novembre 1849.* Paris: Imprimerie Nationale, Première Partie: 148. Url: https://books.google.fr/books?id=ubMJtAEACAAJ&printsec=frontcover&hl=fr&source=gbs_ge_summary_r&cad=0#v=onepage&q&f=false

Archives

PAPER

Journal officiel de la Martinique, Volume XXXI. N°55, Mercredi 5 Juillet 1848, Parti non officielle. Url: http://gallica.bnf.fr/ark:/12148/bpt6k56032781.item

Journal officiel de la Martinique, Volume XXXI. N°48, Samedi 10 Juin 1848 Url: http://gallica.bnf.fr/ark:/12148/bpt6k5603272j/f1.item

Archives Nationales de l'Outre-Mer (ANOM)

GENERALITY CATEGORY

Carton 79, Dossier 650: Martinique Gouvernement Générale, lettre de l'amiral Gouverneur au Ministre datant du 17 décembre 1850.

Carton 79, Dossier 652: note du Gouverneur Vaillant datant du 9 Octobre 1852.

Carton 119, Dossier 1061: Gouvernement Provisoire, Décret de Formation et composition des jurys cantonaux, Fait à Paris en Conseil de Gouvernement, le 27 avril 1848.

Carton 145, Dossier 1226: Commission Coloniale, Répression du Vagabondage, Rapport au nom de la Sous-Commission de la Police du Travail et Projet de la loi ou de décret, sans date.

Carton 145, Dossier 1226: Décret sur les Immigrations et les Engagements de Travail dans les colonies, Rapport au Prince Président de la République Française, p. 3.

Carton 145, Dossier 1229: Gouvernement de la Martinique, lettre du Gouverneur de la Martinique au Ministre daté du 12 Janvier 1853.

Géographic Category, Martinique:

Carton 79, Dossier 652: Gouvernement de la Martinique, Fort-de-France le 9 Octobre 1852 par ampliation A. Vaillant.

Carton 79, Dossier 652: Présentation d'un arrêté d'ensemble sur la police du travail et l'immigration, le 8 Septembre 1855, Rapport à Monsieur le Gouverner en Conseil Privé.

Martinique Carton 79, Dossier 652: Martinique direction de l'Intérieur, Extrait des Procès-Verbaux, Fort-de-France, le 9 octobre 1852, Rapport à Monsieur le Gouverneur en Conseil Privé.

Carton 125, Dossier 1121: Gouvernement de la Martinique, Extrait des Procès-Verbaux, document daté du 4 avril 1850.

Carton 179, Dossier 1649: M. Liottier, Directeur de l'exploitation du Galion et de l'exploitation du François, Note sur les évènements de la Martinique, fait à Fort-de-France le 23 Mars 1900.

National Archives of Pierrefitte

376AP/58: Papiers Pécoul Martinique, Procuration, instruction, inventaire général 1832-1899.

376AP/53-376AP/54: État des lieux évaluation des Troupeaux et Inventaire d tous les effets appartenant à Messieurs les Propriétaires de l'Habitation La Montagne 1886, État nominatif des Noirs employés et logeant dur l'Habitation la Montagne.

376AP/53-376AP/54: La Montagne et Basse Pointe Inventaire 1886-1897, Habitation Pécoul, Basse-Pointe à Messieurs les Héritiers Pécoul, Nom des travailleurs créole casés sur la propriété au 31 Aout 1894.

376AP/53-376AP/54: 1886. Inventaire des constructions états des troupeaux avec leurs estimations et de tous les efforts appartenant à l'Habitation de Messieurs les Héritiers Pécoul à la Basse-Pointe, Martinique, Liste nominative des travailleurs Créoles logeant sur l'habitation Pécoul Casse-Pointe année 1896.

SEVEN

Identity Construction of the White Creoles of Martinique through Networks and Mobility during the Second Half of the Nineteenth Century

Archipelago Families

ADÉLAÏDE MARINE-GOUGEON

Introduction

The white creoles living in Martinique during the second part of the nineteenth century were never really the main objects of historical study. Previous research on the islands focused on general histories of the island or justifiably aimed to consider the new workers who had just come out of slavery and were finally embracing freedom (Fallope 1992). Nevertheless, the white creoles have created a considerable number of archival sources such as private papers or private diaries. The group of the white creoles in Martinique is particularly interesting for a study of the post-slavery era, as they are also directly affected by the decline of the productive system that initially established their wealth and social status.

In my previous research I studied how the former Martinican slave owners endeavoured to organize around political demands throughout the emancipation during the French Second Republic

(1848-51).[1] I aimed to demonstrate how important the issue of compensation was for them. Indeed, they saw it as the main condition to accept the abolishment of slavery and to implement the new colonial societal conditions based on free labour. The preservation of their dominant social status was also at stake, which was an essential part of their identity.

The year 1848 was a landmark in the building of their identity. The white creole dreaded the February Revolution that established the Republic, and the uprising that occurred in Saint-Pierre on the 22nd and 23rd of May forced the authorities of Martinique to proclaim the emancipation sooner than intended.[2] This event triggered off a reaction of fear and panic that led some white creoles to emigrate towards other American territories such as Puerto Rico or Louisiana. My current research tries to focus on the imperial and trans-imperial identity of the Martinican white creoles, who are far more mobile and open to the American territories than usually thought. My work also questions their attachment to their native island and to what extent it defines them, their relationship to France as the metropole, and finally how they identify themselves to a broader space including the wider Caribbean and the American continent.

Studying white creole families in the Caribbean space and their mobility implies an attempt to search for networks that would be supported by family links. My starting point was to question the idea of the White creoles being firmly rooted only into their plantation and living isolated from the rest of the Caribbean space, and only open to the relationships between colony and metropole. Broadening this scope, I highlight their mobility by looking into their travelling into the Atlantic and Caribbean spaces, and possibly beyond. The network, I intend to define in my study has its origin in

[1] Adélaïde Marine-Gougeon. 2011. 'Les colons martiniquais face à l'abolition de l'esclavage, ou le principe de conservation. L'exemple d'Auguste Pécoul, 1848-1851', Master dissertation, Paris-Sorbonne University.

[2] Letter of the Governor of Martinique Rostoland to the Minister of the Marine and Colonies, 28 May 1848, French National archives of the Outre-Mer (Archives nationales de l'Outre-Mer), Ministerial funds, Série géographique de la Martinique, Carton 56 Dossier 464.

the mobility of some individuals from a certain family background in Martinique to another point of establishment, while maintaining more or less regular links with the family that stayed on the island. The network appears to be highly connected to family relationships, and in close relation with widespread endogamy into the White creole environment. In addition, White creole families are assumed to have developed a strong sentiment of solidarity and cohesion (Kováts Beaudoux & Giraud 2002). In the first place, it seems necessary to identify families and their personal history, subsequently to search for the communications between the different nodes of their networks.

The idea of an archipelago captures the idea of a network that would fit this research: indeed, the families that I am interested in are most of the time firmly settled in Martinique, and however have relatives (and sometimes properties) in France, in other Caribbean islands such as Guadeloupe, Saint Lucia, Trinidad, and even in the United States of America, particularly in New Orleans or New York. The challenge is to identify if the different parts of the archipelago families communicate with each other; it seems difficult indeed to talk of a network without any form of communication. The existence of these communication networks is an important factor to consider as soon as the identification work of families has begun.

In the first part of this paper I will recall the general frame of the emancipation from 1848 and the following years (Adélaïde-Merlande 1989). The identification of the corpus of White creole families will then be developed. In the third section, I will attempt to revive a family network through private archives. Finally, I will evoke a family network and its multiple branches.

1848's Emancipation and the Martinican White Creole Social Fears

A long-dreaded emancipation

Most of the French slave owners knew in 1848 that slavery was not an everlasting institution. They observed—with very careful attention—how the British proceeded with the progressive emancipation in their Caribbean colonies. In France, during the 1830s and the

1840s, the debate about emancipation was intense, especially inside the various governments of the Monarchie de Juillet (1830-48). However, it appears that no clear-cut decision was achieved when the revolution occurred in France in February 1848 and evicted the last king, Louis-Philippe d'Orléans. As a result, the Second Republic was determined to close the debate and to proceed to the abolition of slavery, thanks to the action and expertise of French abolitionist Victor Schoelcher (Schmidt 2009). In his opinion, the emancipation of slavery in French colonies should immediately be implemented and not reproduce what he identified as mistakes in the British process, such as apprenticeship.[3]

The 4th of March 1848 décret stated that 'no French territory could bear any slave'. However, this décret was only a declaration of intent, and did not have the effect of emancipating the slaves as yet (Adélaïde-Merlande 1989). This décret reached Martinique by the end of the month, at the same time as the news about the Revolution. Every member of society knew that the end of slavery would be irreversible. However, the slaves remained slaves and thus had to work and obey their masters until the arrival of an additional law which would establish them as free people and citizens, and would reorganize the entire society.

On the side of the slave owners, the fear of a general uprising was growing, and they remembered what happened to White planters in Saint-Domingue during the first French Revolution, such as massive slaughters and exiles. As most of them were monarchists, they dreaded the republican regime and its egalitarian ideology.[4] However, a certain number of them were prepared to accept emancipation on one condition: the compensation, like the one granted to the British slave owners, this was the main condition for most of them to accept the abolition of slavery.

The former owners perceived the time between the announcement of emancipation and the arrival of the long-awaited effective

[3] Victor Schoelcher, *Des colonies françaises, abolition immédiate de l'esclavage*, 1842, éd. Pagnerre.

[4] A good example can be found in the private journal of Pierre Dessalles, edited as *La vie d'un colon à la Martinique au XIXe siècle*, Désormeaux, 1986.

emancipation as too long to be endured by the slaves. Indeed, they were not formally enslaved anymore, but still had to conform to its institutions. The impatience became agitation when they perceived any form of authority coming from a master as unbearable. The agitation turned to insurrection in Saint-Pierre and Le Prêcheur, when angry mobs protested against the imprisonment of a slave called Romain who had been arrested because he played drum against the will of his master. The governor of Martinique, the admiral Rostoland, decided to declare the general emancipation sooner than expected, and chose, because of the pressure of the events, not to wait for the official décret.[5]

The insurrection resulted in thirty-three victims among the White creoles in Saint Pierre. These violent deaths triggered off great fear and anger amongst White creoles, who no longer felt safe. However, the situation almost went back to normal soon after the anticipated emancipation, anger turning into joy for the liberated ones. But the production and work in the fields was deeply affected during the weeks that followed, which increased financial difficulties for a certain number of indebted White creoles (Adélaïde-Merlande 1989, 52). These events seemed inevitable for many of them, but after the emancipation of their former slaves, they developed another form of social fear. This fear would be at the basis of the new post-slavery Martinican society.

The fear of 'substitution'

Soon after emancipation, the notion of substitution appeared in Martinican White creole public and private writings. This new fear arose when the workers were back at the plantations, and when they did not appear any more to be a threat. The abolition of slavery has had an important effect on another social category, as it caused the disappearance of the intermediary class of the free people of colour as a legal category. Since now everybody was free, skin colour and

[5] Letter of the Governor of Martinique Rostoland to the Minister of the Marine and Colonies, 28 May 1848, French National archives of the Outre-Mer (Archives nationales de l'Outre-Mer).

racially mixed origins became a new form of distinction and assignation. The former free people of colour made up a diverse social category of owners, liberal professions or skilled workers living in Martinican cities rather than in the countryside. The elite of those free people of colour could match the standards of the White creoles in terms of education, wealth and ambition (Schmidt 2003).

When the legal status barrier came to a halt, the trajectories now seemed to open up to the 'socalled mulâtres' (or mulattos) to achieve their social ambitions and to rise in the new Martinican society. This explains why the White creoles developed the concept of 'substitution' to express their anxieties of being overrun by the mulattos in political, economic and social domination. The words used to describe them form an archetype of a threatening man, as ambitious and stupid as unaware of its subaltern place in the society. In the eyes of the White creole elite, the mulatto is also a dangerous politician that would encourage the workers on the plantations, then in factories, to protest against their White creole employers. The social and political alliance between Black workers and mulattoes could thus trigger a similar revolution, as the one that created Haiti, and would cause the lasting exile of all the White creoles, or their oppression. The domination of the coloured people would thus mark the end of French domination in the Caribbean.[6]

Such arguments clearly state that the emancipation had an immediate effect by challenging the racial barriers rather than pacifying the society. Along those transformations and social fears, White creole families elaborated various strategies. One of them was mobility.

Identifying Mobile White Creole Families

Genealogy, a precious tool for historians

Genealogy appears to be a very useful tool to start researches on families. The field of genealogy brings together an important num-

[6] This idea is developped in a Letter of Auguste Pécoul to the editor-in-chief of the French newspaper *Le National*, 11 July 1848.

ber of non-professional scholars who created associations to gather and share their knowledge. In the late 1980s an association called 'Généalogie et histoire de la Caraïbe' or 'Genealogy and History of the Caribbean' (GHC) was created which focused on gathering genealogical data concerning French West Indies families. Their motivation was personal rather than purely scientific. The founders focused first on White creole families, as the names of those families allowed for the admission into the White elite of those islands, especially in Martinique. These names are widely recorded in the archives. Moreover, it is the family name that allows a person to be identified in a socio-racial group. In the French West Indies, to look White is not enough, which means that a white skin colour is not sufficient to be accepted inside the group of the white creole. It is significantly the last name that identifies an individual as a member of the White creole elite. This also explains the importance of genealogy for all those White creole families.

More recently, genealogical researches have been increasingly conducted by all social categories of the French West Indies. They turned their researches to the first bearers of their last name who were supposedly born as slaves and emancipated in 1848, and to whom in the following years a patronymic name was given for the first time. Therefore, genealogy captures extremely important stakes concerning identity for all French West Indies populations.

On the GHC database, complete genealogies of French West Indies families can be found, including Saint-Domingue, Guadeloupe, Martinique, and even islands that used to be French in the eighteenth century before becoming British, during a period of time stretching from the seventeenth to the twentieth century. In addition to this online database, some books can be found in libraries, which are quite a precious help. Their author, Eugène Bruneau-Latouche (Bruneau-Latouche et al. 2001), published an important number of genealogies focusing specifically on Martinican white creole families.

Even though these books are very helpful, some missing information must be considered. Indeed, Bruneau-Latouche mostly selected remaining families in Martinique, and does not always consider the family names that disappeared from the records, which is quite important. Some of them left Martinique during the nineteenth century, but also a lot of them fell victim to the dramatic eruption of the volcano la Montagne Pelée in 1902. This bias therefore probably excludes many interesting families. Nevertheless, after a first glance at these data, several conclusions can be drawn.

Intense mobility since the seventeenth century

The first statement that can be made lies on the considerable mobility of the White creoles from the beginning of the Lesser Antilles's colonization in the seventeenth century. Genealogists state for example that the first French colonists of Saint Christopher (now Saint Kitts) settled in many cases in Martinique, after this island was taken over by the British in 1690. In the eighteenth century, France possessed many islands in the Lesser Antilles and it was quite frequent that some families were established on different islands, such as Martinique and Saint Lucia, which is located to the south.

The Dujon family for example is a family that settled in Saint Lucia as well as in Martinique. Moreover, men of the Saint-Lucian branch came to Martinique to choose a wife, strengthening the ties between the two islands. Another interesting case is the family de Gannes de la Chancellerie who followed the vicissitudes of the French empire in the Americas in the eighteenth century: this family was from Acadie, today part of Canada; some members settled however in Grenada (which used to be French), in Trinidad, and in Martinique, all during the eighteenth century. Many family examples show strong links with France: indeed, an important number of Martinican families chose matrimony with small noble or middle-class families which were locally important. These matrimonial alliances allowed Martinican families to strengthen their links with the metropole and allowed French provincial families to enjoy the considerable incomes of the plantations they inherited.

Such is the case of the family Cours de Thomazeau, from a small village in the southwest of France, of which one member travelled to Martinique, where he married a young woman from an old White creole family. This family grew richer due to the incomes of the plantations of the Martinican based allied family, and this accumulation of wealth shows itself in the architecture of the Hôtel Particulier they built in the village of Castillonès (Lot-et-Garonne), which still exists nowadays (Rossignol & Bernadette 2018).[7]

The case of the Pécoul and Dariste families can also be mentioned. Joseph Pécoul and François Dariste were two young men from the southeast of France who settled in Martinique in the late eighteenth century. They both married the Pairès sisters who inherited some of the largest plantations (almost two hundred or three hundred slaves each) in the island. Their children were born and raised in Martinique but did not stay on in the island after they became adults. They however perceived the incomes of their plantations, and more significantly, they became political representatives of the White creoles' interests in Paris under the Second Republic, in an official or non-official way.[8]

A last interesting case is the one of a merchant family from Guadeloupe, the Vatable family, which soon settled in Martinique but also moved to the United States of America after the 1848 emancipation. This family settled there and prospered.

A first outlook at the history of these families suggests that the mobility depended for the most part on the economic opportunities that arose within the commercial expansion of the eighteenth century. The revolutionary era and the imperial wars triggered off a significant increase in the mobility of these families, who escaped from the turmoil of la Terreur or the imperial rivalries. If Martinique was less affected by the revolutionary Terreur than la Guadeloupe, some Martinican White creole families left the island for New Orleans which became a locale of exiles for an important number of White creoles of the whole French West Indies. In the meantime, some Guadeloupean families settled in a British-dominated Martinique, which was occupied from 1794 to 1802, and again from 1809 to 1815.

It may be concluded that the year 1848 does not seem to be a

[7] Philippe Rossignol and Bernadette, 'De Cours de Thomazeau', *Généalogie et Histoire de la Caraïbe*, 2018, article 01.

[8] All these informations can be found in the private papers of the family stored in the French National archives, AN 376 AP.

significant breaking point concerning the specificity of the White creole mobility and migrations, since this phenomenon tends to be quite common as we go back in time. The movement of emigration that appeared in 1848 among the slave owners can be traced back in a long time period. This emigration movement can be considered as a trajectory amongst others, repeating a pattern that existed in the previous eras. This movement, however, makes it relevant to examine the geographical horizon of the actors and how widespread their networks might have been.

Reviving a Family Network Through Private Archives

The archives belonging to the family Hutteau d'Origny-Pécoul have since the late 1970s been located within the national archives.[9] This find is of primary importance for anyone who wishes to study the history of the eighteenth and nineteenth century Martinique. An important number of documents of various sorts can be consulted. The central character of the family, as appears from the archives, is Auguste Pécoul, who was elected as a député of Martinique in 1849 and represented the interests of the White creoles in Paris amongst the ministers during the Second Republic (1848-51). His personal correspondence is quite considerable and is particularly relevant for anyone who wants to write a social and political history of the island.[10]

Public letters

The social and political history was the main focus of my master research work which was focused on the political history of Martinican White creoles. The people who corresponded with Auguste Pécoul are for the most parts other White creoles who relied on him to defend their cause with the Ministry of Marine and Colonies, even before he was elected as député, and of course after his election. It was well-known in Martinique that Auguste Pécoul was well

[9] French National archives, Pierrefitte-sur-Seine, 376 AP.
[10] AN 376 AP.

informed and that he had networks inside the circles of power on the island. Therefore, some creoles asked him to defend their case in order to obtain a position in courts for instance. More significantly, he was informed by his correspondents of the important news of Martinique, and he discussed with them the points he had to argue with the French government. During the four years of the Second Republic, he spent considerable time and energy claiming the compensation (of other planters) that would appear fair to the former slave owners, as they judged the payment delayed and insufficient.

His correspondence states the existence of a network between the White creoles of Martinique and the circles of power in France. Soliciting Auguste Pécoul meant trying to be integrated into his network, and could be considered a way to closer approach to central power. Pécouls position is the reason why we can find many interesting letters, among which those of an important character that drew my attention. Jean François Antoine Huc owned a plantation in Le Prêcheur and was the mayor of this community near Saint Pierre, and was involved in the uprising of May 1848. He wrote to Pécoul an important number of letters during his exile in Puerto Rico, which are particularly interesting.

The archives are not only political, they display a very comprehensive outlook on the life of an entire family, a transatlantic family.

Family documents

Auguste Pécoul personal correspondence stemming from the first half of the ninettenth century is very rich: many documents from the 1820s to the 1840s were preserved. Not only the correspondence but also documents about accounts enable researchers to trace the ties that unite this transatlantic family. Auguste Pécoul studied law in Paris in the late 1810s and graduated in 1820. He spent most of the 1820s at his sister at Bernadets, near Pau (Basses-Pyrénées): she was married to the baron de Laussat, son of the last governor of French Louisiana who completed the retrocession of that territory to the United States of America; he was then governor of la Martinique and Guyane. Auguste Pécoul went back to Martinique in 1824 and stayed in Saint Pierre for most of the 1830s. He exchanged a very important number of letters with his uncle Louis, who lived mostly between Paris and Marseille, and with his sister and her husband in the countryside of Pau. Accountancy documents demonstrate that the two brothers and a sister shared the income of their two plantations in the north of Martinique, La Montagne near Saint-Pierre, and l'Habitation Pécoul in Basse-Pointe.

Additional documents offer an interesting point of view and are related to the passing of Auguste Pécoul since he was not married and had no children, he established in his will a list of the persons to whom he wanted to grant some money, including his many godsons and goddaughters.[11]An interesting fact is that one of them, Auguste de Massias de Bonne, lived in the United States of America with his parents, which is mentioned explicitly in the will. Two letters of that godson can be found in the archives. In one of these letters, he writes that his parents have taken the resolution of 'selling at Madison [New Jersey], and to withdraw towards the South'. As far as he is concerned, he prefers staying in New York City and 'struggling to make a living'.[12] A few months later, he explains that he considers establishing a school in Richmond (Virginia) which he would manage with the help of his parents, who 'do not acclimatize to New Orleans'.[13] He requests from his godfather some money to help him achieving this plan. It is impossible to continue the story of that man at that point of my investigation, as there are no other letters in the Pécoul's papers.

However, these small signs prove that the links between Martinique and the United States of America existed and they are an interesting theme to study. They bring additional information to bring this network to life, which seemed active and communicating, even with little frequency. Exchanges of services, money or information are the proofs that link members of this family between Paris,

[11] AN 376 AP 20.

[12] Letter of Auguste de Massias de Bonne, from New York to Auguste Pécoul, 24 September 1852, AN 376 AP 22.

[13] Letter of Auguste de Massias de Bonne, from New York to Auguste Pécoul, 12 January 1853, AN 376 AP 22.

Martinique and the United States of America, and thus created an archipelago family.

As it was previously mentioned, these private archives enable to evoke another important character of the events of 1848, which happened to be at the centre of mobility in the Caribbean area.

An Example of a Family Network and its Multiple Branches: the Families Huc-Dujon-Lalung

Jean François Antoine Huc and his exile in Puerto Rico

Jean François Antoine Huc is a crucial character of the May 1848 uprising. As mentioned earlier, he owned a plantation in Le Prêcheur and was the mayor of that commune. He is described by the historian Jacques Adélaïde-Merlande (1989) as a pro-slavery partisan and one of the most conservative defenders of the colonial order. As he felt threatened by the agitation from the enslaved workers, he sent for police forces on the 22nd of May to prevent insurgents from trespassing into the community of Le Prêcheur.

At the same time, and partly because of his intransigent attitude, his son-in-law Saint-Clair-Dujon was murdered on that same day. According to a number of scholars such as Jacques-Adélaïde Merlande (1989) or Myriam Cottias (2007), his reaction was radically contrasting the one shown by the Saint-Pierre municipality, who did what they could to calm down the agitation. On the contrary, his violent repression caused the violent reaction of the insurgents and led to the tragic death of thirty-three white creoles in a house that was set on fire in Saint-Pierre.

After the uprising and the anticipated emancipation, the governor Rostoland estimated that he was not able to guarantee the safety of Huc and his family. This is the reason why he chose to leave Martinique by the end of May for Puerto Rico, at that time Spanish territory.[14] He was not the only one to leave: he shared his exile with

[14] From his exile in Puerto Rico, Jean François Antoine Huc wrote a long text to explain the events according to his point of view to the Marine and colonies minister, the 24th of July 1848, Archives Nationales

his family, including his wife, his widowed daughter and her three children, and his son. He was accompanied by his son-in-law's relatives and other White creoles of Le Prêcheur.

According to a letter written in August 1848 by the French ambassador in Madrid the Puerto Rican authorities confirmed they had welcomed about fifty people, 'refugees' from Martinique.[15] Jean François Antoine Huc left many traces of his exile in Puerto Rico as he wrote many letters to Auguste Pécoul and to the minister of Marine and Colonies to defend his cause. He often argued to Pécoul that the provisional government, the first government of the Second Republic, had been unfair to him and that he was persecuted by the Director of the colonies, called Henri-Joseph Mestro, who was assisting the Marine and colonies minister. He constantly claimed what he thought was his right, which is of course the compensation for his former slaves, and also for his plantation that he had lost in the course of the events.

The provisional government was indeed a very specific political institution in French history: it was a short political experience when republicans of different trends worked together. But the influence of the left wing, the 'democrat-socialists' was quite considerable, and their influence in Martinique among the 'mulâtres' and the former slaves was also quite important (Adélaïde-Merlande 1989). This is the reason why Huc anxiety is so evident in his letters, as he considered the attitude of the minister as a form of political repression. However, the republican left wing was progressively defeated in France during the year 1848, and especially after the 'journées de juin', which was a major working class uprising that was quelled in a bloodbath in Paris between the 22nd and the 26th of June. The Second Republic became much more conservative after these events. This also explains why Huc insists on writing to Pécoul to defend his cause.

The correspondence between Huc and Pécoul is very significant

---

de l'Outre-Mer, Fonds ministériels, Série géographique de la Martinique, Carton 7 Dossier 85, 72 pages.

[15] Letter of the French ambassador in Madrid to the Foreign Affairs minister, 22 August 1848, 37 CP, vol. 834.

for several reasons.[16] First, it demonstrates the influence of Pécoul as a representative of the interests of the White creoles in Paris, and states his prominent position in defending them at the time of the abolition. Second, it demonstrates how extended the political spectre of Pécoul was. Indeed, he was much more liberal than Huc on many points. Before the emancipation he presented himself as a good master, treating his slaves with humanity and allowing them to receive a religious education and to marry in the catholic religion. Such an attitude was unusual among slave owners. He was aware that slavery would be abolished sooner or later, and he insisted on the slave masters to prepare themselves to this inevitable and necessary change. His views did not prevent Huc from addressing him his demands, and it was not problematic for Pécoul to defend him in front of the minister. Thirdly, it is likely that Huc adjusted his political discourse to Pécoul's views, as he described himself as ready for the emancipation before the uprising, which in retrospect seems a re-writing of the entire story.

The content of Huc's letters is very instructive in another perspective. During his exile Huc was deprived of his income as his plantation was destroyed by fire and looting, and it was expropriated by his creditors. In his letters Huc repeatedly asked Pécoul to help him to be appointed as consul in the West Indies, for instance in Saint Thomas which was a Danish possession near Puerto Rico, or in Puerto Rico itself in case of the departure of the current consul. The interesting aspect is the geographical horizon of Huc as he does not intend to establish himself in France. He essentially projects himself in the Spanish West Indies. He also considers settling in Puerto Rico and aims to start a business if he receives enough funds from the French government, in case returning to Martinique becomes impossible.

The exiled families in Puerto Rico who accompanied Huc stayed only a few months with him and returned to Martinique the next year, in 1849. Yet Huc remained in Puerto Rico until the end of the Second Republic. He returned to Martinique only in 1854 and

[16] AN 376 AP 20.

remained there until his death in 1877. During and after this exile, no settlement in France was ever considered.

The Caribbean Sea remained the anchor of this family. As Huc mentioned in a letter: 'Saint Thomas, Puerto Rico, Santiago, Cienfuegos were the only points that I met.'[17] He projected himself as the '*commis voyageur*' of French diplomacy of the Caribbean and wanted to be 'protected everywhere under the glorious banner of France'. These quotes reveal that he ambitioned to represent France in the Caribbean, especially among Spanish possessions. We can argue that these Spanish territories were interesting to him because slavery was still established there. The Spanish authorities refused to consider any change towards emancipation. This is particularly visible at the arrival of the 'exiled' from Martinique, when the Governor of Puerto Rico Juan Prim takes measures of protections for the White populations of Puerto Rico by threatening slaves and free people of colour of death penalty if they assaulted White people.[18] The fact that Huc's ambitions proved unsuccessful is of little importance. What matters are the ties created with the Spanish in Puerto Rico and his hopes for his and his family's future during his exile. His horizon is Caribbean, even in times of crisis.

Fortunately for the historians, this family left other traces of a very different nature.

'Mémoires de Békées' (Békées's memories) (Lalung & Dujon-Jourdain, 2006): an example of an archipelago family

Two members of this family, Irmisse de Lalung and later Elodie Dujon-Jourdain, wrote about this exile in Puerto Rico and more generally about the story of their relatives during several generations. These writings, focusing on White creole families, were published in two volumes, even if their authors did not intend to make them

[17] Letter of Jean François Antoine Huc to Auguste Pécoul, 15th and 16th December 1848, AN 376 AP 20: 'Saint Thomas, Puerto Rico, Santiago, Cienfuegos étaient les seuls points que je rencontrais'.

[18] Proclamations of the Governor of Puerto Rico, May and June 1848, Gaceta del Gobierno de Puerto Rico, n°67, 31st May et 9th June 1848.

public. The tales were originally produced only for family use. Their reading is particularly rich with information which gives a more lively perspective on these archipelago families (Lalung & Dujon-Jourdain 2006), (Dujon-Jourdain et al., 2002).

These accounts are more interesting since they were written by women and they bring to light another focal point on the life of these families, more centred on intimacy and the relationships within the circle of family members, or genealogy. This is a way for the authors to pay tribute to the glorious ancestors and the prominent characters, male or female, of the families. They mention the important mobility of the branches of the family, ranging from an ancestor who used to be governor of Grenada, to another one who settled in Saint-Lucia, without forgetting to mention the vicissitudes of a brave woman of the family during the revolutionary terroir. The writing highlights the important mobility of the different branches of those families. They also evoke stories that could seem unimportant on first sight, but tend to be relevant for historians.

Two of the anecdotes reveal how the family networks operated, and during which circumstances they were activated. The anecdotes selected for this article revolve around one and the same character: Jean-Baptiste Lalung, also known as Montrop Lalung. He is depicted as an entrepreneur, ambitious and reckless, occasionally a smuggler, doing business with the recently independent Venezuela in the 1820s. The narrator, Elodie Dujon-Jourdain, depicts him as a man who loved taking risks, even in the face of losing everything. After several unsuccessful businesses, he left Martinique for the United States of America and settled in Boston where he opened a candle factory. It was quite successful, until it was ruined by a fire. He died in Boston ruined and far from his family.

The other story is related to that same man. Long before leaving Martinique for Boston, he was married twice. He had a daughter from his first marriage, but the mother died. He then married Irmisse de Rancé, who tried desperately to get on with the first wife's daughter. However, the young girl could not bear to see her father married to another woman. Montrop Lalung had a sister who was married to an American citizen, and had left Martinique. He informed Mrs Walley, his sister, of his domestic misfortunes. On her own initiative, she suggested the young girl should join her in the United States of America for a stay. This stay that was supposed to last for but a few months, lasted a few years. When she came back to Martinique, the grumpy and angry young girl had turned into an adorable and grateful young woman, thanks to her American aunt.

This American stay is indicative of the existence of a tight family network and renders tangible the archipelago dimension of the Martinican white creole families, as being open to the Atlantic Ocean as well as to the Caribbean Sea.

Conclusion

In their introduction to *Tensions of Empire*, Ann Laura Stoler and Frederick Cooper (2013) invited scholars to adopt a broader scale in their studies and to dare to focus on how the empires worked. One of the aims of my research is to attempt to draw a portrait of a colonial elite on an imperial scale. French historiography is scarce on imperial studies in general. Therefore, it is relevant to focus on the imperial scale and on non-metropolitan actors.

The White creole families selected in my study are doubtlessly rooted in Martinique. However, a first glance at various data such as genealogy or family papers show a wide range of relationships stretching from the traditional link between metropole and colony to Caribbean and American oriented mobilities. Even if the 'exile' of some white creole families towards the United States of America after the uprising of 1848 is not the first of the sort, it shows an important reminiscence of previous patterns of circulations typical of the revolutionary era. The choice of the locale of the exile also highlights the importance of the attachment to slavery, as Puerto Rico and the United States of America were still pro-slavery territories in 1848. Family documents reveal some clues about the existence of a link between the individuals forming different parts of a network, essentially formed by relatives. Despite how scarce those tracks may be, they indicate the existence of communications between different parts of families circulating at different points of the Caribbean Sea and the Atlantic Ocean.

These archipelago families are contributing to the writing of an imperial history also considering colonial elites and actors through their mobility and networks. Of course, the ocean is wide, and there is a lot of work to be done, still.

Bibliography

Books and articles

Adélaïde-Merlande, J. 1989. '1848-1852, L'abolition de l'esclavage', in *Historial antillais, tome IV,* (Vols. 1-6). Editions Dajani.

Bruneau-Latouche, E., Cordiez, C. & Cordiez, P. 2001. *209 anciennes familles subsistantes de la Martinique: Notices généalogiques, acquisitions, ventes, échanges, alliances et descendances antérieurs à 1901. Tome 1, A-G.*, tome 2, G-W, Aix-en-Provence.

Cottias, M. 2007. "Ces « hommes dangereux » de 1848",. *Genèses, n°* 66(1): 30-50.

Dujon-Jourdain, É., Dormoy-Léger, R., & Levillain, H. 2002. *Mémoires de békées: Textes inédits: Vol. I.* l'Harmattan.

Fallope, J. 1992. *Esclaves et citoyens: les Noirs à la Guadeloupe au dix-neuvième-siècle, dans les processus de résistance et d'intégration, 1802-1910.* Basse-Terre: Société d'histoire de la Guadeloupe.

Kováts Beaudoux, É., & Giraud, M. 2002. *Les blancs créoles de la Martinique: Une minorité dominante.* Paris: L'Harmattan.

Lalung, I. de, & Dujon-Jourdain, É. 2006. *Mémoires de Békées: Textes inédits. II* (H. Levillain & C. Thiébaut, Éds.).

Rossignol, Philippe and Bernadette, « De Cours de Thomazeau », *Généalogie et Histoire de la Caraïbe*, 2018, article 01

Schmidt, N. 2003. *Histoire du métissage* (A. Corbin, Éd.). Éd. de La Martinière.

______. 2009. *La France a-t-elle aboli l'esclavage?: Guadeloupe-Martinique-Guyane (1830-1935).* Perrin.

Stoler, Ann Laura and Frederick Cooper. 2013. *Repenser le colonialisme* (tr. Christina Jeanmougin). Paris: éd. Payot.

Archives

French National Archives, AN 376 AP 20; 22;.

French National Archives, Pierrefitte-sur-Seine, 376 AP.

Private papers of the Pécoul and Dariste families, stored in the French National Archives, AN 376 AP.

French National Archives of the Outre-Mer (Archives nationales de l'Outre-Mer).

French National Archives of the Outre-Mer (Archives nationales de l'Outre-Mer), Minis-terial funds, Série géographique de la Martinique, Carton 56 Dossier 464

Archives Nationales de l'Outre-Mer, Fonds ministériels, Série géographique de la Martinique, Carton 7 Dossier 85, 72 pages.

Newspapers

Proclamations of the Governor of Puerto Rico, May and June 1848 *Gaceta del Gobierno de Puerto Rico*, n°67, 31st May et 9 June 1848.

Le National, 11 July 1848 (French Newspaper).

EIGHT

Pas d'ombres chinoises
Jews in French Caribbean Literature

KATHLEEN GYSSELS

> Just what is a 'group' anyway? (...) To a passerby (...), I am white. To an anti-Semite, I am simply a Jew. To a German Jew, I may be one of the *Ostjuden*, to Sephardim, an Askenazi Jew, to an Israeli Jew, American, to a religious Jew, secular; to a right-wing Zionist, an apostate, or no Jew at all. Tod Gitlin.
>
> –Tod Gitlin in *The Twilight of Common Dreams* (1995, 208): 'Where we're coming from'.

Introduction: The Chosen Place, the Timeless People

Although Jews have been migrating to the Caribbean since the arrival of Columbus, critical attention to Black-Jewish cultural relations in the Caribbean and Guianese context has been sparse. Recent scholarship (Ben-Ur 2013; Gerber 2013) has confirmed the dearth of interest in the forced or free emigration of Jews to the New World. While they have never been deported to the Americas like the Africans, strong similarities could have translated into literary representations of their respective place and function in this multilingual and multicultural region. While the Holocaust and *Middle Passage,* the transatlantic deportation of millions of Africans, calls for strong convergences in visual culture (see Gyssels 2016; Mirzoeff 2000) both have given rise to extensive, yet separate treatment in the literary sphere; postcolonial studies and cultural memory studies have ignored the intersections between Jewish and African Diasporas. Conversely, Jewish studies have until recently bluntly ignored the Caribbean diasporic imagination. Cheyette explains this compartmentalization as 'disciplinary thinking' and 'supersessionist thinking' (Cheyette 2017). Concepts such as 'multidirectional memory' (Rothberg 2009) and post-memory (Hirsch 2012) have been applied to colonial contexts such as the Algerian War of Independence, the Middle East conflict, but may be equally applied to the Caribbean in a large number of cases.

While some critics pretend that a rare study of the Jew as literary character in West Indian fiction by Sue Greene (1986) is too pessimistic and that 'in the English-speaking Caribbean' the depiction of the Jew gives rise to 'sincere sympathy, empathy even, on the part of postwar Caribbean writers' (Ledent 2017, 202), my survey of a selection of French-Caribbean novelists suggests, on the contrary, that the interaction between blacks and Jews in French-Caribbean literature is problematic to say the least. When it does occasionally appear, it mostly serves as an illustration of the memory wars, the competition of memories, and gives rise to debates about who suffered most, the Jew or the Black enslaved or the unchained. As I have shown elsewhere (Gyssels 2001), the example of the Guadeloupean novel *Moi, Tituba* by Maryse Condé forces the Jew in the role of the good master who even falls in love with his Black slave whom he bought and liberated from her shackles. Benjamin Cohen de Azevedo is the '*planteur*' who will convert to Tituba's black magic and who discusses History as a record of persecution and massacre. Hearing this dreadful history, Tituba admits his people suffered most. A mock epic, Condé does not fear to stereotype the Jew as an ugly yet sexually very hungry male. Naming her character Benjamin Cohen de Azevedo is enough to highlight the role of the Jew in the Black Atlantic slave trade. One might ask why Condé does so, especially as later novels flirt with suspicions of antisemitic characters: one example is Dieudonné in *La Belle Créole*. In contrast to the Black master's mistress Tituba, Condé now stages a love affair between a '*béké*' Lo[r]raine—a name hinting at l'Alsace-Lorraine, a region in France with a high level of Ashkenazi Jews—and her younger Black gardener whose name clearly refers to the actor who radicalized even after the 9/11 attacks of 2001. Dawn Fulton reads Condé's fourteenth novel as a crime fiction with Fanonian accents as the fatal attraction between Black and White has indeed led to murder (think of Bigger Thomas in Richard Wright's *Native Son*). Dieudonné is accused of murdering his employer and lover Loraine, a wealthy White woman descended from plantation owners (Fulton 2008). His only refuge is a sailboat, *La Belle Creole*, a relic of times gone by. Dieudonné is the name of an openly antisemitic actor who has been accused in France for his virulent sketches and invited to Martinique, has been defended by Raphaël Confiant. Condé plays hide and seek with competitive memories (Gyssels 2010) and discusses whom of both communities suffered the most.

Another Anglo-Caribbean novelist, Paule Marshall, is much subtler as I conclude in a comparative analysis with Condé's neo slave narrative and *Beloved* (Morisson 1987) respectively. In *The Chosen Place, the Timeless People* (1969), Marshall embeds a Biblical echo, and stages a mixed couple: Saul, an American Jew, and Merle Kimbona (Gyssels 2001). Inverting the myth of the Jews as 'chosen ones', Marshall audaciously portrays the Caribbean, descendants of Africans neither chosen people, neither willingly sailing to the Caribbean archipelago: they are persecuted by Cham's curse and endured centuries of slavery and colonialism. The Jews, on the contrary, have never been enslaved in this part of the world. Their hazardous migration to the Caribbean archipelago as a place to start all over began, with Columbus discovering the New World. They mostly settled as plantation owners, hence the designation 'Plantation Jews' (Casteel-Phillips 2016). Jews fleeing fascist Europe before, during and even after WW II to this part of the world, have generally kept their Jewishness hidden. In other words, they became 'marranos' and have globally remained very discrete.

The reluctance of Caribbean literature to embrace knotted intersections are manifold. First, a minor percentage of the Jews who settled in colonial times took part in the slave trade and plantation economy. Second, a disproportionate number of Jewish settlers is to be observed between the cluster of islands, with a minor percentage of Jews and Suriname. The former 'Dutch Guiana' indeed is a continental enclave where Jews are numerous. Compared to the French, Spanish and English 'lesser Antilles', the Dutch Caribbean (and ABC-islands) also count an important number of Sephardic Jews who settled there after having fled the Iberian Peninsula in the fifteenth century and the Netherlands during the sixteenth and seventeenth centuries. Jewish refugees who came to the Caribbean, following or just prior to the Shoah Holocaust, often left quickly for the United States or Canada, leaving few literary traces of their transit (Behar 1996). Fiction from the Dutch-speaking Caribbean and Guyana's not only remains peripheral but also untranslated, hence the limited international reputation.

Most of all, Jews who migrated to this part of the archipelago or continent chose to obscure their Judaism. In the beginning of the twenty-first century, some of the most promising Haitian novelists like Louis-Philippe Dalembert and Caryl Phillips belatedly reclaim this hidden heritage or come out for their conversion (Jamaica Kincaid, Gyssels 2021a). One wonders: why have authors dealt so late with the issue? How come critics did not pay more attention to that component of the 'kaleidoscopic mosaic'? Claiming to be equally attentive to all components of the Creole society, Raphaël Confiant and his co-authors don't illustrate in which way Chinese or Jews contributed to their complex multi-religious or confessional fabric. Authors rarely trespass ethnic and religious boundaries and together with 'postcolonial Jews' like Cynthia Ozick and André Schwarz-Bart (1928-2006), Caribbean fiction and criticism should no longer overlook fruitful exchanges and productive dialogues.

Absent Interface

While striking similarities between the two groups assimilation, 'whitening', alienation, the urge to travel back to the homeland, etc. call for the trope of 'reversibility' between the Jewish and Black condition (Gyssels 2014), authors rarely addressed these issues in Caribbean and Guianese fiction where French immigrants/settlers are the most important number and while France has the largest percentage of Jews from European countries. The tiny Jewish populations on various islands, a mere 400 today in Martinique, but three times more in the English-speaking Caribbean islands due to greater religious tolerance among Protestants, is clearly a handicap to develop a Jewish subculture in the '*Belles Lettres*'.

The blindness of Jews and Blacks vis-à-vis one another in the overseas departments French Guiana, Martinique and Guadeloupe is further paradoxical since one of its most influential intellectuals, the Martinican Frantz Fanon, stressed that scapegoating concerned similarly the Black and the Jew in the Republic. So, one of the most famous and leading French-Caribbean theorists advocating a decolonization of the mind, warned for the blindness between two familiar cases of mockery, oppression, and discrimination. This warning by Fanon springs from reading J.P. Sartre's *Réflexions sur la question juive* (1948): Fanon was quick to make a strong remark in his Chapter 'The Fact of Blackness': as the Black could not hide his blackness, he endured an even worse ostracism, while the Jew could always try to pass for a Goy (Fanon 1952, 122). This goes to the heart of the troubled relationship between the condition of the coloured people Afro-Caribbean and Caribbean Jewishness, be they of colour or not. Thanks to Fanon prominent Caribbean thinkers call for an awareness of their shared condition of oppression. Stuart Hall claims Jewish, as well as Scottish, African and Amerindian heritage (1999, 2000). His spiritual son, Paul Gilroy, addresses Jewish and Black diasporic issues in his sequels to *The Black Atlantic* (1993). Both *Postcolonial Melancholia* (2000) and *Between Camps* (2000) call for the dissolution of boundaries between different communities of suffering. Gilroy has not cut off critical insight into the Jewish-Blacks relationship as part of a 'convivial culture' (Gilroy et al. 2019) and community building together in the new context of European colonialism in the New World was imposed upon both communities. Although Caribbean thinkers Césaire, Fanon, Hall and Gilroy have underscored the interconnectedness of Jews and Blacks, literary practices in the various islands have barely spurred creative writing. While novelists such as Caryl Phillips, Ledent (2002) and David Dabydeen (Pagnoulle 2007) prove a vibrant area of Anglophone-Caribbean literature, the intertwined traumas of extreme violence and deportation (Raiskin 1996, Casteel-Phillips 2016, Sundquist 2005) that stimulates the dialogue between both communities, remained peripheral until the 'multidimensional turn' spurred by Rothberg's seminal essays in which precisely André Schwarz-Bart is the key example of linking the Holocaust to other genocidal violences worldwide, in the colonies and under dictatorships.

French Caribbean

Nuée ardente

The 'gift of fiction' allows any oddity to be proffered in the narrative on the pretext it is invention, fabulation, imagination. The narrator a fictional mediator and not the author nor his public person is to be blamed for despicable formulations and heinous messages. One knows this very old excuse which L.F. Céline to name just one example in French literature invoked to speak out loud his hatred of Jews. He who can be considered responsible for discourses which can be considered inappropriate or even simple radically racist. One is familiar with famous examples by Céline who in spite of being a great writer was a notorious anti-Semite with *Bagatelles pour un massacre*, to give but one example.

Since the very inception of his novels, Raphaël Confiant is the 'Rabelais of the tropics', a fierce defender of Creole as a language and of Creole identity as a fusion or synthesis of many elements. A first example occurs in *Nuée ardente* 2004, the novel which deals with the commemoration of the Centennial of the Destruction of Saint-Pierre de la Martinique by the eruption of the volcano Mont Pelée in 1903. This disaster supposedly takes place at the same time as the premiere of *La Juive*, an opera by the Jewish composer Fromentin Halévy. *Nuée ardente* mixes pure invention and a historical fact: an opera banned during the Occupation Vichy régime, never performed in the Antilles at the beginning of the twentieth century (and later), both the Jewish composer as an outburst of enthusiasm by the public spur suspicion. Set in 1903, the novel deals with the death by fire of thousands of islanders, supposedly at the moment when this performance took place. Confiant suggests that this city, the 'Sodom and

Gomorrah of the tropics' was punished by God. Its entire population perished in the furnace and that was divine's will. The Confiantian narrator adds that the audience was shrieking: '*Vive les Juifs*!' (Long live the Jews!), but this is highly ironic. The exclamation has to be on the contrary be read as synonymous with 'To hell with the Jews') The sentence (*Nuée* 132) is the very opposite of the slogan heard all over France before, during (and rapidly after) the disaster of WW II and the Shoah: whereas the French were shouting '*A mort les Juifs*!' (Death to the Jews!), the satiric narrator fictionalizes the opposite. During violent eruptions of anti-Semitism and in the writings of some of the most famous, yet openly anti-Semitic authors: Louis-Ferdinand Céline *Guignols Band*, for instance, is in fact partially rewritten in *Chronique des sept misères* by Patrick Chamoiseau (Cornille 2013).

This leads me once again to suspect Confiant of resentment towards an invisible minority in the Caribbean. Indeed, Confiant's fictional adornment (*Nuée* 131) suggests that the natural catastrophe was a curse placed upon Jews, with the deaths of other inhabitants of Saint-Pierre de la Martinique as collateral damage. Note that Wagner praised this opera, of which the aria, 'Rachel Quand du Seigneur', reveals the impossible love between the Jewish Rachel and a Gentile. Following seasons in London, Vienna and Paris, La Juive was censored for many years and performed again at the Opera de Lyon in 2007, Ghent 2019 and other cities in Europe.

In his own grotesque and pathetic way Confiant seems to take revenge of history and more precisely to accuse Jews as being responsible partly for the slave trade[1] and today to occupy Palestine.[2] Of course, Confiant's attitude goes unnoticed by colleagues in Martinique and France. Critical views on the matter have been downplayed by

[1] https://www.myjewishlearning.com/article/jews-and-the-african-slave-trade/

[2] Confiant defended the sketches of Dieudonné on his website and even invited him to Martinique. This blend of Israeli politics, Holocaust fatigue, and anti-Semitism crystallized in the shows of Dieudonné, a French-African comic performer who dressed up as a Hasidic Jew and did the Nazi salute while shouting 'Heil Hitler!'. Anti-Semitism peaked in France under the presidencies of Hollande, and even Nicolas Sarkozy himself having Jewish ancestry.

the excuse of imagination. Intellectual probity of the novelist who is also a scholar and professor are not to be examined. That his fiction is not innocent and his allusions far from neutral reappears in Eau de Café (1991). Here a taxi is called '*la corne du "Golem*"', a clear double reference to Jewish culture: the horn (*shofar*) being an instrument to alert and communicate, the Golem the monstruous 'Geek'. If the name of the collective taxi is not sufficient enough to raise eyebrows, the narrator describes its velocity spreading terror among the local population: '*La corne du Golem qui passait à grand ballant fit sursauter les badauds*': the trump of the taxi scares off passengers who jump up. But the reference to the Golem sounds as an omen of bad luck and imminent danger. In Jewish folklore, the Golem is the demonic clay figure causing havoc in the Jewish ghetto; he is the madman, stupid and dangerous. The symbolic is the exact opposite of the hand of Fatima in Arabic culture. In the novel, the narrator further polarizes and opposes the passengers of the Golem are 'feminized' reproducing homophobic and sexist discourses spoken through his hypermasculine fictional characters. As Harrod states in *Queer Roots for the Diaspora: Ghosts in the Family Tree*, the *Créolistes* are often criticized for their *misogynoir* but in this novel, the Jew is mocked as subaltern, effeminate, '*macoumé*,' a Creole word for homosexual (the French '*ma commère*' being a woman who gossips). In this respect, it might count that Confiant converted to Islam and called one of his sons with an Arabic first name. *Eau de café* hints at the destructive power of this mad vehicle swinging wildly, making bystanders panic. Confiant hints at Israel's military superpower.

Raised in a multi-ethnic society, Raphaël Confiant saw in his childhood movies on the Roman Empire in which exceptionally Jews were playing a major role: in his childhood memories, *Cahier de romances*, Jews have been lapidated and crucified, while the Jewish resistance against Roman oppression has been embodied in the Masada massacre (*Cahier* 18). References to the Holocaust occur in the second tome, *Ravines du devant-jour*, mentions during the siege of Jerusalem under Titus (*Cahier* 181).

In many respects, Confiant resembles the Nobel Laureate from Trinidad: Like V.S. Naipaul who Confiant mocked as a '*couli-saxon*' who betrayed his Indian grandfather (see Gyssels 2010). Confiant makes fun of the Jew. So far, Confiant's allosemitism stereotyping and fixing identity (see Bassi 2004), implies quite the opposite 'encensement' of the Arabic characters. Syrian characters are also nicknamed 'le Sarrasin' (*Cahier* 60), and are portrayed with sympathy. These people came after the Ottoman Empire was dismantled and are called 'Levantine riff raff' which spread to the Caribbean, America, Europe. For instance, Mansour is a '*drivailleur de la rue des Syriens et des alentours du Grand Marché*' vagabond in the Rue des Syriens and in the area surrounding the Central Market. Earlier on, the narrator makes clear that:

Tous les Syriens respectaient tes grands-parents. Ton grand-père, que vous la marmaille, appeliez tous Papa Parrain, avait un ascendant naturel sur la piétaille nègre et levantine du quartier à cause de son air de maharadjah (Cahier 48).

[All Syrians respected their grandparents. Your grandfather, who all the kids called Papa Parrain, had a natural forebear amongst the Negro and Levantine riff raff of the neighbourhood, which explained his maharajah-style appearance.]

Confiant's own phenotype is a mix of four races:

[L]es quatre demi-sœurs de ton père (…) étaient le fruit d'un croisement proprement inouï. Elles tenaient, en effet, du Chinois et du Noir du côté de ta grand-mère et du Blanc et de l'Hindou du côté de ton grand-père (*Cahier* 48-9).

[The four half-sisters of your father were the fruits of a highly unusual cross-breeding. In effect, they inherited Chinese and Black blood from your grandmother's side of the family and White and Hindu blood from your grandfather's side] (translation by the author).

Staging the complex ethnic fabric of Martinique, Confiant thus simplifies the various groups: Abdallah (*Cahier* 49) reinforces the complexity of family makeups (*Cahier* 23) and are portrayed as '*Lapin échaudé*' ('scalded rabbit', a reference to the Tar Baby character of the Uncle Remus stories in African American folklore, *Cahier* 209). Another simplification is that he automatically considers them Muslim. In fact, Syrians might also include Jews and Christians, as Abdallah corrects the neighbourhood:

Pestant contre Mansour en particulier et les musulmans en général – 'Je suis maronite, moi, c'est-à-dire phénicien!, ronchonna [Abadallah], contre les cargos et leurs éternels passagers clandestins, contre la négraille (…), contre ce foutu soleil de merde qui lui ramollissait les nerfs', Abdallah finit par offrir son couloir en location à son présumé cousin (*Cahier* 45).

[Pesting against Mansour in particular and Muslims in general—'I am a Maronite, I, that is to say a Phoenician!, grumbled [Abadallah], against the freighters and their eternal stowaways, against the negroes (…), against this damn shit sun that softened his nerves', Abdallah ended up offering his hallway for rent to his presumed cousin] (Translation by the author).

Simplistic and reductive, Confiant's view of the pre- and post-abolition indenture labour (see Gyssels in Hassankhan, Gounder et al.), the new flux of migrants and strangers, the animosity between the groups truncates the authentic portrayal of French-Caribbean society.

Moreover, the Jewish minority is only occasionally evoked through details, or worse, jokes or mocking remarks. Confiant rejects Fanon's statement about segregation in the French Caribbean, mistakenly quoting *Peaux noires, masque blanc sic*, he tends rather to contradict Fanon's 'color prejudice' as a major problem in the Caribbean society. There is no such thing as racial compartmentalization in Martinique: '*aucune ségrégation ni exaction particulière*', no particular segregation or outlandish claim (*Cahier* 239).

In *La vierge du grand retour* (1996), Confiant mocks religion and stages Mathieu Salem as a hero of the cross. This Mathieu Salem reads like Mathusalem, the grandfather of Noah, believed to have been 969 years old. Legend has it he had hundreds of women and thousands of children. Yet Confiant amuses his reader by making him the zealous multiplier of faith, symbolising:

(…) la mémoire historique d'une époque ancienne, mais non révolue, rattachée au présent et transmise à la jeune génération; l'Évêque incarne l'esprit de direction et de surveillance d'une Église exploiteuse, acoquinée avec les béké dans un colonialisme qui n'en finit plus de sévir.

[(…) the historical memory of an ancient, but not bygone era, linked to the present and transmitted to the younger generation; the Bishop embodies the spirit of leadership and oversight of an exploiting Church, acquined with the béké in a colonialism that continues to rage] (translation by the author).

La vierge du grand retour is another example, among many, of Confidant's irreverence when it comes to religious practices and more specifically Jewish characters.

Le fabuleux destin d'Ivan et d'Ivana

After her portrait of a Black witch, Condé's last novel has been inspired by the terrorist attacks in Paris Charlie Hebdo' and the shooting of a Black police-woman who turned out to come from Guadeloupe. In *Le fabuleux destin d'Ivan et d'Ivana*, she turns to the Jihad in its ramifications with Black and mixed population from Guadeloupe. The author of *Ségou* (1984-5) returns to her native island of Guadeloupe to deal with current problems concerning the radicalization of youth growing up in France, in French-Caribbean families and those who have been in touch with the terrorists following the different attacks in the 'metropole'. Fifty French Jihadists were identified in the Antilles and Guyana in 2016, while some left for the Middle East to join IS and become martyrs for the Jihad. Some of these youngsters are originating from the Caribbean, and have an African parent through whom they come in contact with Islam, and radicalize to the point of participating in terrorist attacks.

Islamophobia and Judeophobia go hand in hand and form the kernel of this novel, in which Condé endeavours to unearth links between these 'fighters' and the 'indépendantistes des années 1970-1980', a militant movement to which she felt closely connected. Is it, as one reviewer wonders, also a battle against 'la métropole et le néocolonialisme', France and neocolonialism? The twin protagonists are intruders into other belief systems. When Ivan, who develops an incestuous relationship with his sister Ivana, discovers she dates a Jew, he becomes extremely jealous over Ivana's boyfriend Ariel Zeni. Ivan admits he knew little about the conflict in the Middle East:

> Jusqu'alors il n'éprouvait ni sympathie ni antipathie pour les Juifs. Il n'avait jamais compris pourquoi les Nazis s'étaient acharnés contre eux et avaient recherché la solution finale. A présent il ne comprenait pas ce que beaucoup

leur reprochaient. Former une communauté soudée et solidaire, est-ce un crime? Brusquement être Juif prenait l'apparence d'un rival. Ariel était-il un rival? (*Fabuleux destin* 302)

[Up to this point he had neither sympathy for nor antipathy towards Jews. He had never understood why the Nazis were so unremitting against them and why they had looked for a final solution. At present he didn't understand what a lot of people had against them. Is forming a solidly welded community a crime? Jewish people suddenly looked like rivals. Was Ariel a rival?] (translation by the author).

Le fabuleux destin picks up the turbulent and troublesome relationship between Blacks and Jews which have regularly upset American society (Sundquist 1995) and which tends to intensify in the world at large, because of the global war on terror and the planetary scale of islamophobia and anti-Semitism.

Adieu Bogota

No French-Caribbean author has been more involved in the interethnic dialogue and transcultural memory of trauma than Simone Schwarz-Bart as she co-authored novels with her husband André Schwarz-Bart. The Polish-Guadeloupean authors André and Simone Schwarz-Bart defend the strong links and reveal the sympathy between two groups of people who share much more than they think: oppression and colonialism, assimilation and the question of the return to the native land. Signing separately and together novels dealing with uprooted Blacks and Jews (Gyssels 1996, 2014), their posthumous novel bridges universes from the tropics to cold Europe. *Adieu Bogota* is set partly in French Guiana, famous for its 'Green Hell' in Saint-Laurent de Maroni. Here French Guiana figures as a place of transit for the main character of the novel, Mariotte, who is fleeing Saint-Pierre de la Martinique after the volcano disaster of 1903.

He befriends an ex-prisoner nicknamed 'La Commune'.[3] This

[3] The Paris Commune of 1871 was one of the greatest and most inspiring episodes in the history of the working class. In a tremendous revolutionary movement, they replaced the capitalist state with their own

white outlaw, a pariah whose name is never mentioned, spent years of internment in the Transportation Camp, in the company of Algerian dissidents and other communists. The authors make a strong statement about the Transportation Camp being analogous to the concentration camps of the Nazis: famine, torture and rampant mistreatment dehumanize the inmates.[4] *Adieu Bogota* defines the penal colony as a forebode of Buchenwald:

Saint-Laurent-du-Maroni était une ville bâtie par le bagne et pour le bagne, comme Buchenwald le serait plus tard pour d'autres damnés (*Adieu Bogota* 185).

[Saint-Laurent-du-Maroni was a town constructed as a result of the prison camp and for the prison camp, as Buchenwald would later be for other damned prisoners]

[D]e rallonge en rallonge, il devint un 'perpète' et finit par atterrir au camp disciplinaire du Maroni. 'La Commune', quant à lui, parvint à rester un homme à l'intérieur, tout juste. Il considérait les gardiens et les prisonniers comme deux variétés d'une même espèce, dont faisaient partie les Bonis, les Indiens, les Créoles

---

organs of government and held political power until their downfall in the last week of May. 130 years later the lessons of these events are of fundamental importance for socialists today. The arrested 'communards' have been imprisoned and many of them deported to the 'Bagnes'. Schwarz-Bart hasbeen a convinced communist and illustrates in *The Last of the Just* the important communist branch of East-European Jewry in the nineteenth century. To Schwarz-Bart, both Russian and African American and Caribbean are entangled by the historically fact of bondage. In this respect, Dale E. Peterson's epic *Up from Bondage. The Literatures of Russian and African American Soul* comes to mind (2000).

[4] Schwarz-Bart's first novel, *Le Dernier des Justes (The Last of the Just)* has an overlooked torture scene in which Ernie Lévy is arrested by the Gestapo and left for dead, 'gigot[ant] comme une chenille blesse dans ses liquides' writhing in his bodily fluids like a wounded grub (310). In the eyes of his perpetrators, he was merely 'une de ces merde[s] [...] qui sortaient d'un "trou" et qui venaient tranquillement à la fosse ou au camion et qui voulaient aussile "Traitement spécial"' – ('One of these pieces of shit who crawled out of a hole and who came without bother to the pit or the truck, and who wanted "special Treatment" as well' (*Dernier des Justes,* 311).

et les blancs de Guyane, comme si au fond toutes ces différences étaient minimes entre les uns et les autres (*Adieu Bogota* 178).

[As the extensions increased, he became a prisoner for life and ended up at the Maroni disciplinary camp. 'The Commune', according to him, allowed him to remain a man on the inside, just. He considered the wardens and the prisoners as two varieties of the one species, made up of Bonis, Indians, Creoles and whites from Guyane as if, in the end, all differences between them were minimal][5] (translation by the author).

Je ressentais confusément qu'à part la question de couleur, beaucoup de noirs américains étaient des vrais nègres blancs, des déracinés par cette grande file en faisait une foule non solidaire, frappée d'une double solitude (*Adieu Bogota* 198).

[I vaguely felt that, apart from the colour question, many Black Americans were really White Negroes, uprooted by this great chain which formed them into an unstable aggregation struck doubly by solitude.]

Mariotte, in fact, is the descendant of one of the rare survivors of the Mont Pelé catastrophe. In certain respects, she is like a Holocaust survivor. Her cohabitation with an ex-prisoner may have been a deliberate knotting of Black and Jewish Diasporas by the authors, given that the *bagne* is a crime against humanity (Badinter 2017), and people released or escaping from this place have no place to go or endure ostracism by the Creole population in Guyane.

Rendez-vous avec l'heure qui blesse

One of the important historical heroes from Martinique could have captured Confiant's or Chamoiseeau's, Condé's or Glissant's attention, especially as the latter does stage the figure of the '*tirailleur sénégalais*' in a long episode in *Tout-monde* 1994. Glissant's attention goes instead to the miraculously saved Martinican by a sympathetic 'officer' by the name of Mulher. In the concluding remarks upon such an incredible story, Glissant's semi-fictional double compares

[5] Boni is an ethnic group which claim to be descendants of Maroons who fled from Suriname in the 1800s and live in the interior.

numbers and ways in which Black and Jewish survivors lived after the war. Such a take is ambiguous to say the least. Hence the avoidance of close reading of Glissant's chapters, and if one does so (Gyssels 2013) it comes at the cost of criticism by some *aficionados* at the 'ITM' (Institut du Tout-Monde, founded by Glissant and François Noudelmann).

Notwithstanding some symbolic crossroad figures at the intersection of Black and Jewish diasporas, Martinican literature does not venture into the 'resolution' of the tensions. To give but two examples: Black WW II hero Raphaël Elizée, originally from a family in Saint-Pierre de la Martinique, became before the outbreak of the war the first Black mayor of a small town in France, Sablé-sur-Sarthes. The Elizée family had escaped Saint-Pierre at the threat of the volcano eruption and settled in France. Raphaël Elizée was a much-admired vet in the rural city and joined the Resistance. Betrayed, he was deported to Buchenwald, and killed by the bombings of the allies at the very end of the war. It is the Franco-Cameroun's novelist and philosopher Gaston-Paul Effa who unravels this forgotten chapter in *Rendez-vous avec l'heure qui blesse* (Gyssels 2016a). Effa matches Haitian author L.P. Dalembert who in *Avant que les ombres s'effacent* recalls how Paris was a meeting place for many African American expats and Afro-Caribbean intellectuals and artists in exile. They were all under attack for the simple reason of their pigmentation and risked deportation (Gyssels 2019).

Each time the Palestinian conflict reaches a peak, anti-Semitic feelings and outbursts inflame in Martinique and Guadeloupe. Defending ambiguity as a veil for opacity, Glissant's equivocal passages in subsequent essays are not scrutinized. Promoting '*Tout-monde*', it is a cultural diversity and an encounter of diverse and even oppressed cultures in a time of globalization, some of the most prominent Antillean authors give in to resentment and even anti-Israelism, amalgamating Jewishness and Zionism. A growing number of scholars (Adler, Slamovich, Kokken-Benedicty) start to challenge upfront this conflation between the political and the fictional on highly polemical issues, and while intellectuals are bestowed with the responsibility of uttering their views on loaded debates such as the 'Question of Palestine' (to use a title by Edward Said), Glissant and his 'spiritual sons' do have the right to disapprove with the political crisis in Israel, but that does not allow them to look down upon authors with a Jewish background. According to Hallward (2006) and Bongie (2010), paradoxes and contradictions are numerous in Glissant's ethics of Relation. Unlike most admirers, ambiguity in this and subsequent essays prove skepticism towards the Middle East crisis but that should not reverberate in pseudo-fictional accounts as *Tout-monde* (Gyssels 2017). On the contrary, and the one does not exclude the other, Glissant organized tributes to Mahmoud Darwich, the Palestinian poet who died in exile in 2008, and awarded the Carbet Prize to Israel's filmmaker which leads me to conclude that some of the most prominent Antillean authors understandably give in to anti-Israelism but have on the other hand marginalized authors like the Schwarz-Barts. Poet Léon-Gontran Damas already targeted in a long sketch in a posthumous collection of poetry, '*A la rubrique des chiens crevés*', the neglected 'commemoration' and 'tribute' of Black victims during the War but did not dare to publish it during his lifetime (Gyssels 2018a). While Serge Bilé's work documented the Black presence in the concentration camps (2005) and the role of Black collaborators or on the contrary resistant fighters (2011), it has barely been embraced by French-Caribbean critics.

Conclusion

Peau noire, masques blancs warned in Chapter 5 that whenever Jews are mocked, the Black man is also ridiculed. This Fanonian statement echoes large in the sparse fiction from the Antilles dealing with the Black-Jew relationship. This overview leads us to conclude that Fanon's warning has not materialized in cross-cultural fiction. On the contrary, Confiant's blasphemy has been covered up by leading intellectual Edouard Glissant in his function of 'president du Prix Carbet'. In Martinique however, a humble praise for the deceased author André Schwarz-Bart in *Tribune des Antilles*, guest edited by Diana Ramassamy and me (Gyssels & Ramassamy 2008) met with fierce insults by Raphaël Confiant, not admitting the slightest rehabilitation of the Jewish author in 'his journal'. Having immediately alerted Glissant of the matter, the latter was quick to attribute, albeit belatedly, both André and Simone Schwarz-Bart 'le Prix Carbet' in December 2008. It is this micro-historical incident that accounts heavily for the fraught relationship between prominent Martinican writers and the Jewish outsider in their midst.

Little exchange between Jewish and postcolonial theory further endangers the literary engagements and portrayals. While there are outstanding authors mostly publishing in English, like Michelle Cliff (Raiskin 1996) and Caryl Phillips (Phillips-Casteel 2015), the French-speaking Caribbean have occasionally portrayed the Jewish minority only to recycle clichés (Confiant, Condé). Exceptions are the Schwarz-Barts (Block-Lazarus 1999), and posthumous poetry by the French-Guianese Leon Damas (Gyssels 2018). To link the 'Black Atlantic' to the Jewish history and its diaspora, to implement '*noeuds de mémoire*' (Rothberg 2009) are illustrative of 'Diasporas of the mind' (Cheyette, 2014) which forge the Caribbean as the crossroad of those invisible migrants. According to Miles (2010), Adler (2014) and Taguieff (2004), anti-Israelism and Judeophobia easily spill over into its overseas departments in the Antilles.

Bibliography

Adler, Alexandre. 2014. 'Phénoménologie de l'antisémitisme.' *L'Arche*, 31(03). Online. https://larchemag.fr/2014/03/31/1022/1022/. Accessed 2 March 2015.

Behar, Ruth. 1996. *The Vulnerable Observer. Anthropology That Breaks Your Heart*. Boston: Beacon Press.

Ben-Ur, Aviva. 2020 (2013). *Jewish Autonomy in a Slave Society. Suriname in the Atlantic World, 1651-1825*. Philadelphia: Pennsylviana University Press.

Fulton, Dawn. 2008. *Signs of Dissent. Maryse Condé and Postcolonial Criticism*. Charlottesville: Virginia University Press.

Badinter, Georges. 2017. 'Le bagne de Guyane, crime contre l'humanité.' *Le Monde*, 24 November. Online. http://www.lemonde.fr/idees/article/2017/11/24/robert-badinter-le-bagne-de-guyane-un-crime-contre-l-humanite_5219546_3232.html. Accessed 7 April 2018.

Bassi, Shaul. 2004. 'Resisting Jews: Allosemitism and the Dialectics of Assimilation', in Marco Fazzini (ed.), *Resisting Alterities. Wilson Harris and Other Avatars of Otherness*. Amsterdam: Rodopi: 209-24.

Bénédicty-Kokken, Alessandra. 2019. 'Raphaël Confiant and Jewishness, or the Fraught Landscapes of French, Martinican and Franco-Martinican Intellectualisms', in Sarah Casteel-Phillips et Heidi Kaufman (eds.), *Caribbean Jewish Crossings. Literary History and Creative Practice.* Charlottesville: Virginia University Press: 220-47.

Bilé, Serge. 2005. *Noirs dans les camps*. Paris: Serpent à Plumes.

______. 2011. *Sombres bourreaux*. Paris: Ed. Pascal Galodé.

Block-Lazarus, Joyce. 1999. *Strangers and Sojourners. Jewish Identity in Contemporary Francophone Fiction.* New York, Berlin: Peter Lang.

Bongie, Chris. 2010. *Friends and Enemies: The Scribal Politics of Post/Colonial Literature*. Liverpool: Liverpool University Press.

Britton, Celia. 2014. *Language and Literary Form in French Caribbean Writing*. Liverpool: Liverpool University Press.

Casteel-Phillips, Sarah. 2016. *Calypso Jews. Jewishness in the Caribbean Imagination*. New York: Columbia University Press.

Céline, Louis-Ferdinand. 1938. *Bagatelles pour un massacre*. Paris: Gallimard.

______. 1951. *Guignols band.* Paris: Payot.

Cheyette, Bryan. 2014. *Diasporas of the Mind. Jewish and Postcolonial Writing and the Nightmare of History.* Yale: Yale University Press.

______. 2017. 'Against Supersessionist Thinking: Old and New, Jews and Postcolonialism, the Ghetto and Diaspora.' *The Cambridge Journal of Postcolonial Literary Inquiry*, 4(3): 424-39. doi:10.1017/pli.2017.31.

Condé, Maryse. 1986. *Moi, Tituba sorcière noire de Salem*. Paris: Mercure.

______. 2000. *Célanire cou-coupé.* Paris: Laffont.

______. 2001. *La Belle Créole*. Paris: Laffont.

______. 2017. *Le Fabuleux et Triste Destin d'Ivan et Ivana.* Paris: Lattès.

Confiant, Raphaël. 2021. 'The Israëli conflict this year', *Montray Kréol.* 16 mai: https://www.montraykreyol.org/comment/4752#comment-4752.

______. 1992. *La Vierge du Grand Retour.* Paris: Mercure.

______. 1993. *Ravines du devant-jour.* Tome I. Paris: Gallimard.

______. 2000. *Le Cahier de Romances.* Tome II. Paris: Gallimard.

______. 2003. *Nuée ardente.* Paris: Mercure.

______. 2006. *La panse du chacal.* Paris: Mercure.

______. 2007. *Case à Chine.* Paris: Mercure.

Cornille, Jean-Louis. 2013. 'Soul Limbo féérique Chamoiseau avec Céline.' *Nouvelles Études Francophones*, 28(1): 32–43. www.jstor.org/stable/24244748. Accessed 2 June 2021.

Couti, Jacqueline. 2011. '*Friends and Enemies: The Scribal Politics of Post/Colonial Literature.*' Review Chris Bongie. Liverpool: Liverpool University Press, 2010.

Nieuwe West Indische Gids, 85.1: 152-4. https://www.jstor.org/stable/41850647?seq=1#page_scan_tab_contents

Fanon, Frantz. 1952. *Black Skin; White Masks*, translation Charles Lam Markman, New York: Grove Press, 1967.

Fulton, Dawn. 2008. *Signs of Dissent: Maryse Conde and Postcolonial Criticism*. Charlottesville and London: Virginia University Press.

Gallagher, Mary. 2002. *Soundings in French Caribbean Writing. Since 1950; the Shock of Space and Time.* Oxford: Oxford University Press.

Garcin, Jérôme. 2015. 'A la mémoire d'André Schwarz-Bart, le Blanc qui avait osé écrire sur les Antilles.' *Le Nouvel Observateur*, 22 février. Accessed 7 July 2017.

Gilroy. Paul. 1994. *The Black Atlantic. Modernity and Double Consciousness.* London: Pluto.

_____. 2000. *Between Camps. Race, Identity and Nationalism at the End of the Colour Line.* London: Allen Lane, Penguin Press.

Gilroy, Paul, Tony Sandset, Sindre Bangstad & Gard Ringen Høibjerg. 2019. 'A diagnosis of contemporary forms of racism, race and nationalism: a conversation with Professor Paul Gilroy', *Cultural Studies*, 33(2): 173-97, DOI: 10.1080/09502386.2018.1546334

Gitlin, Todd. 1995. *The Twilights of Common Dreams. Why America is Wracked by Culture Wars.* New York: Henry Holt and Company.

Gyssels. Kathleen. 1996. *Filles de Solitude. Essai sur les [auto-]biographies fictives de Simone et André Schwarz-Bart*. Paris: L'Harmattan.

_____. 2001. *Sages sorcières? Révision de la mauvaise mère dans Beloved (T Morrison), Praisesong for the Widow (P Marshall) et Moi, Tituba (Condé).* New York/Lanham: America University Press.

_____. 2007. '*La dernière des races après les crapauds ladres*': Confiant's Citizens and Terroir in *Mamzelle Libellule*' in Rivke Jaffe. *The Caribbean City*, Kingston: Ian Randle Publishers: 324-41. https://www.potomitan.info/bibliographie/rivke_jaffe.php

_____. 2010. 'Tour d'horizon de V.S. Naipaul dans l'archipel caribéen', in Florence Labaune-Demeule (ed.), *V.S. Naipaul: écriture de l'altérité, altérité de l'écriture.* Paris: Houdiard: 153-76.

_____. 2013a. 'Communautarisme dans l'outre-mer.' *Bulletin de l'Académie des Sciences d'Outre-Mer,* 59: 229-42.

_____. 2013b. 'André Schwarz-Bart à Auschwitz et Jérusalem.' *Image et Narrative*, 14(2). Special issue guest ed. Gyssels and Ledoux-Beaugrand, 16-28. https://www.academia.edu/6574557/_Repr%C3%A9sentations_r%C3%A9centes_de_la_Shoah_Image_and_Narrative. Accessed 7 July 2017.

———. 2014. *Marrane et marronne: la co-écriture d'André et de Simone Schwarz-Bart.* Leiden: Brill.

———. 2016a. '*Rendez-vous avec l'heure qui blesse* ou l'élégie d'Elizé de Gaston-Paul Effa', *Etudes Caribéennes*, 33-34 avril-août. Consulté le 2 juin 2021. http://journals.openedition.org/etudescaribeennes/9463 .

———. 2016b. 'Shoah et esclavage à l'écran', in *Mémoires transmédiales. Geschichte und Gedächtnis in der Karibik und ihrer Diaspora*, Gisela Febel, Natascha Ueckmann, Hgs., Berlin: Frank & Timme, 159-84.

———. 2017. '*Rendez-vous avec l'heure qui blesse ou l'élégie d'Elizée de G.P. Effa.*' *Etudes Caribéennes* mars, 33-34, 1-8. https://journals.openeditioon. rg/etudescaribeennes/9463. Accessed 7 July 2017.

———. 2018a. 'The Raceless and Restless Novels of Caryl Phillips: *The Nature of Blood* on French Ground', *Yod*, 21. Accessed 18 May 2021. http://journals.openedition.org/yod/2631; https://doi.org/10.4000/yod.263

———. 2018b. 'Leon Damas Facing Memory Wars' in Anja Bandau, Anne Brüske, Natascha Ueckmann (eds.), *Reshaping Glocal Dynamics of the Caribbean.* Heidelberg: Heidelberg University Press.

———. 2019a. 'Knots of memory in French Caribbean literature: Edouard Glissant's "Nous ne mourions pas"', in Dagmar Vandebosch & Theo D'haen (eds.). *Literary Transnationalism(s).* Leiden: Brill: 245-63.

———. 2019b. 'From Shtetl to Settler Colony and Back: André Schwarz-Bart's *The Morning Star*', in Sarah Phillips Casteel & Heidi Kaufman, *Caribbean-Jewish Crossings, Literary History and Creative Practice*, Charlottesville: Virginia University Press: 198-219.

———. 2020. 'Jubanidad dans *Avant que les ombres s'effacent*', *African Studies in South Africa,* 50: 38-59.

———. 2021a. 'The Oriental Other in *Mr Potter* (Jamaica Kincaid)', *Shofar*, 39(2).

———. 2021b. 'The Enigma of Denial: Raphaël Confiant and Maryse Condé Facing "Sinitude"' *Caribbean Quarterly,* special double issue on Sino-Caribbean art and literature, 67.1 March: 80-95.

Gyssels, Kathleen, Diana Ramassamy, 2008. "Hommage à André Schwarz-Bart". *Tribune des Antilles*. 30 November.

Hall, Stuart. 1999. 'Un-settling "the heritage", Re-imagining the post-nation: Whose heritage?' *Third Text*, 13(49): 3-13.

Hallward, Peter. 2006. 'Review of Nick Nesbitt, *Voicing Memory. History and Subjectivity in French Caribbean Literature*'. *French Forum*, 31(3) Fall: 171-3.

Hirsch, Marianne. 2012. *The Generation of Postmemory: Writing and Visual Culture After the Holocaust*. Columbia University Press.

Kaufman, Jonathan. 2018. *Broken Alliances. Turbulent relations Blacks and Jews in America*. New York: Charles Scribner's Sons.

Ledent, Bénédicte. 2002. *Caryl Phillips*. Manchester: Manchester University Press.

_____. 2017. 'Caribbean Writers and the Jewish Diaspora.', in Gordon Collier, et al. (eds.), *The Cross-Cultural Legacy. Critical and Creative Writings in Memory of Hena Maes-Jelinek*. Leiden: Brill: 201-18.

Marival, Gladis. 2017. 'Maryse Condé et le djihadiste antillais.' *Le Monde*. http://www.lemonde.fr/livres/ article/ 2017/07/06/maryse-conde-et-le-djihadiste-antillais_5156467_3260.html#Jt0UQMZQu47lUz Tt.99. Accessed 7 July 2017.

Miles, William F. 2010. 'Les juifs et la créolité à la Martinique.' *Pouvoirs de la politique,* 16: 129-62.

_____. 2021. 'How the Slave Trade and the Shoah Gave Birth to a Musical Marvel: Interview with Jacques Schwarz-Bart', in *RELIEF*, December. Special issue guest edited by Kathleen Gyssels.

Miller, Christopher L. 1993. 'Nationalism as Resistance and Resistance to Nationalism in the Literature of Francophone Africa.' *Yale French Studies* 82: 62–100. www.jstor.org/stable/2930212. Accessed 18 May 2021.

Mirzoeff, Nicolas. 2000. *Diaspora and Visual Culture. Representing Africans and Jews*, London, New York: Routledge.

Morrison, Toni. 1987. *Beloved*. New York: Knopf.

Nesbitt, Nick. 2003. *Voicing Memory. History and Subjectivity in French Caribbean Literature*. Charlottesville: University Press Virginia.

Ozick, Cynthia. 1983. *Art & Ardor*. New York: A. Knopf.

Pagnoulle, Christine. 2007. 'David Dabydeen's A Harlot's Progress: Memories in Knots and Stays', in Karra Kampla & Macedo Lynn (eds.), *No Land, no Mother: Essays on David Dabydeen*. Leeds: Peepal Tree Press, 181-203.

Paduro, Leonardo, *Herejes*, 2013. London: Bitter Lemon Press; New York: Farrar, Strauss and Giroux, 2017.

Peterson, Dale, E. 2000. *Up from Bondage. The Literatures of Russian and African American Soul*. Dunham: Duke University Press.

Phillips, Caryl. 1997. *The Nature of Blood*. London: Faber and Faber.

Phillips-Casteel, Sarah. 2016. *Calypso Jews. Jewishness in the Literary Caribbean Imagination*. New York: Columbia University Press.

Plapp, Laurel. 2008. *Zionism and Revolution in European-Jewish Literature*, Berlin, New York: Peter Lang.

Raiskin, Judith. 1996. *Snow on the Cane Fields, With the Logic of a Creole.* Minnesota: Minnesota University Press.

Rothberg, Michael. 2009. *Multidimensional Memory: Remembering the Holocaust in the Age of Postcolonialism.* Stanford: Stanford University Press.

______. 2010 «From *Lieux de mémoire* to *Nœuds de mémoire* », *Yale French Studies*, 118-19: 3-12.

Sartre, Jean-Paul. 1948. *Réflexions sur la question juive*. Paris: Gallimard.

Schwarz-Bart, Simone et André. 2017. *Adieu Bogota.* Paris: Seuil.

Slamovitch, Jean. 2017. 'Raphaël Confiant face aux Juifs "innommables": obsession et denegation', *Controverses,* 5 juin: 175-92. http://www.controverses.fr/pdf/n5/szlamouwicz5.pdf .

Stovall, Styler. 2005. 'Universalisme, différence et invisibilité. Essai sur la notion de race dans l'histoire de la France contemporaine', *Cahiers d'histoire. Revue d'histoire critique*, 96-7. Connection on 18 May 2021. http://journals.openedition.org/chrhc/956; DOI: https://doi.org/10.4000/chrhc.956

Sundquist, Eric. 2005. *Strangers in the Land. Blacks and Jews in American Literature*. Harvard: Harvard University Press.

Taguieff, Pierre-André. 2004. 'Anti-israélisme et judéophobie: l'exception française.' *Outre-Terre,* 9: 385-404.

Valens, Keja. 2021. 'Caribbean Jewish Crossings: Literary History and Creative Practice' by Sarah Phillips Casteel & Heidi Kaufman eds.', *New West Indian Guide/Nieuwe West-Indische Gids*, 951.2:154-5. https://doi.org/10.1163/22134360-09501051.

Wright, Richard. 1940. *Native Son*. Paris: Albin Michel, *Un enfant du pays.* 1947, 1973.

Contributors

Burrowes, Nicole is an Assistant Professor in the Department of History at Rutgers University. Her scholarly interests include social justice movements, comparative histories of racialization and colonialism, and Black Internationalism. Her current book project, *Seeds of Solidarity: African-Indian Relations and the 1935 Labor Rebellions in British Guiana,* explores the historical possibility of a movement forged by those at the edges of empire in the midst of economic, environmental and political crises. Dr. Burrowes earned her Ph.D. in Latin American and Caribbean History from the City University of New York Graduate Center. Email: nb740@history.rutgers.edu

Choenni, Chan E.S. was born in Paramaribo (Suriname). He emigrated to The Netherlands in 1972 and studied Political Science and Science of Philosophy at the University of Amsterdam. He qualified himself also as a social researcher and an historian. He received his Ph.D in 1995 from the University of Utrecht and his thesis was on Conscripts in the Dutch Military and Integration. In 2010 he was appointed as professor at the Free University of Amsterdam. He has published about integration, racism and extensively about Hindustanis. His latest work is on the Afro-Surinamese. Email: c.choenni@kpnmail.nl

Egger, Jerome L. is a historian and has specialized in the twentieth-century history of Suriname. He is presently Head of the History Department of the Faculty of Humanities of the Anton de Kom

University of Suriname. He has published on ethnicity, politics in Suriname and the history of Creoles in Suriname after the abolition of Slavery. He is one of the founding members and member of the editorial board of the journal *His/Her Tori*. E-mail: jlegger@yahoo.com

Gyssels, Kathleen is Professor of Caribbean and African American Literatures at the University of Antwerp. As a comparatist, she focusses on questions of cultural memory and intertwined Diasporas (Black and Jewish) in contemporary postcolonial literatures. She has published several monographs and special issues on authors such as Léon-Gontran Damas, Hélène Cixous, André and Simone Schwarz-Bart and René Maran. She is the author of *Filles de Solitude. Essai sur l'identité antillaise dans les [auto-]biographies fictives de Simone et André Schwarz-Bart* (1996) and *Marrane et marronne: la co-*écriture *réversible d'André et Simone Schwarz-Bart (*2014). Email: kathleen.gyssels@uantwerpen.be

Jagdew, Eric R. is a senior researcher at the Faculty of Humanities of the Anton de Kom University of Suriname. For his M.A. thesis in New History (2007-8) and his Ph.D. dissertation (2009-14). He did research about Indigenous and Maroon Treaties in Suriname, between 1650 and 1863. Since then he worked as Researcher (2008-15) and Director of the Research Institute for Social Sciences (IMWO) (2015-18), Interim Director of the Bureau (2017-19) and (Interim) Chair of the Board (2019-20) of the Anton de Kom University of Suriname. He is now developing a Master programme in History at the FdHum-AdeKUS and is working on a comparative study about Suriname and Guyana after 1834/1863. Email: eric.jagdew@uvs.edu

Leconte, David is a Ph.D. student in history in the University of Le Havre–Normandie (France). His research is entitled: 'The administration of the indentured migrations in the Mascarene islands between the 1830s and the 1860s'. He explores how the French and British imperial and colonial administrations elaborated imperial and local regulations on indentured migrations in Mauritius and

Réunion island. He underlines the influence of local and imperial elites on the making of those regulations, but also the influence of other administrations. Email: leconte.david.ld@gmail.com

Marine-Gougeon, Adélaïde is associated to the Centre d'histoire du XIXème siècle and the CIRESC, and is a Ph.D. student in History. The title of her Ph.D. thesis is: *Circulations, networks and identity of White créole families from Martinique in the 19th century: between transcolonialism and nationalist affirmatio*n. Her advisers are Myriam Cottias (CNRS/CIRESC) and Jacques-Olivier Boudon (Sorbonne Université). Her research focus is on an imperial and transimperial perspective regarding the white creoles of Martinique as colonial actors. She is also currently teaching modern history at Sorbonne Université. Email: adelaide.marine.gougeon@gmail.com

Neus-van der Putten, Hilde writes regular book reviews for the daily newspaper *De Ware Tijd*, and articles on history in *Museumstof*. She taught Colonial and Modern Literature at the Advanced Teacher Training College and is currently in an editing job at the Research Institute for Social Sciences, Anton de Kom University of Suriname. She published 'Susanna du Plessis. Portret van een slavenmeesteres', and is researching free and coloured women in eighteenth-century Suriname. She edited, co-wrote and co-produced several publications, mostly on literature or history. Email: heneus@sr.net

Noémie, Marie-Rose is a Ph.D. student at l'EHESS under the supervision of Myriam Cottias. After a bachelor's degree at the Université des Antilles-Guyane, she obtained a master's degree in History at the University of Paris-Sorbonne. Her Ph.D. focuses on the 'attached worker', who remained on the plantations after the abolition of slavery in Martinique between 1848 and 1948. Email: marierosenoemie@outlook.fr

Schalkwijk, Marten is professor emeritus of Social Change and Development at the Anton de Kom University in Suriname. He studied in Jamaica, Suriname and the United States (Ph.D. Cornell University). His research interests include development issues and planning, the Colonial State, Elites, democracy, Civil Society, and Tribal Societies. He knows the interior of Suriname very well and has done much field research. He also does a lot of policy related research and writing, and teaches courses in research methods, statistics, project management and leadership. Email: martennikos@yahoo.com

Toussaint, Michael F. is a lecturer at The University of the West Indies, St. Augustine, Trinidad and Tobago. He is specialized in the history of the African Diaspora, European Imperialism, West Indian and Latin American History, and Migration Studies. He has written extensively on these areas and pioneered research on nineteenth-century Asian migration from the Caribbean to the Spanish Main. He is the current editor of *History in Action*, the Online Peer Reviewed Journal of the History Department of The University of the West Indies, St Augustine Campus. Email: Michael.Toussaint@sta.uwi.edu

Index